WORD 6
for Windows™
SIMPLIFIED

IDG's
3-D Visual™
Series

by: maranGraphics' Development Group

IDG
BOOKS

IDG Books Worldwide, Inc.
An International Data Group Company

Foster City, California ✦ Indianapolis, Indiana ✦ Boston, Massachusetts

Word 6 for Windows™ Simplified

Published by
IDG Books Worldwide, Inc.
An International Data Group Company
919 E. Hillsdale Blvd., Suite 400
Foster City, CA 94404
(415) 655-3000

Library of Congress Catalog Card No.: 94-079410

ISBN: 1-56884-660-6

Printed in the United States of America

10 9 8 7 6 5 4 3

Distributed in the United States by IDG Books Worldwide, Inc.

Distributed by Computer and Technical Books in Miami, Florida, for South America and the Caribbean; by Longman Singapore in Singapore, Malaysia, Thailand, and Korea; by Toppan Co. Ltd. in Japan; by IDG Communications HK in Hong Kong; by WoodsLane Pty. Ltd. in Australia and New Zealand; and by Transworld Publishers Ltd. in the U.K. and Europe.

For general information on IDG Books in the U.S., including information on discounts and premiums, contact IDG Books at 800-762-2974 or 317-895-5200.

For U.S. Corporate Sales and quantity discounts, contact maranGraphics at 800-469-6616, ext. 206.

For information on international sales of IDG Books, contact Helen Saraceni at 415-655-3021, Fax number 415-655-3295.

For information on translations, contact Marc Jeffrey Mikulich, Director of Rights and Licensing, at IDG Books Worldwide. Fax number 415-655-3295.

For sales inquiries and special prices for bulk quantities, write to the address above or call IDG Books Worldwide at 415-655-3000.

For information on using IDG Books in the classroom, or ordering examination copies, contact Jim Kelly at 800-434-2086.

Trademark Acknowledgments

©1994
maranGraphics, Inc.

The animated characters are the copyright of maranGraphics, Inc.

U.S. Corporate Sales	U.S. Trade Sales
Contact maranGraphics at (800) 469-6616, ext. 206 or Fax (905) 890-9434.	Contact IDG Books at (800) 434-3422 or (415) 655-3000.

About IDG Books Worldwide

Welcome to the world of IDG Books Worldwide.

IDG Books Worldwide, Inc., is a subsidiary of International Data Group, the world's largest publisher of business and computer-related information and the leading global provider of information services on information technology. IDG was founded more than 25 years ago and now employs more than 5,700 people worldwide. IDG publishes more than 200 computer publications in 63 countries (see listing below). Forty million people read one or more IDG publications each month.

Launched in 1990, IDG Books is today the fastest-growing publisher of computer and business books in the United States. We are proud to have received 3 awards from the Computer Press Association in recognition of editorial excellence, and our best-selling ...For Dummies series has more than 10 million copies in print with translations in more than 20 languages. IDG Books, through a recent joint venture with IDG's Hi-Tech Beijing, became the first U.S. publisher to publish a computer book in the People's Republic of China. In record time, IDG Books has become the first choice for millions of readers around the world who want to learn how to better manage their businesses.

Our mission is simple: Every IDG book is designed to bring extra value and skill-building instructions to the reader. Our books are written by experts who understand and care about our readers. The knowledge base of our editorial staff comes from years of experience in publishing, education, and journalism — experience which we use to produce books for the '90s. In short, we care about books, so we attract the best people. We devote special attention to details such as audience, interior design, use of icons, and illustrations. And because we use an efficient process of authoring, editing, and desktop publishing our books electronically, we can spend more time ensuring superior content and spend less time on the technicalities of making books.

You can count on our commitment to deliver high-quality books at competitive prices on topics customers want to read about. At IDG, we value quality, and we have been delivering quality for more than 25 years. You'll find no better book on a subject than an IDG book.

John Kilcullen
President and CEO
IDG Books Worldwide, Inc.

IDG Books Worldwide, Inc., is a subsidiary of International Data Group. The officers are Patrick J. McGovern, Founder and Board Chairman; Walter Boyd, President. International Data Group's publications include: ARGENTINA'S Computerworld Argentina, Infoworld Argentina; AUSTRALIA'S Computerworld Australia, Australian PC World, Australian Macworld, Network World, Mobile Business Australia, Reseller, IDG Sources; AUSTRIA'S Computerwelt Oesterreich, PC Test; BRAZIL'S Computerworld, Gamepro, Game Power, Mundo IBM, Mundo Unix, PC World, Super Game; BELGIUM'S Data News (CW) BULGARIA'S Computerworld Bulgaria, Ediworld, PC & Mac World Bulgaria, Network World Bulgaria; CANADA'S CIO Canada, Computerworld Canada, Graduate Computerworld, InfoCanada, Network World Canada; CHILE'S Computerworld Chile, Informatica; COLOMBIA'S Computerworld Colombia, PC World; CZECH REPUBLIC'S Computerworld, Elektronika, PC World; DENMARK'S Communications World, Computerworld Danmark, Macintosh Produktkatalog, Macworld Danmark, PC World Danmark, PC World Produktguide, Tech World, Windows World; ECUADOR'S PC World Ecuador; EGYPT'S Computerworld (CW) Middle East, PC World Middle East; FINLAND'S MikroPC, Tietoviikko, Tietoverkko; FRANCE'S Distributique, GOLDEN MAC, InfoPC, Languages & Systems, Le Guide du Monde Informatique, Le Monde Informatique, Telecoms & Reseaux; GERMANY'S Computerwoche, Computerwoche Focus, Computerwoche Extra, Computerwoche Karriere, Information Management, Macwelt, Netzwelt, PC Welt, PC Woche, Publish, Unit; GREECE'S Infoworld, PC Games; HUNGARY'S Computerworld SZT, PC World; HONG KONG'S Computerworld Hong Kong, PC World Hong Kong; INDIA'S Computers & Communications; IRELAND'S ComputerScope; ISRAEL'S Computerworld Israel, PC World Israel; ITALY'S Computerworld Italia, Lotus Magazine, Macworld Italia, Networking World, PC Shopping, PC World Italia; JAPAN'S Computerworld Today, Information Systems World, Macworld Japan, Nikkei Personal Computing, SunWorld Japan, Windows World; KENYA'S East African Computer News; KOREA'S Computerworld Korea, Macworld Korea, PC World Korea; MEXICO'S Compu Edicion, Compu Manufactura, Computacion/Punto de Venta, Computerworld Mexico, MacWorld, Mundo Unix, PC World, Windows; THE NETHERLANDS' Computer! Totaal, Computable (CW), LAN Magazine, MacWorld, Totaal "Windows"; NEW ZEALAND'S Computer Listings, Computerworld New Zealand, New Zealand PC World, Network World; NIGERIA'S PC World Africa; NORWAY'S Computerworld Norge, C/World, Lotusworld Norge, Macworld Norge, Networld, PC World Ekspress, PC World Norge, PC World's Produktguide, Publish& Multimedia World, Student Data, Unix World, Windowsworld; IDG Direct Response; PAKISTAN'S PC World Pakistan; PANAMA'S PC World Panama; PERU'S Computerworld Peru, PC World; PEOPLE'S REPUBLIC OF CHINA'S China Computerworld, China Infoworld, Electronics Today/Multimedia World, Electronics International, Electronic Product World, China Network World, PC and Communications Magazine, PC World China, Software World Magazine, Telecom Product World; IDG HIGH TECH BEIJING'S New Product World; IDG SHENZHEN'S Computer News Digest; PHILIPPINES' Computerworld Philippines, PC Digest (PCW); POLAND'S Computerworld Poland, PC World/Komputer; PORTUGAL'S Cerebro/PC World, Correio Informatico/Computerworld, Informatica & Comunicacoes Catalogo, MacIn, Nacional de Produtos; ROMANIA'S Computerworld, PC World; RUSSIA'S Computerworld-Moscow, Mir - PC, Sety; SINGAPORE'S Computerworld Southeast Asia, PC World Singapore; SLOVENIA'S Monitor Magazine; SOUTH AFRICA'S Computer Mail (CIO),Computing S.A.,Network World S.A., Software World; SPAIN'S Advanced Systems, Amiga World, Computerworld Espana, Communicaciones World, Macworld Espana, NeXTWORLD, Super Juegos Magazine (GamePro), PC World Espana, Publish; SWEDEN'S Attack, ComputerSweden, Corporate Computing, Natverk & Kommunikation, Macworld, Mikrodatorn, PC World, Publishing & Design (CAP), Datalngenjoren, Maxi Data,Windows World; SWITZERLAND'S Computerworld Schweiz, Macworld Schweiz, PC Tip; TAIWAN'S Computerworld Taiwan, PC World Taiwan; THAILAND'S Thai Computerworld; TURKEY'S Computerworld Monitor, Macworld Turkiye, PC World Turkiye; UKRAINE'S Computerworld; UNITED KINGDOM'S Computing /Computerworld, Connexion/Network World, Lotus Magazine, Macworld, Open Computing/Sunworld; UNITED STATES' Advanced Systems, AmigaWorld, Cable in the Classroom, CD Review, CIO, Computerworld, Digital Video, DOS Resource Guide, Electronic Entertainment Magazine, Federal Computer Week, Federal Integrator, GamePro, IDG Books, Infoworld, Infoworld Direct, Laser Event, Macworld, Multimedia World, Network World, PC Letter, PC World, PlayRight, Power PC World, Publish, SWATPro, Video Event; VENEZUELA'S Computerworld Venezuela, PC World; VIETNAM'S PC World Vietnam

Credits

Author and Architect:
Ruth Maran

Technical Consultant:
Wendi Blouin Ewbank

Designer:
Jim C. Leung

Layout and Screens:
Lance Pilon

Illustrator:
Dave Ross

Editor:
Kelleigh Wing

Post Production:
Robert Maran

Acknowledgments

Thanks to Hilaire Gagne and Matthew Price of Microsoft Canada Inc. for their support and consultation.

Deepest thanks to Wendi B. Ewbank for her dedication and support in ensuring the technical accuracy of this book.

Thanks to José F. Pérez and Saverio C. Tropiano for their assistance and expert advice.

Thanks to the dedicated staff of maranGraphics, including David de Haas, Peters Ezers, David Hendricks, Jill Maran, Judy Maran, Maxine Maran, Robert Maran, Dave Ross, Christie Van Duin, Carol Walthers and Kelleigh Wing.

Finally, to Richard Maran who originated the easy-to-use graphic format of this guide. Thank you for your inspiration and guidance.

TABLE OF CONTENTS

Save and Open Your Documents

Using Multiple Documents

Print Your Documents

Change Your Screen Display

Format Characters

Format Paragraphs

Format Pages

Smart Formatting

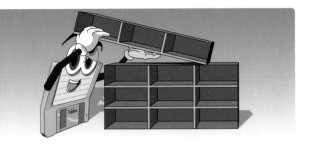

verview

GETTING STARTED

◆ This chapter will show you everything you need to know to start using Word. You will learn how to use a mouse and how to move through your document.

Getting Started

| Edit Your Documents | Smart Editing | Save and Open Your Documents | Using Multiple Documents | Print Your Documents | Change Your Screen Display |

Introduction
Mouse Basics
Start Word
Enter Text

Using the Menus
Move Through a Document
Select Text
Help

What You Can Create With Word for Windows

PERSONAL AND BUSINESS LETTERS

Word for Windows helps you to produce letters quickly and accurately.

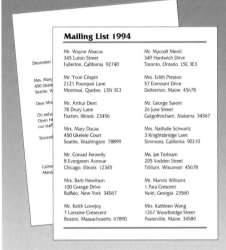

MAILING LISTS

Word for Windows can merge documents with a list of names and addresses to produce personalized letters.

REPORTS AND MANUALS

Word for Windows provides editing and formatting features that make it ideal for producing longer documents such as reports and manuals.

Let's Assume...

◆ You have installed the Word for Windows program on your hard drive.

◆ You are using a mouse with Word for Windows.

MOUSE BASICS

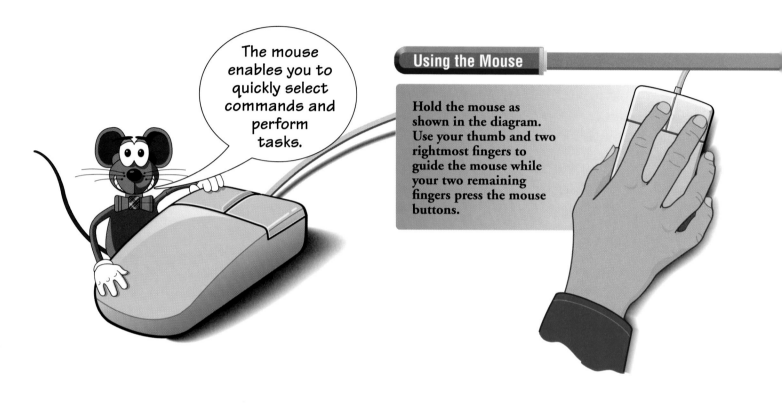

The mouse enables you to quickly select commands and perform tasks.

Using the Mouse

Hold the mouse as shown in the diagram. Use your thumb and two rightmost fingers to guide the mouse while your two remaining fingers press the mouse buttons.

Moving the Mouse Pointer

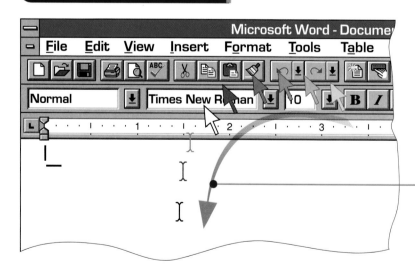

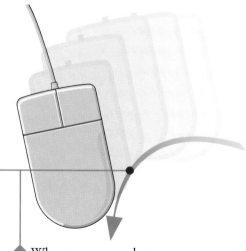

◆ When you move the mouse on your desk, the mouse pointer (⇖ or I) on your screen also moves. The mouse pointer changes shape depending on its location on your screen.

◆ The mouse has a left and right button. You can use these buttons to:

• open menus
• select commands
• choose options

Note: You will use the left button most of the time.

◆ Under the mouse is a ball that senses movement. To ensure smooth motion of the mouse, you should occasionally remove and clean this ball.

Mouse Terms

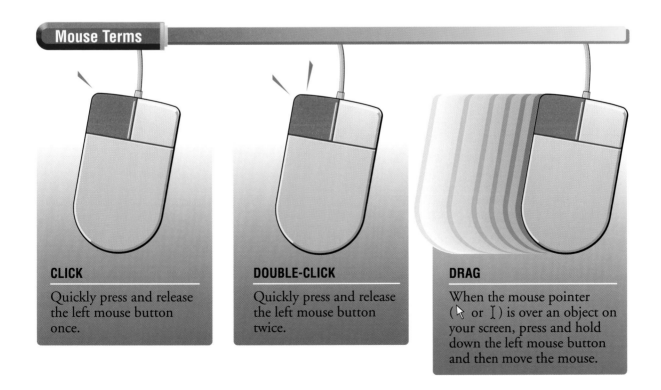

CLICK

Quickly press and release the left mouse button once.

DOUBLE-CLICK

Quickly press and release the left mouse button twice.

DRAG

When the mouse pointer (⇖ or I) is over an object on your screen, press and hold down the left mouse button and then move the mouse.

START WORD

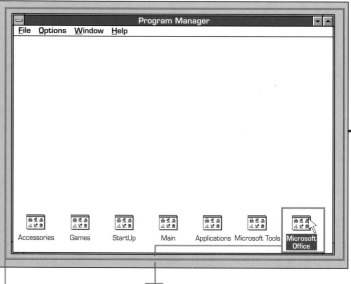

When you start Word for Windows, a blank document appears. You can now begin to type text into this document.

Start Word for Windows

C:\> WIN _

Program Manager

File   Options   Window   Help

Accessories   Games   StartUp   Main   Applications   Microsoft Tools   Microsoft Office

1 To start Word for Windows from MS-DOS, type **WIN** and then press Enter .

◆ The **Program Manager** window appears.

2 To open the group window that contains Word, move the mouse ⬚ over the icon (example: **Microsoft Office**) and then quickly press the left button twice.

| Getting Started | Edit Your Documents | Smart Editing | Save and Open Your Documents | Using Multiple Documents | Print Your Documents | Change Your Screen Display |

Introduction
Mouse Basics
Start Word
Enter Text

Using the Menus
Move Through a Document
Select Text
Help

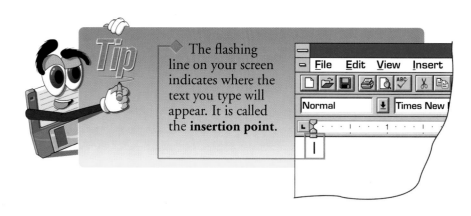

The flashing line on your screen indicates where the text you type will appear. It is called the **insertion point**.

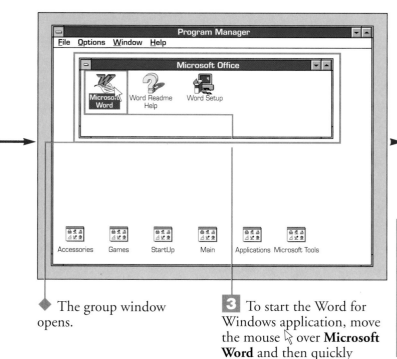

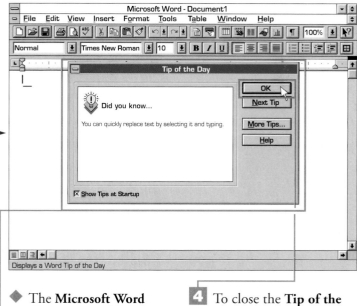

◆ The group window opens.

3 To start the Word for Windows application, move the mouse ⬚ over **Microsoft Word** and then quickly press the left button twice.

◆ The **Microsoft Word** window appears, displaying a blank document.

◆ Each time you start Word, a tip about using the program appears.

4 To close the **Tip of the Day** dialog box, move the mouse ⬚ over **OK** and then press the left button.

ENTER TEXT

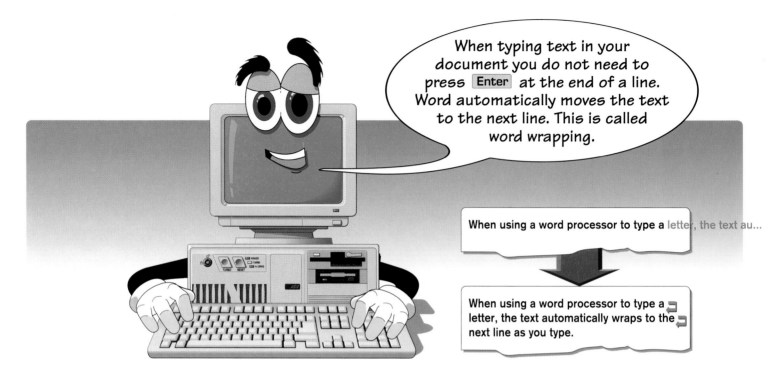

When typing text in your document you do not need to press **Enter** at the end of a line. Word automatically moves the text to the next line. This is called word wrapping.

When using a word processor to type a letter, the text au...

When using a word processor to type a letter, the text automatically wraps to the next line as you type.

Enter Text

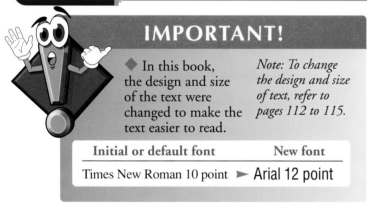

IMPORTANT!

◆ In this book, the design and size of the text were changed to make the text easier to read.

Note: To change the design and size of text, refer to pages 112 to 115.

Initial or default font	New font
Times New Roman 10 point ►	Arial 12 point

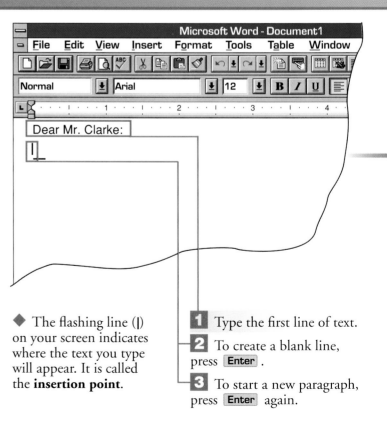

Microsoft Word - Document1

File   Edit   View   Insert   Format   Tools   Table   Window

Normal   Arial   12   B I U

Dear Mr. Clarke:

◆ The flashing line (|) on your screen indicates where the text you type will appear. It is called the **insertion point**.

1 Type the first line of text.

2 To create a blank line, press **Enter** .

3 To start a new paragraph, press **Enter** again.

INTRODUCTION TO WORD

| Getting Started | Edit Your Documents | Smart Editing | Save and Open Your Documents | Using Multiple Documents | Print Your Documents | Change Your Screen Display |

Introduction | Using the Menus
Mouse Basics | Move Through a Document
Start Word | Select Text
Enter Text | Help

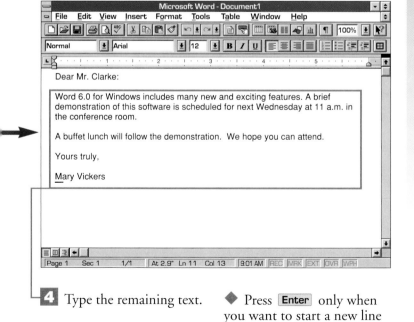

STATUS BAR

The status bar provides information about the position of the insertion point and the text displayed on your screen.

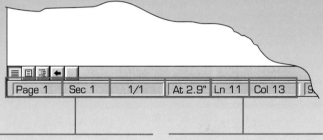

◆ **Page 1**
The page displayed on your screen.

◆ **Sec 1**
The section of the document displayed on your screen.

◆ **1/1**
The page displayed on your screen. / The total number of pages in your document.

◆ **At 2.9"**
The distance (in inches) from the top of the page to the insertion point.

◆ **Ln 11**
The number of lines from the top of the page to the insertion point.

◆ **Col 13**
The number of characters from the left margin to the insertion point, including spaces.

4 Type the remaining text.

◆ Press **Enter** only when you want to start a new line or paragraph.

USING THE MENUS

You can open a menu to display a list of related commands. You can then select the command you want to use.

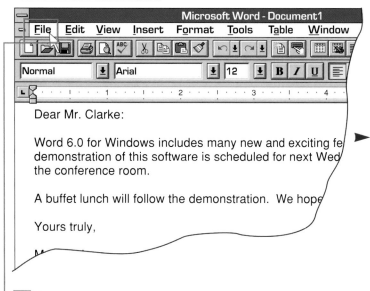

1 To open a menu, move the mouse ⌖ over the menu name (example: **File**) and then press the left button.

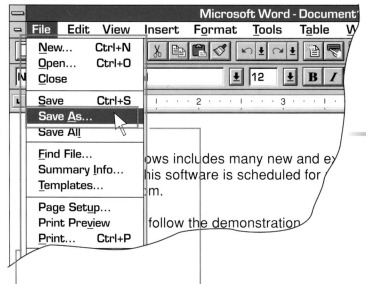

◆ A menu appears displaying a list of related commands.

Note: To close a menu, move the mouse ⌖ anywhere over your document and then press the left button.

2 To select a command, move the mouse ⌖ over the command name (example: **Save As**) and then press the left button.

Getting Started	Edit Your Documents	Smart Editing	Save and Open Your Documents	Using Multiple Documents	Print Your Documents	Change Your Screen Display

Introduction
Mouse Basics
Start Word
Enter Text

Using the Menus
Move Through a Document
Select Text
Help

Edit

Underline Typing	Ctrl+Z
Repeat Typing	**Ctrl+Y**
Cut	Ctrl+X
Copy	Ctrl+C
Paste	Ctrl+V
Paste Special...	

◆ If a command is dimmed (example: **Cut**), it is currently unavailable.

◆ If key names are separated by a plus sign (+), press and hold down the first key before pressing the second key (example: Alt + F4).

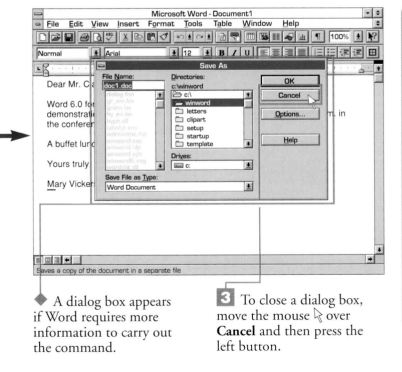

◆ A dialog box appears if Word requires more information to carry out the command.

3 To close a dialog box, move the mouse ⌖ over **Cancel** and then press the left button.

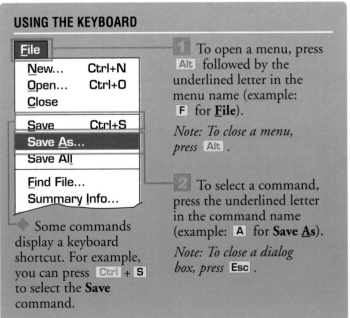

USING THE KEYBOARD

1 To open a menu, press Alt followed by the underlined letter in the menu name (example: **F** for **File**).

Note: To close a menu, press Alt .

◆ Some commands display a keyboard shortcut. For example, you can press Ctrl + S to select the **Save** command.

2 To select a command, press the underlined letter in the command name (example: **A** for **Save As**).

Note: To close a dialog box, press Esc .

MOVE THROUGH A DOCUMENT

If you create a long document, your computer screen cannot display all the text at the same time. You must scroll up or down to view other parts of your document.

IMPORTANT!

You cannot move the insertion point past the horizontal line (_) displayed on your screen. To move this line, position the insertion point after the last character in your document and then press Enter .

Move to Any Position on Your Screen

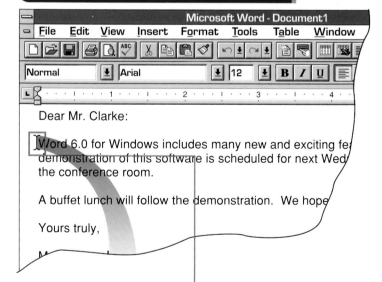

Microsoft Word - Document1

File   Edit   View   Insert   Format   Tools   Table   Window

Normal   Arial   12   B I U

Dear Mr. Clarke:

Word 6.0 for Windows includes many new and exciting fe demonstration of this software is scheduled for next Wed the conference room.

A buffet lunch will follow the demonstration. We hope

Yours truly,

The insertion point indicates where the text you type will appear in your document.

1 To position the insertion point at another location on your screen, move the mouse I over the new location and then press the left button.

| Getting Started | Edit Your Documents | Smart Editing | Save and Open Your Documents | Using Multiple Documents | Print Your Documents | Change Your Screen Display |

Introduction | Using the Menus
Mouse Basics | **Move Through a Document**
Start Word | Select Text
Enter Text | Help

Scroll Up or Down

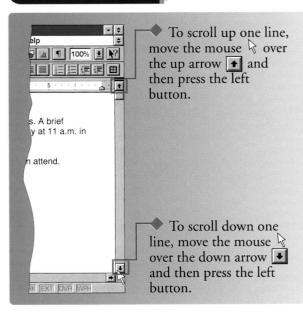

◆ To scroll up one line, move the mouse Ⓚ over the up arrow ⬆ and then press the left button.

◆ To scroll down one line, move the mouse Ⓚ over the down arrow ⬇ and then press the left button.

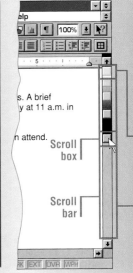

Scroll box

Scroll bar

The location of the scroll box on the scroll bar indicates which part of your document is displayed on the screen.

For example, when the scroll box is in the middle of the scroll bar, you are viewing the middle part of your document.

1 To move the scroll box, position the mouse Ⓚ over the box and then press and hold down the left button.

2 Still holding down the button, drag the scroll box down the scroll bar. Then release the button.

Keyboard Shortcuts

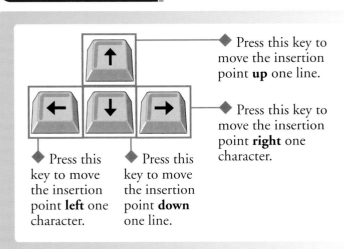

◆ Press this key to move the insertion point **up** one line.

◆ Press this key to move the insertion point **right** one character.

◆ Press this key to move the insertion point **left** one character.

◆ Press this key to move the insertion point **down** one line.

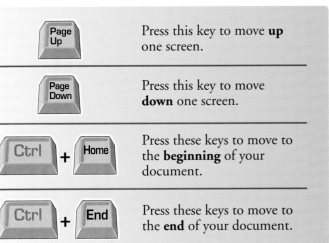

Press this key to move **up** one screen.

Press this key to move **down** one screen.

Press these keys to move to the **beginning** of your document.

Press these keys to move to the **end** of your document.

SELECT TEXT

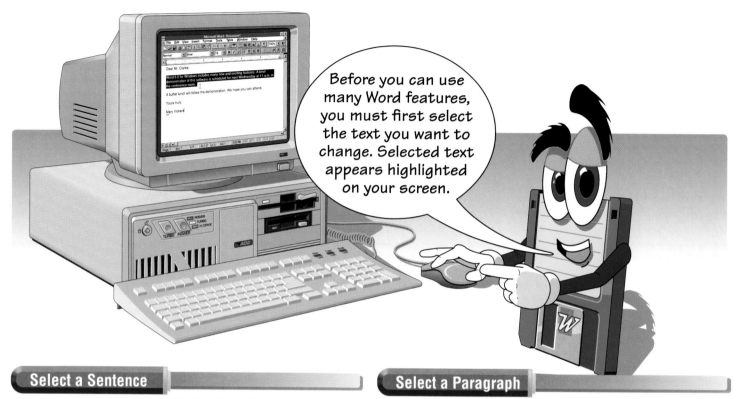

Before you can use many Word features, you must first select the text you want to change. Selected text appears highlighted on your screen.

Select a Sentence

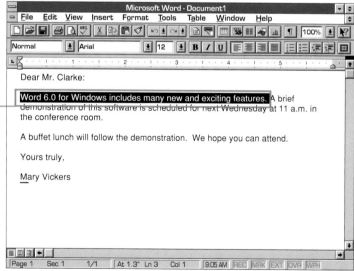

1 Press and hold down `Ctrl`.

2 Still holding down `Ctrl`, move the mouse I anywhere over the sentence you want to select and then press the left button. Release `Ctrl`.

TO CANCEL A TEXT SELECTION

Move the mouse I outside the selected area and then press the left button.

Select a Paragraph

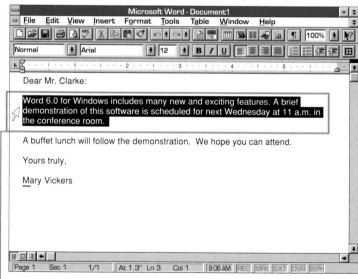

1 Move the mouse I to the left of the paragraph you want to select (I changes to ⌐) and then quickly press the left button twice.

14

Getting Started

Edit
Your
Documents

Smart
Editing

Save and
Open Your
Documents

Using
Multiple
Documents

Print
Your
Documents

Change
Your Screen
Display

Introduction	Using the Menus
Mouse Basics	Move Through a Document
Start Word	**Select Text**
Enter Text	Help

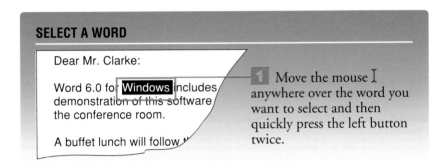

SELECT A WORD

Dear Mr. Clarke:

Word 6.0 for Windows includes demonstration of this software the conference room.

A buffet lunch will follow

1 Move the mouse I anywhere over the word you want to select and then quickly press the left button twice.

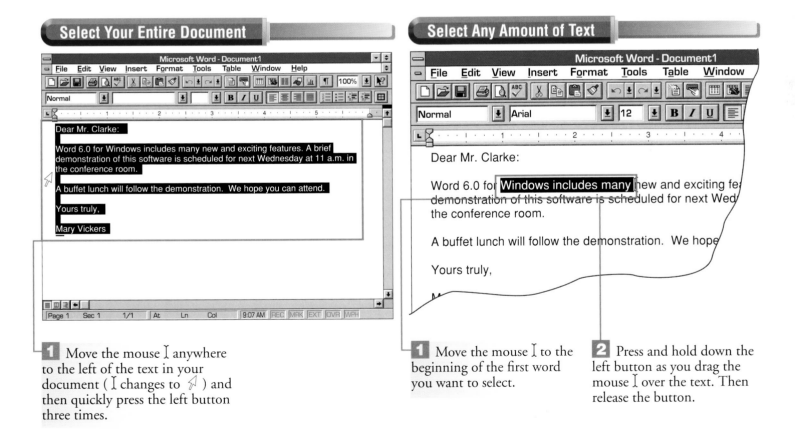

Select Your Entire Document

1 Move the mouse I anywhere to the left of the text in your document (I changes to) and then quickly press the left button three times.

Select Any Amount of Text

1 Move the mouse I to the beginning of the first word you want to select.

2 Press and hold down the left button as you drag the mouse I over the text. Then release the button.

If you forget how to perform a task, you can use the Word Help feature to obtain information. This can save you time by eliminating the need to refer to other sources.

Help

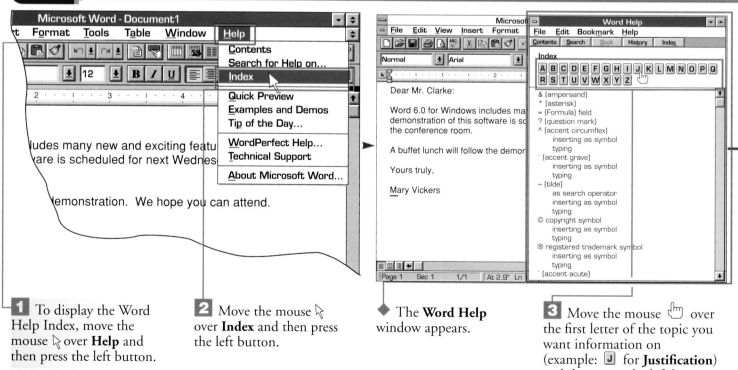

1 To display the Word Help Index, move the mouse ⬚ over **Help** and then press the left button.

2 Move the mouse ⬚ over **Index** and then press the left button.

◆ The **Word Help** window appears.

3 Move the mouse ⬚ over the first letter of the topic you want information on (example: **J** for **Justification**) and then press the left button.

INTRODUCTION TO WORD

| Getting Started | Edit Your Documents | Smart Editing | Save and Open Your Documents | Using Multiple Documents | Print Your Documents | Change Your Screen Display |

Introduction
Mouse Basics
Start Word
Enter Text

Using the Menus
Move Through a Document
Select Text
Help

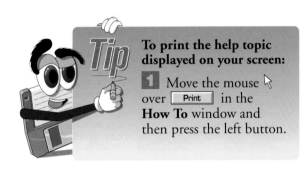

To print the help topic displayed on your screen:

1 Move the mouse over Print in the **How To** window and then press the left button.

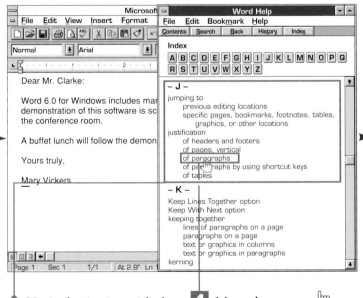

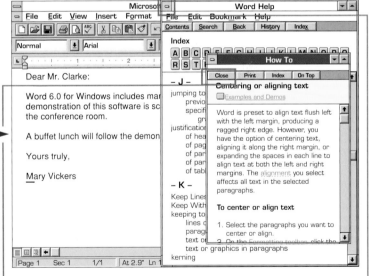

◆ Topics beginning with the letter you selected appear.

◆ To view more topics beginning with that letter, press PageDown on your keyboard.

4 Move the mouse over the topic of interest (example: **justification of paragraphs**) and then press the left button.

◆ Information on the topic you selected appears.

5 To close the **How To** window, move the mouse over **Close** and then press the left button.

6 To close the **Word Help** window, move the mouse over its **Control-menu** box and then quickly press the left button twice.

17

You can use the Word Help feature to receive information on any button or command.

Receive Help on a Button

The Word buttons enable you to quickly select the most commonly used commands.

For example, you can use 💾 to quickly select the Save command.

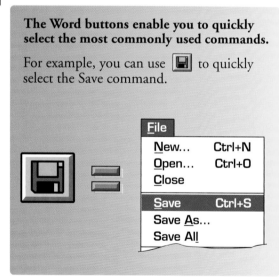

File	
New...	Ctrl+N
Open...	Ctrl+O
Close	
Save	Ctrl+S
Save **A**s...	
Save Al**l**	

1 To display a description of a button displayed on your screen, move the mouse ▷ over the button of interest (example: 💾).

◆ After a few seconds, the name of the button appears (example: **Save**).

◆ A short description of the button also appears at the bottom of your screen.

| Getting Started | Edit Your Documents | Smart Editing | Save and Open Your Documents | Using Multiple Documents | Print Your Documents | Change Your Screen Display |

Introduction
Mouse Basics
Start Word
Enter Text

Using the Menus
Move Through a Document
Select Text
Help

RECEIVE HELP ON A MENU COMMAND

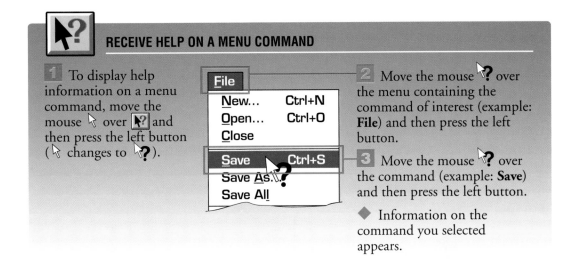

1 To display help information on a menu command, move the mouse ⩗ over 🔲 and then press the left button (⩗ changes to ⩗?).

2 Move the mouse ⩗? over the menu containing the command of interest (example: **File**) and then press the left button.

3 Move the mouse ⩗? over the command (example: **Save**) and then press the left button.

◆ Information on the command you selected appears.

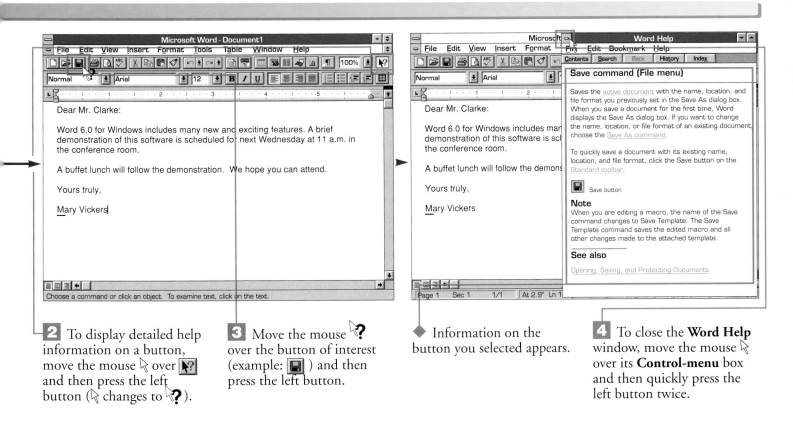

2 To display detailed help information on a button, move the mouse ⩗ over 🔲 and then press the left button (⩗ changes to ⩗?).

3 Move the mouse ⩗? over the button of interest (example: 🔲) and then press the left button.

◆ Information on the button you selected appears.

4 To close the **Word Help** window, move the mouse ⩗ over its **Control-menu** box and then quickly press the left button twice.

Overview

EDIT YOUR DOCUMENTS

Insert Text

Delete Text

Replace Selected Text

Undo Changes

Redo Changes

Change the Case of Text

Move Text

Copy Text

◆ This chapter will show you how to make changes to your document. You will learn how to insert and delete text and how to make many other quick and easy changes.

INSERT TEXT

Insert a Blank Line

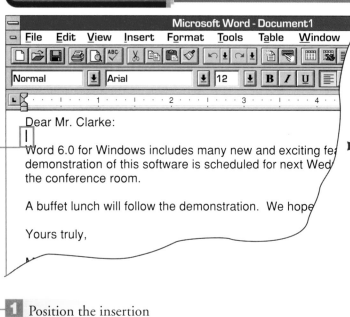

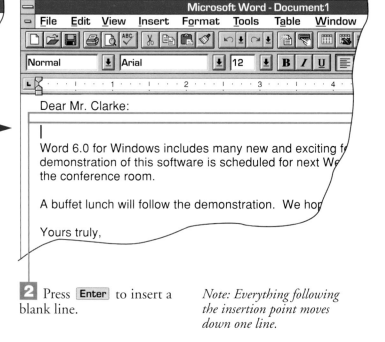

1 Position the insertion point where you want to insert a blank line.

2 Press **Enter** to insert a blank line.

Note: Everything following the insertion point moves down one line.

Getting
Started

**Edit
Your
Documents**

Smart
Editing

Save and
Open Your
Documents

Using
Multiple
Documents

Print
Your
Documents

Change
Your Screen
Display

Insert Text	Redo Changes
Delete Text	Change the Case of Text
Replace Selected Text	Move Text
Undo Changes	Copy Text

IMPORTANT!

Make sure you save your document to store it for future use. If you do not save your document, it will disappear when you turn off your computer.

Note: To save a document, refer to page 64.

Split and Join Paragraphs

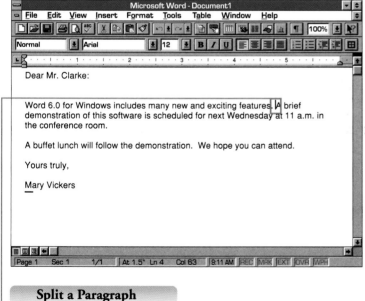

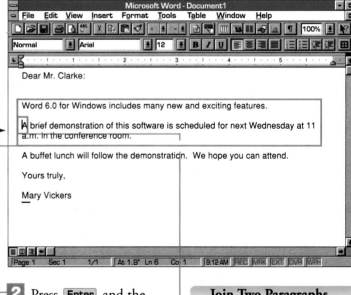

Split a Paragraph

1 Position the insertion point where you want to split a paragraph in two.

2 Press **Enter** and the paragraph is split in two.

3 To insert a blank line between the two paragraphs, press **Enter** again.

Join Two Paragraphs

1 Position the insertion point to the left of the first character in the second paragraph.

2 Press **◆Backspace** until the paragraphs are joined.

23

INSERT TEXT

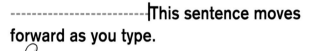

This sentence moves forward as you type.

------------------------------This sentence moves forward as you type.

In the Insert mode, the text you type appears at the current insertion point location. Any existing text moves forward to make room for the new text.

Insert Text

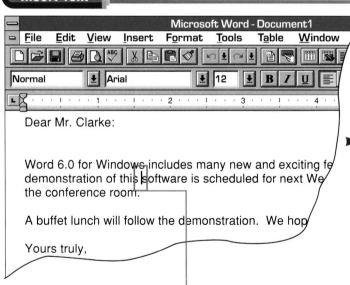

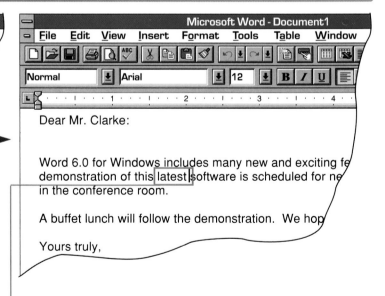

When you start Word, the program is in the Insert mode.

1 Position the insertion point where you want to insert the new text.

*Note: If the letters **OVR** appear in black (OVR) at the bottom of your screen, press* Insert *on your keyboard to switch to the **Insert** mode.*

2 Type the text you want to insert (example: **latest**).

3 To insert a blank space, press the **Spacebar**.

Note: The words to the right of the inserted text are pushed forward.

24

Getting
Started

**Edit
Your
Documents**

Smart
Editing

Save and
Open Your
Documents

Using
Multiple
Documents

Print
Your
Documents

Change
Your Screen
Display

Insert Text	Redo Changes
Delete Text	Change the Case of Text
Replace Selected Text	Move Text
Undo Changes	Copy Text

In the Overtype mode, the text you type appears at the current insertion point location. The new text replaces (types over) any existing text.

This sentence disappears as you type.

xxxxxxxxxxxxxxxxxxxpears as you type.

Overtype Text

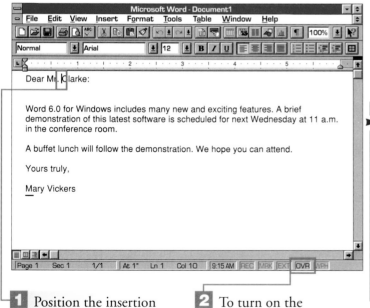

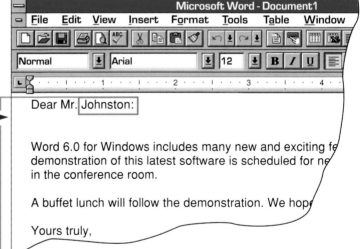

1 Position the insertion point to the left of the first character you want to replace.

2 To turn on the **Overtype** mode, move the mouse over OVR and then quickly press the left button twice (OVR changes to OVR).

3 Type the text you want to replace the existing text with (example: **Johnston:**).

Note: The new text types over the existing text.

4 To turn off the **Overtype** mode, repeat step **2** (OVR changes to OVR).

Note: You can also press Insert *on your keyboard to turn on or off the* **Overtype** *mode.*

25

DELETE TEXT

You can use Delete to remove the blank line the insertion point is on. The remaining text moves up one line.

Delete — **Delete a Blank Line**

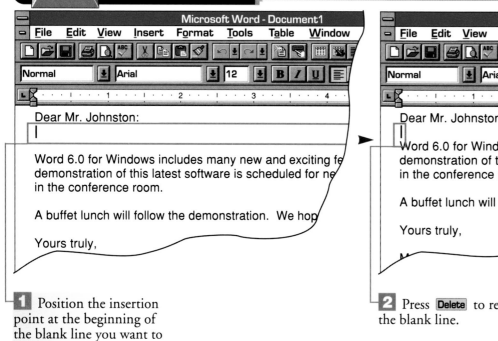

1 Position the insertion point at the beginning of the blank line you want to delete.

2 Press Delete to remove the blank line.

Note: The remaining text moves up one line.

Getting
Started

Edit
Your
Documents

Smart
Editing

Save and
Open Your
Documents

Using
Multiple
Documents

Print
Your
Documents

Change
Your Screen
Display

Insert Text	Redo Changes
Delete Text	Change the Case of Text
Replace Selected Text	Move Text
Undo Changes	Copy Text

You can use Delete to remove the character to the right of the insertion point. The remaining text moves to the left.

Delete — Delete a Character

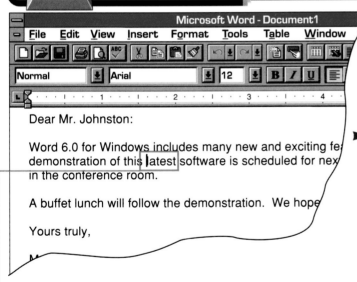

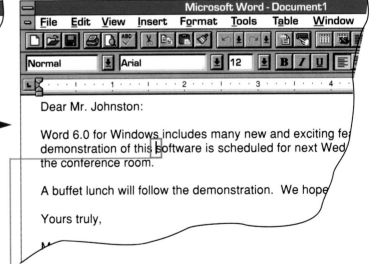

1 Position the insertion point to the left of the character you want to delete (example: **l** in **l**atest).

2 Press Delete once for each character you want to delete (example: press Delete seven times).

You can also use this key to delete characters. Position the insertion point to the right of the character(s) you want to delete and then press ←Backspace.

You can use Delete to remove text you have selected. The remaining text moves up or to the left.

Delete Selected Text

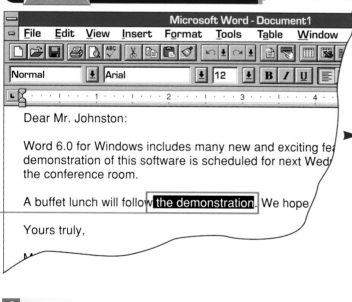

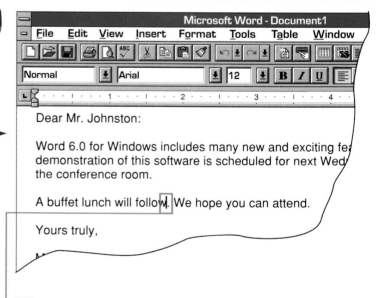

1 Select the text you want to delete.

Note: To select text, refer to page 14.

2 Press Delete to remove the text.

INTRODUCTION TO WORD

Getting
Started

Edit
Your
Documents

Smart
Editing

Save and
Open Your
Documents

Using
Multiple
Documents

Print
Your
Documents

Change
Your Screen
Display

Insert Text
Delete Text
Replace Selected Text
Undo Changes

Redo Changes
Change the Case of Text
Move Text
Copy Text

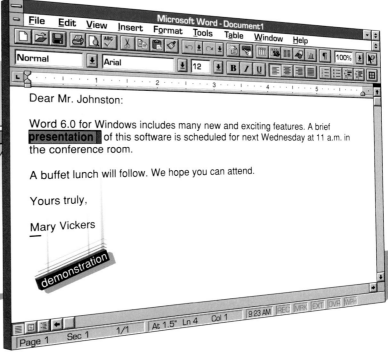

Word allows
you to replace text
you have selected
with new text.

Replace Selected Text

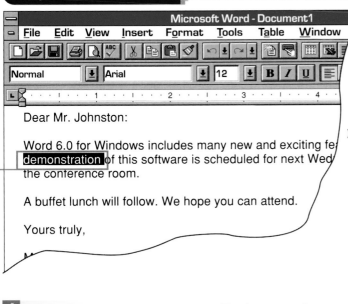

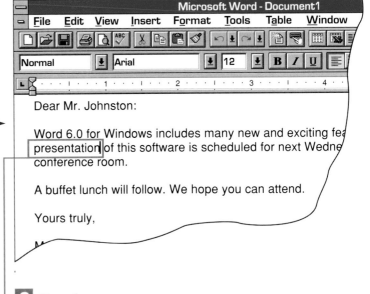

1 Select the text you want to replace with new text.

Note: To select text, refer to page 14.

2 Type the text (example: **presentation**). This text replaces the text you had selected.

29

Word remembers the last 100 changes you made to your document. If you regret these changes, you can cancel them by using the Undo feature.

Undo Changes

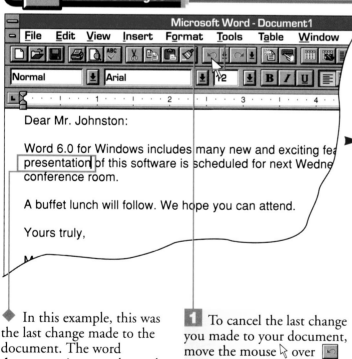

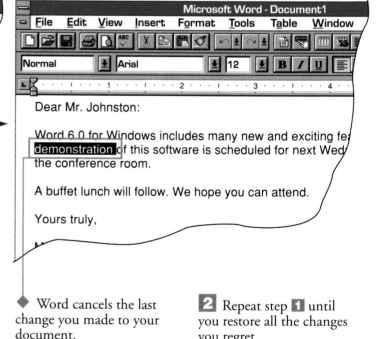

◆ In this example, this was the last change made to the document. The word **demonstration** was changed to **presentation**.

1 To cancel the last change you made to your document, move the mouse ⌖ over 🔙 and then press the left button.

◆ Word cancels the last change you made to your document.

2 Repeat step **1** until you restore all the changes you regret.

Getting
Started

Edit
Your
Documents

Smart
Editing

Save and
Open Your
Documents

Using
Multiple
Documents

Print
Your
Documents

Change
Your Screen
Display

Insert Text
Delete Text
Replace Selected Text
Undo Changes

Redo Changes
Change the Case of Text
Move Text
Copy Text

The Undo and Redo features are very helpful, but there are some commands that Word cannot undo.

For example, you cannot use the Undo feature to cancel the save and print commands.

Redo Changes

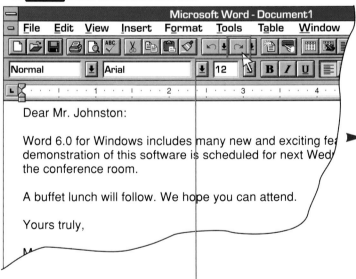

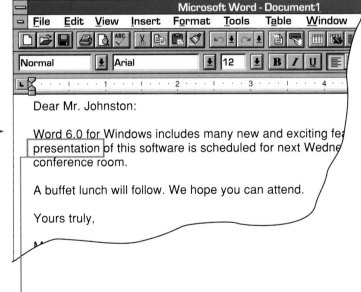

If you are not satisfied with the results of the Undo feature, you can use the Redo feature to return the document to the way it was.

1 To reverse the results of using the Undo feature, move the mouse ⟑ over and then press the left button.

◆ Word reverses the results of the last undo command.

2 Repeat step **1** until you reverse the results of all the undo commands you regret.

Note: For the remaining examples in this book, the word **presentation** *was returned to* **demonstration.**

CHANGE THE CASE OF TEXT

> You can change the case of text in your document without having to retype the text. Word offers five case options.

Change the Case of Text

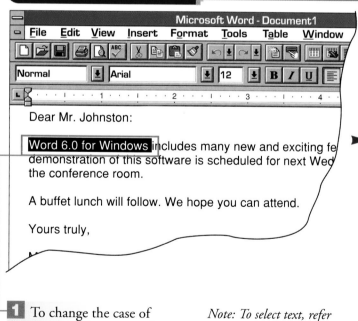

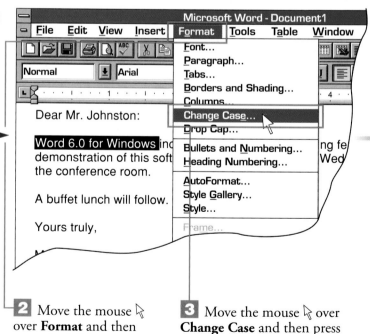

1 To change the case of text in your document, select the text you want to change.

Note: To select text, refer to page 14.

2 Move the mouse ⌖ over **Format** and then press the left button.

3 Move the mouse ⌖ over **Change Case** and then press the left button.

INTRODUCTION TO WORD

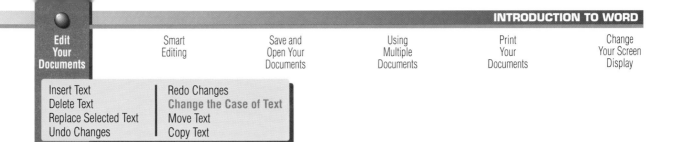

Getting
Started

Edit
Your
Documents

Smart
Editing

Save and
Open Your
Documents

Using
Multiple
Documents

Print
Your
Documents

Change
Your Screen
Display

Insert Text
Delete Text
Replace Selected Text
Undo Changes

Redo Changes
Change the Case of Text
Move Text
Copy Text

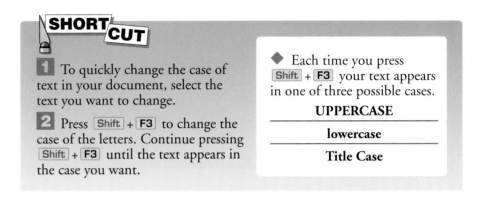

SHORT CUT

1 To quickly change the case of text in your document, select the text you want to change.

2 Press Shift + F3 to change the case of the letters. Continue pressing Shift + F3 until the text appears in the case you want.

◆ Each time you press Shift + F3 your text appears in one of three possible cases.

UPPERCASE

lowercase

Title Case

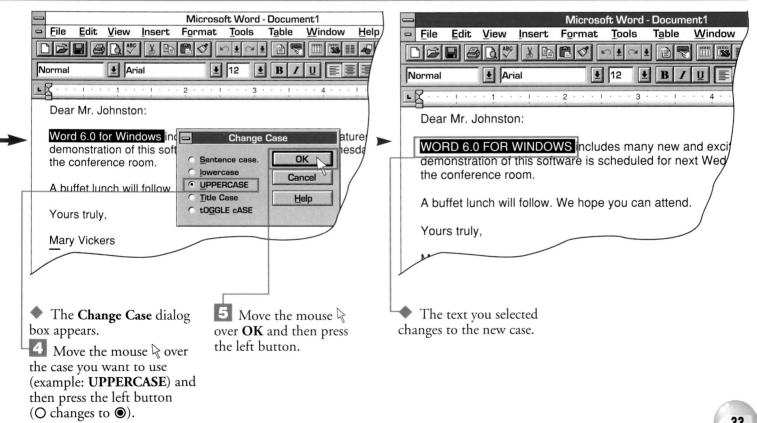

◆ The **Change Case** dialog box appears.

4 Move the mouse over the case you want to use (example: **UPPERCASE**) and then press the left button (○ changes to ◉).

5 Move the mouse over **OK** and then press the left button.

◆ The text you selected changes to the new case.

MOVE TEXT

You can move text from one location in your document to another. Word "cuts" the text and "pastes" it in a new location. The original text disappears.

Move Text

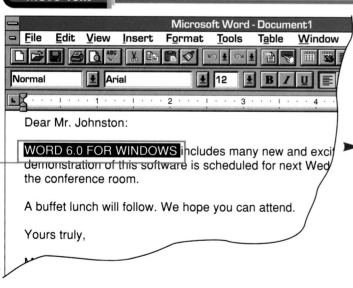

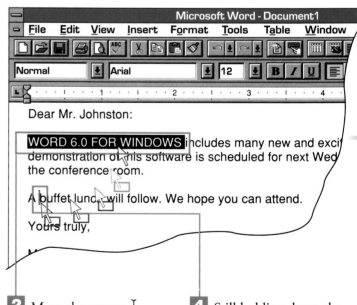

1 Select the text you want to move.

Note: To select text, refer to page 14.

2 Move the mouse I anywhere over the selected text (I becomes ⇗).

3 Press and hold down the left button (⇗ becomes ⛶).

4 Still holding down the left button, move the mouse ⛶ where you want to place the text.

Note: The text will appear where you position the dotted insertion point on your screen.

Getting Started	Edit Your Documents	Smart Editing	Save and Open Your Documents	Using Multiple Documents	Print Your Documents	Change Your Screen Display

Insert Text
Delete Text
Replace Selected Text
Undo Changes

Redo Changes
Change the Case of Text
Move Text
Copy Text

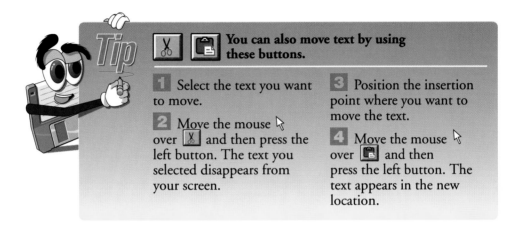

You can also move text by using these buttons.

1 Select the text you want to move.

2 Move the mouse over ✂ and then press the left button. The text you selected disappears from your screen.

3 Position the insertion point where you want to move the text.

4 Move the mouse over 📋 and then press the left button. The text appears in the new location.

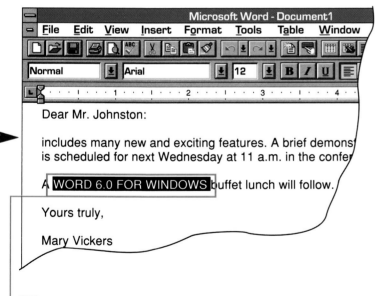

You can cancel the last change you made to your document.

◆ To move the text back to its original location, move the mouse over ↶ and then press the left button.

Note: For more information on canceling changes made to your document, refer to page 30.

5 Release the button and the text moves to the new location.

You can copy text from one location in your document to another. Word "copies" the text and "pastes" the copy in a new location. The original text remains in its place.

Copy Text

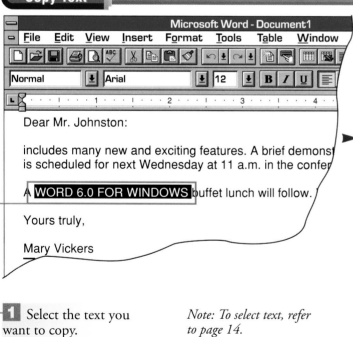

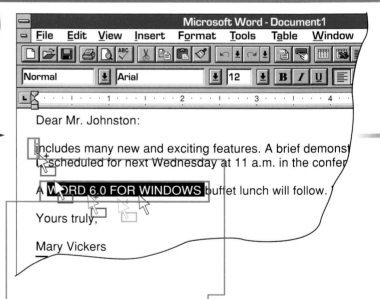

1 Select the text you want to copy.

Note: To select text, refer to page 14.

2 Move the mouse I anywhere over the selected text (I becomes ☝).

3 Press and hold down Ctrl and press and hold down the left button (☝ becomes ☝⁺).

4 Still holding down Ctrl and the left button, drag the mouse ☝⁺ where you want to place the copy.

Note: The text will appear where you position the dotted insertion point on your screen.

Getting
Started

**Edit
Your
Documents**

Smart
Editing

Save and
Open Your
Documents

Using
Multiple
Documents

Print
Your
Documents

Change
Your Screen
Display

Insert Text	Redo Changes
Delete Text	Change the Case of Text
Replace Selected Text	Move Text
Undo Changes	Copy Text

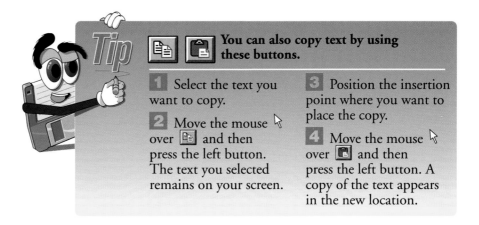

Tip

You can also copy text by using these buttons.

1 Select the text you want to copy.

2 Move the mouse over 📄 and then press the left button. The text you selected remains on your screen.

3 Position the insertion point where you want to place the copy.

4 Move the mouse over 📋 and then press the left button. A copy of the text appears in the new location.

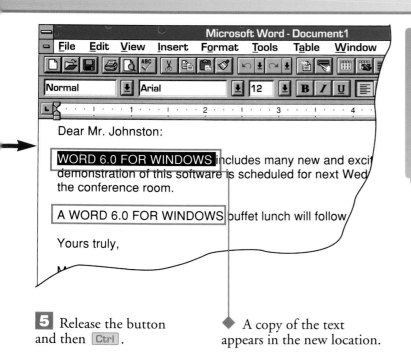

You can cancel the last change you made to your document.

◆ To remove the copy, move the mouse over ↶ and then press the left button.

Note: For more information on canceling changes made to your document, refer to page 30.

5 Release the button and then `Ctrl`.

◆ A copy of the text appears in the new location.

verview

SMART EDITING

Insert the Date

Find Text

Replace Text

Check Spelling

Using AutoCorrect

Using AutoText

Using the Thesaurus

Check Grammar

◆ This chapter will show you Word's powerful editing features. You will learn how to find and replace text and how to check your document for spelling and grammatical errors.

INSERT
THE DATE

You can have Word insert the current date into your document and automatically update it each time you print the document.

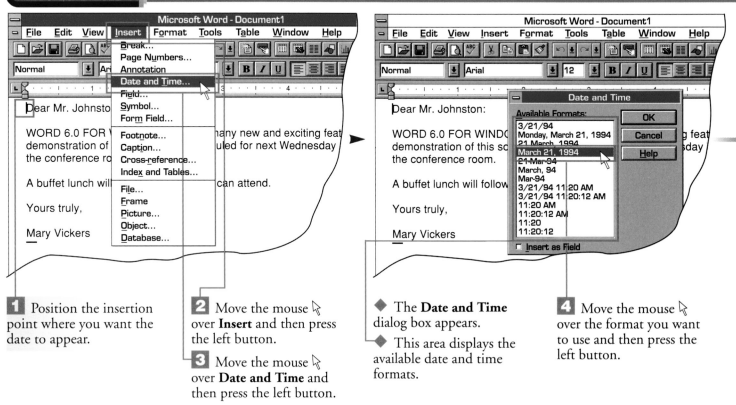

Insert the Date

1 Position the insertion point where you want the date to appear.

2 Move the mouse over **Insert** and then press the left button.

3 Move the mouse over **Date and Time** and then press the left button.

◆ The **Date and Time** dialog box appears.

◆ This area displays the available date and time formats.

4 Move the mouse over the format you want to use and then press the left button.

INTRODUCTION TO WORD

| Getting Started | Edit Your Documents | **Smart Editing** | Save and Open Your Documents | Using Multiple Documents | Print Your Documents | Change Your Screen Display |

Insert the Date   Using AutoCorrect
Find Text   Using AutoText
Replace Text   Using the Thesaurus
Check Spelling   Check Grammar

◆ If Word inserts the wrong date in your document, you must change the date set in your computer.

Note: For information on changing the date set in your computer, refer to your Windows manual.

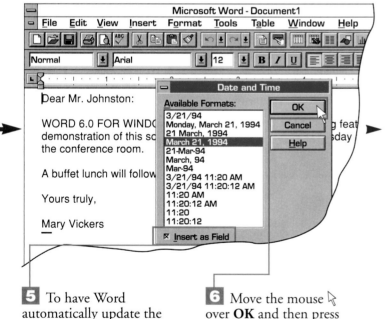

5 To have Word automatically update the date each time you print your document, move the mouse ⬚ over **Insert as Field** and then press the left button (□ becomes ⊠).

6 Move the mouse ⬚ over **OK** and then press the left button.

◆ The date appears in your document.

Note: To delete the date, select the entire date and then press Delete *. To select text, refer to page 14.*

You can use the Find feature to locate a word or phrase in your document.

Find Text

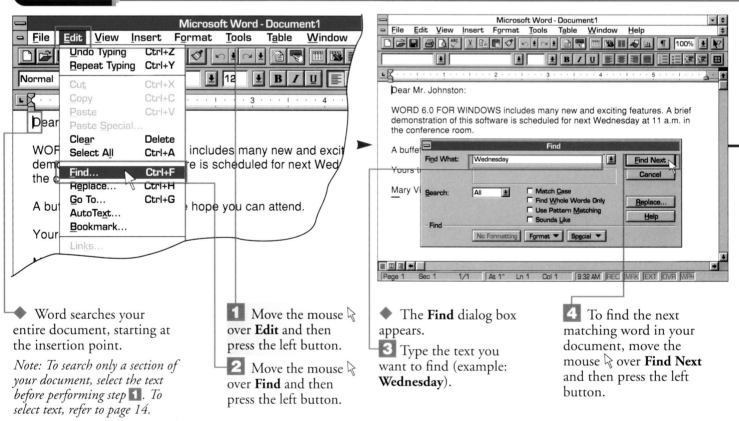

◆ Word searches your entire document, starting at the insertion point.

Note: To search only a section of your document, select the text before performing step 1. To select text, refer to page 14.

1 Move the mouse ⇖ over **Edit** and then press the left button.

2 Move the mouse ⇖ over **Find** and then press the left button.

◆ The **Find** dialog box appears.

3 Type the text you want to find (example: **Wednesday**).

4 To find the next matching word in your document, move the mouse ⇖ over **Find Next** and then press the left button.

Getting
Started

Edit
Your
Documents

Smart
Editing

Save and
Open Your
Documents

Using
Multiple
Documents

Print
Your
Documents

Change
Your Screen
Display

Insert the Date | Using AutoCorrect
Find Text | Using AutoText
Replace Text | Using the Thesaurus
Check Spelling | Check Grammar

FIND OPTIONS

You can use the following options to search for a word in your document.

To select an option, move the mouse over the option and then press the left button (□ becomes ⊠).

⊠ Match Case

◆ This option finds words with exactly matching upper and lower case letters.

*For example, if you search for **place**, Word will not find **Place** or **PLACE**.*

⊠ Find Whole Words Only

◆ This option finds a word only if it is not part of a larger word.

*For example, if you search for **place**, Word will not find common**place**, **place**s or **place**ment.*

⊠ Sounds Like

◆ This option finds words that sound the same but are spelled differently.

*For example, if you search for **there**, Word will also find **their** and **they're**.*

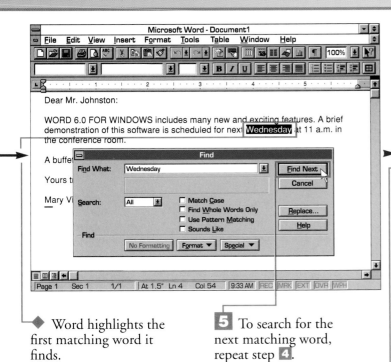

◆ Word highlights the first matching word it finds.

5 To search for the next matching word, repeat step **4**.

Note: To cancel the search at any time, press **Esc**.

◆ This dialog box appears when there are no more matching words in your document.

6 To close the dialog box, move the mouse over **OK** and then press the left button.

7 To close the **Find** dialog box, move the mouse over **Cancel** and then press the left button.

REPLACE TEXT

You can use the Replace feature to locate and replace every occurrence of a word or phrase in your document. This is ideal if you have frequently misspelled a word.

Replace Text in Your Document

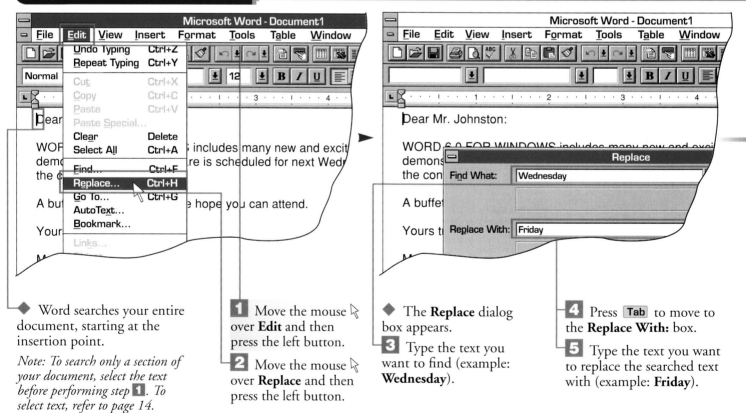

◆ Word searches your entire document, starting at the insertion point.

Note: To search only a section of your document, select the text before performing step 1. To select text, refer to page 14.

1 Move the mouse over **Edit** and then press the left button.

2 Move the mouse over **Replace** and then press the left button.

◆ The **Replace** dialog box appears.

3 Type the text you want to find (example: **Wednesday**).

4 Press **Tab** to move to the **Replace With:** box.

5 Type the text you want to replace the searched text with (example: **Friday**).

Getting
Started

Edit
Your
Documents

Smart
Editing

Save and
Open Your
Documents

Using
Multiple
Documents

Print
Your
Documents

Change
Your Screen
Display

Insert the Date | Using AutoCorrect
Find Text | Using AutoText
Replace Text | Using the Thesaurus
Check Spelling | Check Grammar

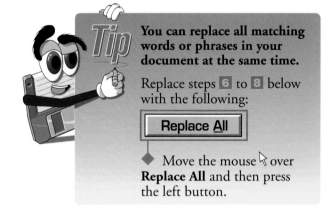

You can replace all matching words or phrases in your document at the same time.

Replace steps **6** to **8** below with the following:

Replace All

◆ Move the mouse ₭ over **Replace All** and then press the left button.

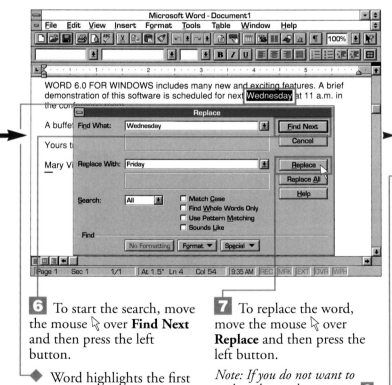

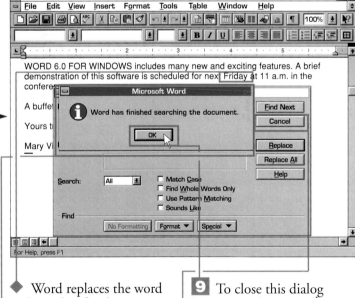

6 To start the search, move the mouse ₭ over **Find Next** and then press the left button.

◆ Word highlights the first matching word it finds.

7 To replace the word, move the mouse ₭ over **Replace** and then press the left button.

Note: If you do not want to replace the word, repeat step **6** *to find the next matching word in your document.*

◆ Word replaces the word and searches for the next matching word.

8 Repeat step **7** for each word you want to replace.

◆ This dialog box appears when there are no more matching words in your document.

9 To close this dialog box, move the mouse ₭ over **OK** and then press the left button.

10 To close the **Replace** dialog box, move the mouse ₭ over **Cancel** or **Close** and then press the left button.

45

You can use Word's spelling feature to find and correct spelling errors in your document.

Word compares every word in your document to words in its dictionary. If a word does not exist in the dictionary, Word considers it misspelled.

Check Spelling

The spell check will find:	Example:
Misspelled words	The girl is six **yeers** old.
Duplicate words	The girl is **six six** years old.
Capitalization errors	**THe** girl is six years old.

The spell check will not find:	Example:
A correctly spelled word used in the wrong context.	The girl is **sit** years old.

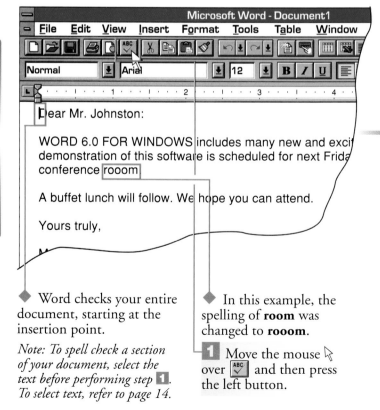

◆ Word checks your entire document, starting at the insertion point.

Note: To spell check a section of your document, select the text before performing step **1**. *To select text, refer to page 14.*

◆ In this example, the spelling of **room** was changed to **rooom**.

1 Move the mouse ⬚ over 🔲 and then press the left button.

Getting
Started

Edit
Your
Documents

**Smart
Editing**

Save and
Open Your
Documents

Using
Multiple
Documents

Print
Your
Documents

Change
Your Screen
Display

Insert the Date
Find Text
Replace Text
Check Spelling

Using AutoCorrect
Using AutoText
Using the Thesaurus
Check Grammar

IMPORTANT!

You should save your document to store it for future use. If you do not save your document, it will disappear when you turn off your computer.
Note: To save your document, refer to page 64.

Once you have stored your document on a disk, save it every ten minutes or so to reduce the possibility of work loss due to system or power failure.

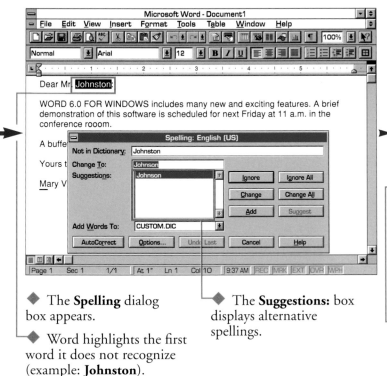

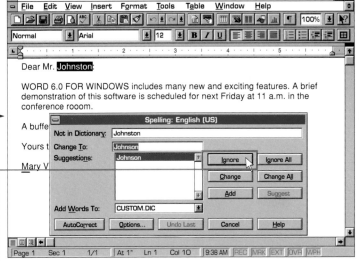

◆ The **Spelling** dialog box appears.

◆ Word highlights the first word it does not recognize (example: **Johnston**).

◆ The **Suggestions:** box displays alternative spellings.

Ignore misspelled word

2 If you do not want to change the spelling of the highlighted word, move the mouse ⮕ over **Ignore** and then press the left button.

Note: To change the spelling of a word and continue the spell check, refer to the next page.

Check Spelling (Continued)

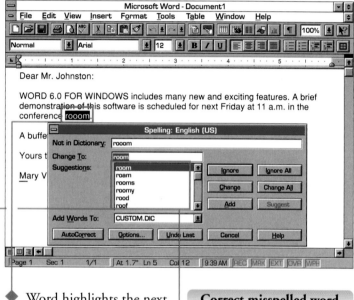

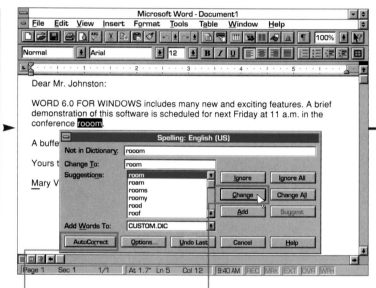

◆ Word highlights the next word it does not recognize (example: **rooom**).

◆ The **Suggestions:** box displays alternative spellings.

Correct misspelled word

3 To select the correct spelling, move the mouse ⇖ over the word you want to use (example: **room**) and then press the left button.

*Note: If the **Suggestions:** box does not display the word you want to use, move the mouse I over the **Change To:** box and then quickly press the left button twice. Type the correct spelling.*

4 To have Word automatically correct the misspelled word every time you type it in your document, move the mouse ⇖ over **AutoCorrect** and then press the left button.

Note: For information on the AutoCorrect feature, refer to page 50.

5 To replace the misspelled word in your document with the correct spelling, move the mouse ⇖ over **Change** and then press the left button.

SPELL CHECK OPTIONS

When Word finds a spelling error in your document, you can choose one of the following options.

Ignore Keeps the current spelling of the word in this instance only.

Change Replaces the misspelled word in your document with the text in the **Change To:** box.

Add Adds the word to the custom dictionary. The spell check then considers the word correctly spelled in all future spell checks.

Ignore All Keeps the current spelling of the word and skips every occurrence in the document.

Change All Replaces the misspelled word with the text in the **Change To:** box every time it appears in your document.

| Getting Started | Edit Your Documents | Smart Editing | Save and Open Your Documents | Using Multiple Documents | Print Your Documents | Change Your Screen Display |

Insert the Date   Using AutoCorrect
Find Text   Using AutoText
Replace Text   Using the Thesaurus
Check Spelling   Check Grammar

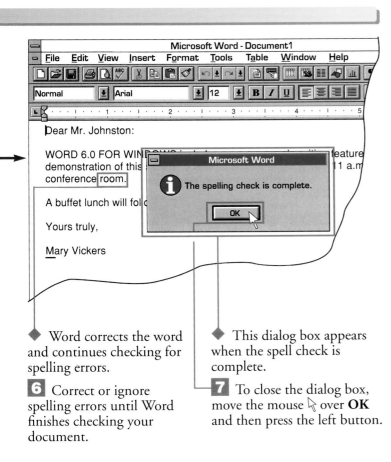

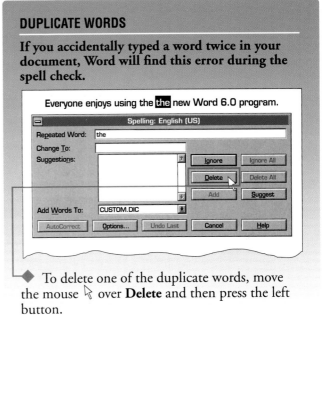

DUPLICATE WORDS

If you accidentally typed a word twice in your document, Word will find this error during the spell check.

◆ Word corrects the word and continues checking for spelling errors.

6 Correct or ignore spelling errors until Word finishes checking your document.

◆ This dialog box appears when the spell check is complete.

7 To close the dialog box, move the mouse ⤷ over **OK** and then press the left button.

◆ To delete one of the duplicate words, move the mouse ⤷ over **Delete** and then press the left button.

To cancel the spell check at any time, move the mouse ⤷ over Close or Cancel and then press the left button.

USING AUTOCORRECT

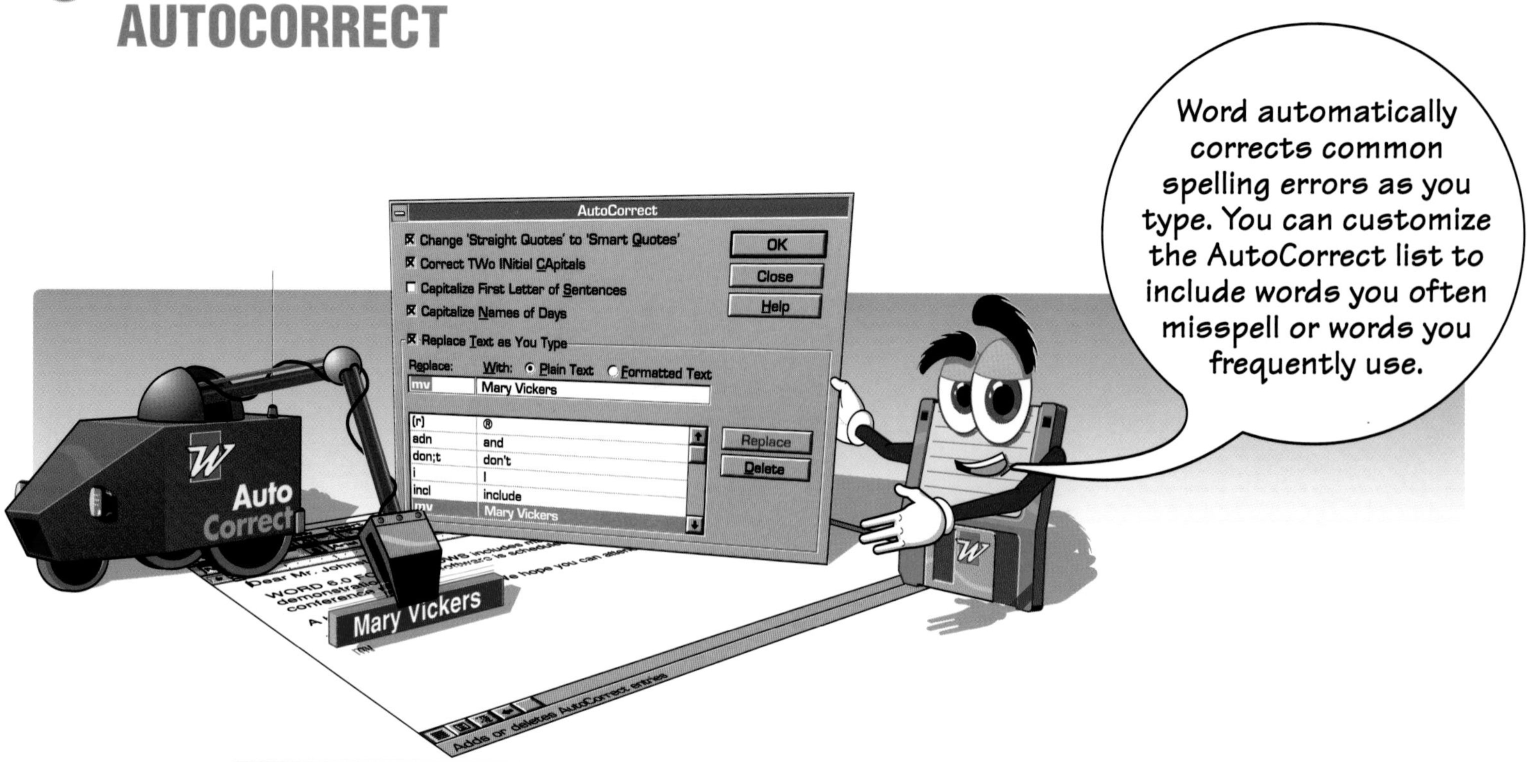

Word automatically corrects common spelling errors as you type. You can customize the AutoCorrect list to include words you often misspell or words you frequently use.
AutoCorrect
Change 'Straight Quotes' to 'Smart Quotes'
Correct TWo INitial CApitals
Capitalize First Letter of Sentences
Capitalize Names of Days
Replace Text as You Type
OK
Close
Help
Replace
Delete
Mary Vickers
Auto Correct

Add Text to AutoCorrect

If you type one of the following words and then press the Spacebar, Word will automatically change the word for you.

Text You Type	Replace With
(r)	®
adn	and
don;t	don't
i	I
incl	include
occurence	occurrence
recieve	receive
seperate	separate
teh	the

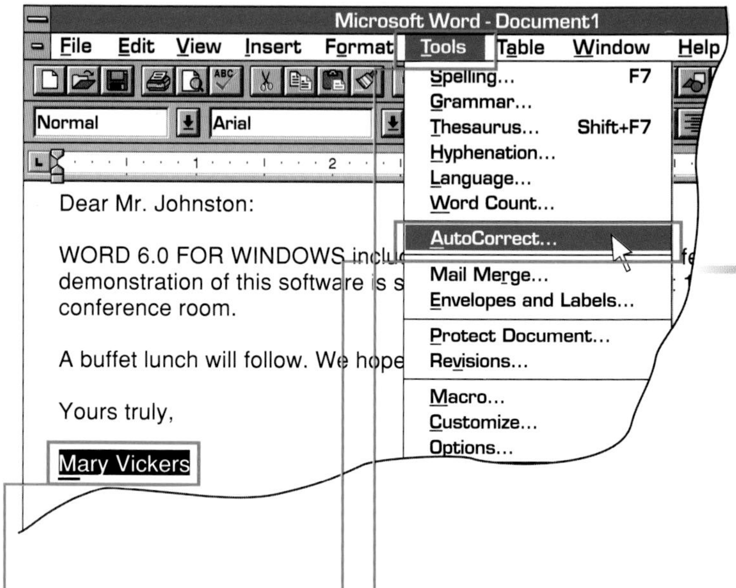

Microsoft Word - Document1
File Edit View Insert Format Tools Table Window Help
Spelling... F7
Grammar...
Thesaurus... Shift+F7
Hyphenation...
Language...
Word Count...
AutoCorrect...
Mail Merge...
Envelopes and Labels...
Protect Document...
Revisions...
Macro...
Customize...
Options...
Dear Mr. Johnston:
A buffet lunch will follow. We hope
Yours truly,
Mary Vickers

1 Select the text you want Word to automatically place in your documents.

Note: To select text, refer to page 14.

2 Move the mouse ↖ over **Tools** and then press the left button.

3 Move the mouse ↖ over **AutoCorrect** and then press the left button.

INTRODUCTION TO WORD

| Getting Started | Edit Your Documents | Smart Editing | Save and Open Your Documents | Using Multiple Documents | Print Your Documents | Change Your Screen Display |

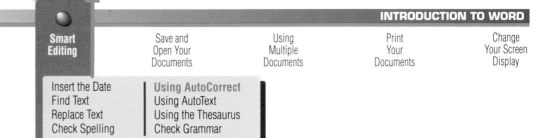

Insert the Date
Find Text
Replace Text
Check Spelling

Using AutoCorrect
Using AutoText
Using the Thesaurus
Check Grammar

USING AUTOCORRECT TO INSERT TEXT

After you add text to the AutoCorrect list, Word will automatically change the text each time you type it in your document.

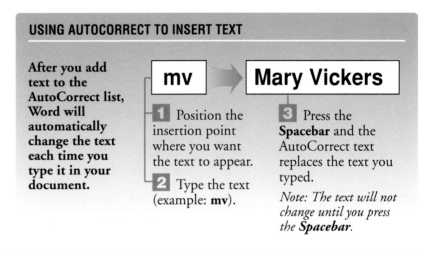

1 Position the insertion point where you want the text to appear.

2 Type the text (example: **mv**).

3 Press the **Spacebar** and the AutoCorrect text replaces the text you typed.

*Note: The text will not change until you press the **Spacebar**.*

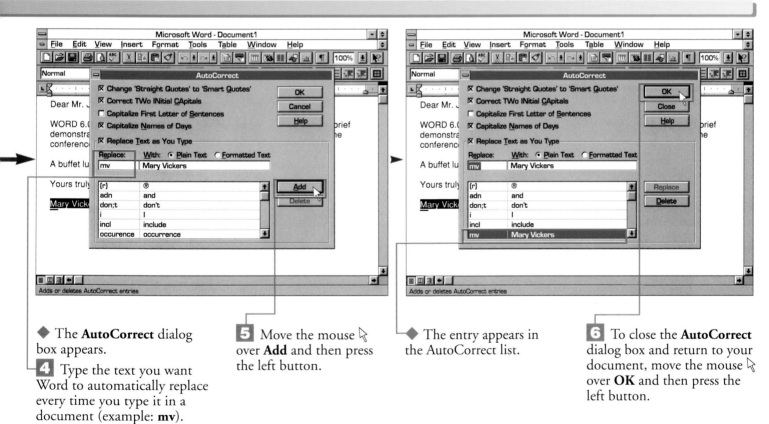

◆ The **AutoCorrect** dialog box appears.

4 Type the text you want Word to automatically replace every time you type it in a document (example: **mv**).

Note: This text cannot contain any spaces. Also, do not use a real word.

5 Move the mouse over **Add** and then press the left button.

◆ The entry appears in the AutoCorrect list.

6 To close the **AutoCorrect** dialog box and return to your document, move the mouse over **OK** and then press the left button.

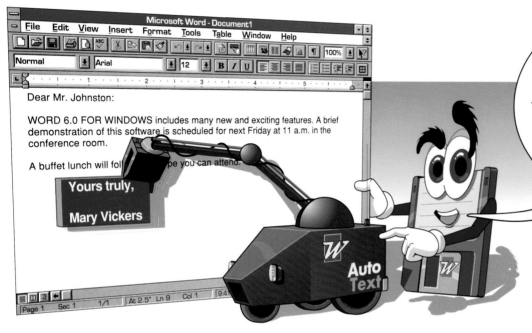

The AutoText feature lets you store frequently used words, phrases and sentences. You can then insert them into your document by typing an abbreviated version of the text.

 **Add Text to AutoText**

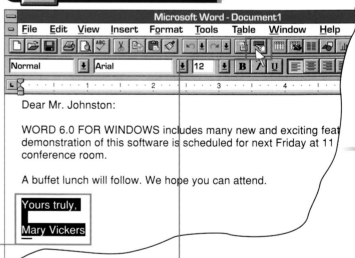

1 Select the text you want to appear in your document each time you type its abbreviated name.

Note: To select text, refer to page 14.

2 Move the mouse ↕ over and then press the left button.

INTRODUCTION TO WORD

| Getting Started | Edit Your Documents | Smart Editing | Save and Open Your Documents | Using Multiple Documents | Print Your Documents | Change Your Screen Display |

The AutoText and AutoCorrect features both insert text into your document. However, there are two distinct differences:

Note: For information on the AutoCorrect feature, refer to page 50.

AUTOTEXT

◆ Use AutoText to insert groups of text or to insert text you use occasionally.

◆ Word inserts the text only when you instruct it to do so.

AUTOCORRECT

◆ Use AutoCorrect to correct your most common spelling errors or to insert text you use frequently (i.e., every day).

◆ Word automatically inserts the text as you type.

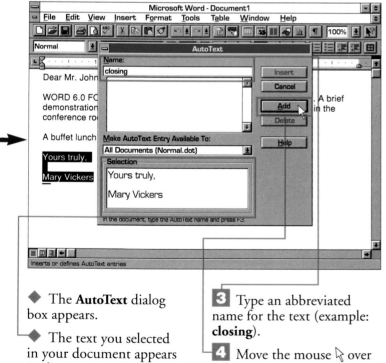

◆ The **AutoText** dialog box appears.

◆ The text you selected in your document appears in the **Selection** box.

3 Type an abbreviated name for the text (example: **closing**).

4 Move the mouse ⍐ over **Add** and then press the left button.

USING AUTOTEXT

After you add text to the AutoText list, you can insert the text into your document.

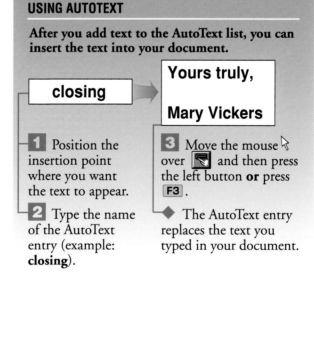

1 Position the insertion point where you want the text to appear.

2 Type the name of the AutoText entry (example: **closing**).

3 Move the mouse ⍐ over 🖎 and then press the left button **or** press **F3**.

◆ The AutoText entry replaces the text you typed in your document.

USING THE THESAURUS

To add variety to your writing, you can use the Thesaurus. This feature enables you to replace a word in your document with one that is more suitable.

Using the Thesaurus

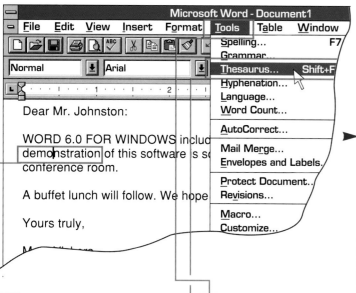

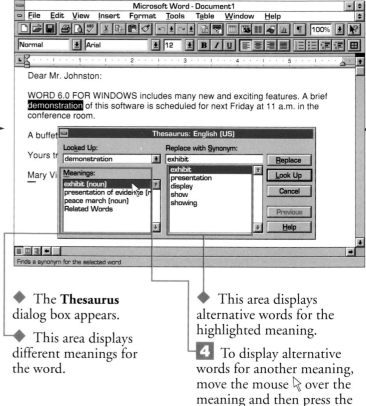

1 Move the mouse I anywhere over the word you want to look up (example: **demonstration**) and then press the left button.

2 Move the mouse ⬡ over **Tools** and then press the left button.

3 Move the mouse ⬡ over **Thesaurus** and then press the left button.

◆ The **Thesaurus** dialog box appears.

◆ This area displays different meanings for the word.

◆ This area displays alternative words for the highlighted meaning.

4 To display alternative words for another meaning, move the mouse ⬡ over the meaning and then press the left button.

| Getting Started | Edit Your Documents | Smart Editing | Save and Open Your Documents | Using Multiple Documents | Print Your Documents | Change Your Screen Display |

Insert the Date · Using AutoCorrect
Find Text · Using AutoText
Replace Text · **Using the Thesaurus**
Check Spelling · Check Grammar

LOOK UP A WORD

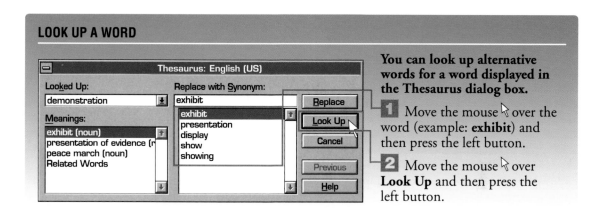

You can look up alternative words for a word displayed in the Thesaurus dialog box.

1 Move the mouse ↖ over the word (example: **exhibit**) and then press the left button.

2 Move the mouse ↖ over **Look Up** and then press the left button.

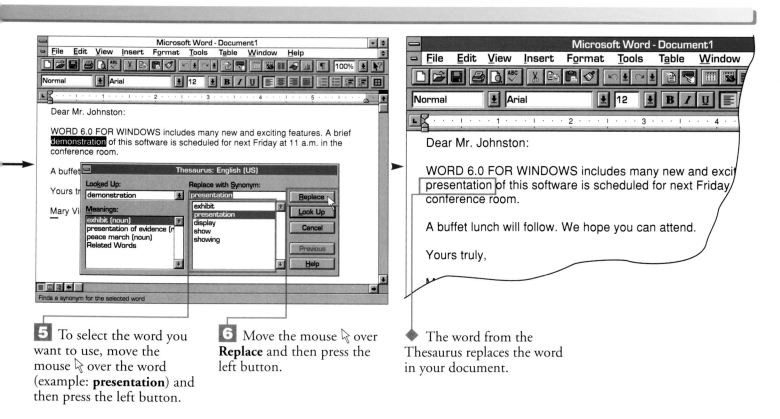

5 To select the word you want to use, move the mouse ↖ over the word (example: **presentation**) and then press the left button.

6 Move the mouse ↖ over **Replace** and then press the left button.

◆ The word from the Thesaurus replaces the word in your document.

You can use Word's grammar feature to look for and correct spelling and grammatical errors. This will improve the readability of your document.

Check Grammar and Spelling

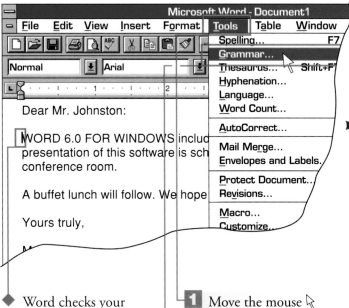

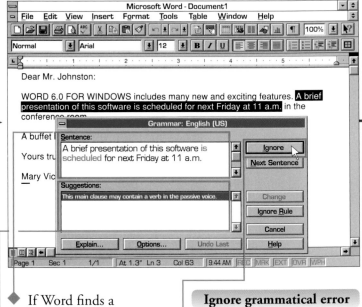

◆ Word checks your entire document, starting at the insertion point.

Note: To check only a section of your document, select the text before performing step 1. To select text, refer to page 14.

1 Move the mouse ⬚ over **Tools** and then press the left button.

2 Move the mouse ⬚ over **Grammar** and then press the left button.

◆ If Word finds a grammatical error, the **Grammar** dialog box appears. This area displays the sentence containing the error.

◆ This area tells you what is wrong with the sentence and may offer a suggestion to correct the error.

Ignore grammatical error

3 If you want to ignore the error and continue checking your document, move the mouse ⬚ over **Ignore** and then press the left button.

INTRODUCTION TO WORD

Getting
Started

Edit
Your
Documents

Smart
Editing

Save and
Open Your
Documents

Using
Multiple
Documents

Print
Your
Documents

Change
Your Screen
Display

Insert the Date   Using AutoCorrect
Find Text   Using AutoText
Replace Text   Using the Thesaurus
Check Spelling   **Check Grammar**

If Word finds a spelling
error in your document, the
Spelling dialog box appears.

For information on using
the **Spelling** dialog box to
correct a misspelled word,
refer to pages 46 to 49.

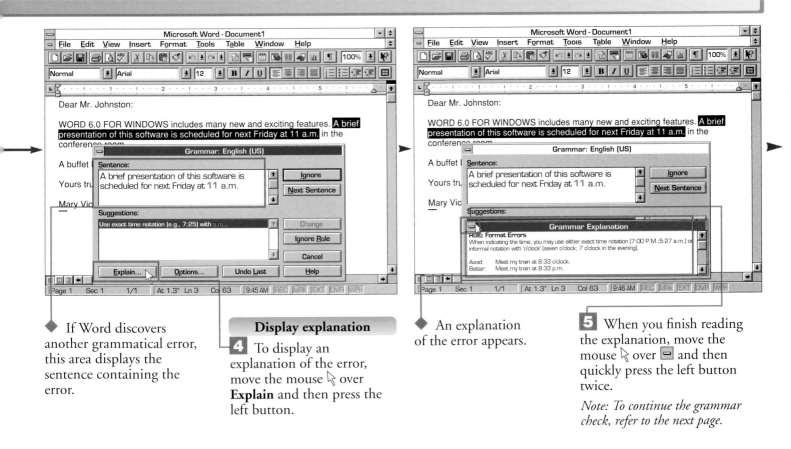

◆ If Word discovers
another grammatical error,
this area displays the
sentence containing the
error.

Display explanation

4 To display an
explanation of the error,
move the mouse ⌖ over
Explain and then press the
left button.

◆ An explanation
of the error appears.

5 When you finish reading
the explanation, move the
mouse ⌖ over ⊟ and then
quickly press the left button
twice.

*Note: To continue the grammar
check, refer to the next page.*

57

CHECK GRAMMAR

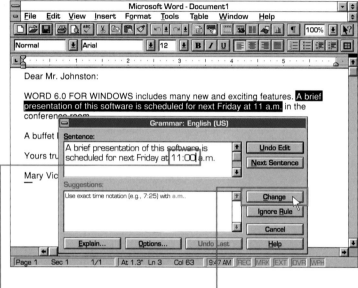

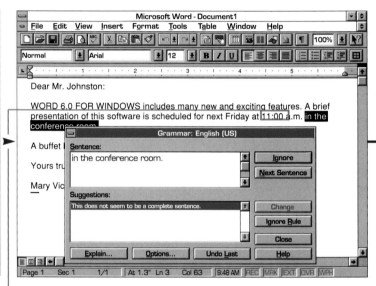

Correct grammatical error

6 You can edit the text as you would any text in your document (example: change **11** to **11:00**).

Note: To insert and delete text, refer to pages 22 to 29.

7 Move the mouse ⌖ over **Change** and then press the left button.

◆ The change appears in your document and Word continues checking for grammatical and spelling errors.

8 Correct or ignore grammatical errors until Word finishes checking your document.

INTRODUCTION TO WORD

| Getting Started | Edit Your Documents | Smart Editing | Save and Open Your Documents | Using Multiple Documents | Print Your Documents | Change Your Screen Display |

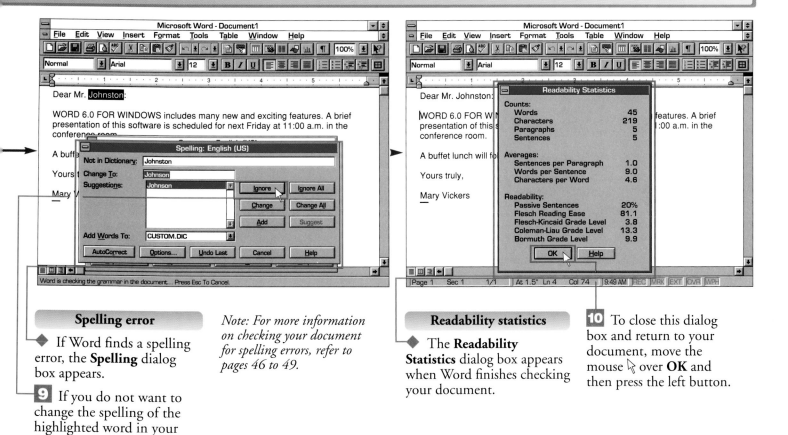

Spelling error

◆ If Word finds a spelling error, the **Spelling** dialog box appears.

9 If you do not want to change the spelling of the highlighted word in your document, move the mouse ▷ over **Ignore** and then press the left button.

Note: For more information on checking your document for spelling errors, refer to pages 46 to 49.

Readability statistics

◆ The **Readability Statistics** dialog box appears when Word finishes checking your document.

10 To close this dialog box and return to your document, move the mouse ▷ over **OK** and then press the left button.

To cancel the grammar check at any time, move the mouse ▷ over Cancel or Close and then press the left button.

Overview

SAVE AND OPEN YOUR DOCUMENTS

Introduction

Save a New Document

Save a Document to a Diskette

Password Protect a Document

Exit Word

Open a Document

Find a Document

◆ This chapter will show you how to save your document for future use and how to exit Word. You will also learn how to find and open your documents.

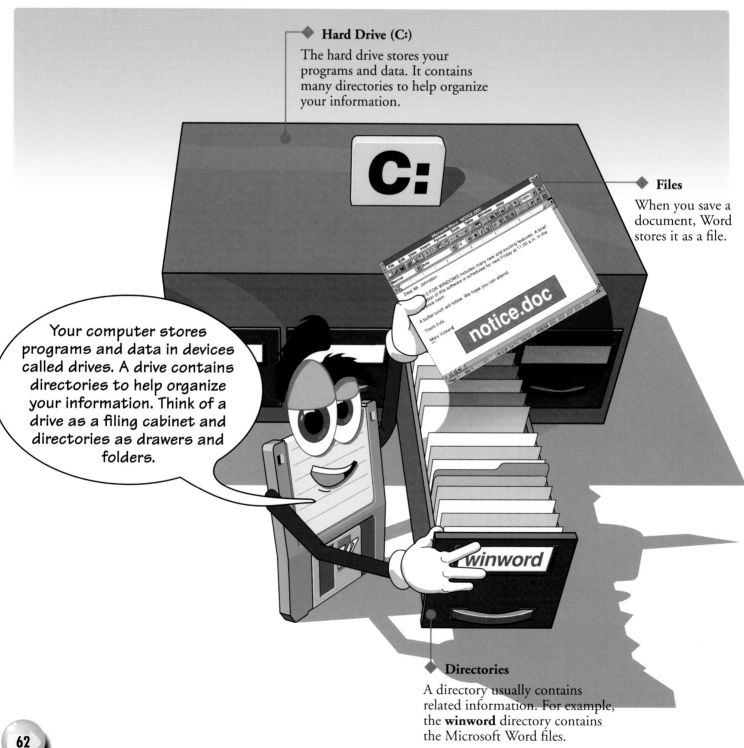

Hard Drive (C:)

The hard drive stores your programs and data. It contains many directories to help organize your information.

Files

When you save a document, Word stores it as a file.

notice.doc

Your computer stores programs and data in devices called drives. A drive contains directories to help organize your information. Think of a drive as a filing cabinet and directories as drawers and folders.

Directories

A directory usually contains related information. For example, the **winword** directory contains the Microsoft Word files.

INTRODUCTION TO WORD

Getting
Started

Edit
Your
Documents

Smart
Editing

**Save and
Open Your
Documents**

Using
Multiple
Documents

Print
Your
Documents

Change
Your Screen
Display

Most computers have one hard drive and one or two floppy drives to store information.

Hard drive (C:)

◆ The hard drive magnetically stores information inside your computer. It is called drive **C**.

*Note: Your computer may be set up to have additional hard drives (example: drive **D**).*

Floppy drives (A: and B:)

◆ A floppy drive stores information on removable diskettes (or floppy disks). A diskette operates slower and stores less data than a hard drive.

Diskettes are used to:

• Load new programs.
• Store backup copies of data.
• Transfer data to other computers.

If your computer has only one floppy drive, it is called drive **A**.

If your computer has two floppy drives, the second drive is called drive **B**.

SAVE A NEW DOCUMENT

You should save your document to store it for future use. This enables you to later retrieve the document for reviewing or editing purposes.

 Save a New Document

When you save a document for the first time, you must give it a name. A file name consists of two parts: a name and an extension. You must separate these parts with a period.

notice . doc

◆ **Name**

The name should describe the contents of a file. It can have up to eight characters.

◆ **Period**

A period must separate the name and the extension.

◆ **Extension**

The extension describes the type of information a file contains. It can have up to three characters.

Note: doc stands for document.

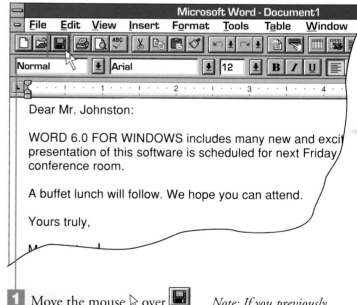

Dear Mr. Johnston:

WORD 6.0 FOR WINDOWS includes many new and exciting presentation of this software is scheduled for next Friday conference room.

A buffet lunch will follow. We hope you can attend.

Yours truly,

1 Move the mouse ⬚ over ⊟ and then press the left button.

*Note: If you previously saved your document, the **Save As** dialog box will not appear since you have already named the file.*

64

Getting Started

Edit Your Documents

Smart Editing

Save and Open Your Documents

Using Multiple Documents

Print Your Documents

Change Your Screen Display

Introduction
Save a New Document
Save a Document to a Diskette
Password Protect a Document

Exit Word
Open a Document
Find a Document

Rules for Naming a File

A file name *can* contain the following characters:

◆ The letters A to Z, upper or lower case

◆ The numbers 0 to 9

◆ The symbols
_ ^ $ ~ ! # % & { } @ ( )

A file name *cannot* contain the following characters:

◆ A comma (,)

◆ A blank space

◆ The symbols
* ? ; [ ] + = \ / : < >

Each file in a directory must have a unique name.

letter.doc
note1q.doc
test.doc
training.doc

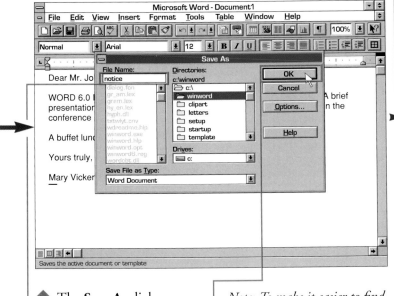

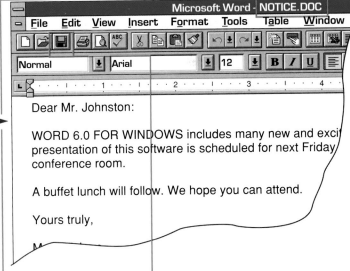

◆ The **Save As** dialog box appears.

2 Type a name for your document (example: **notice**).

*Note: To make it easier to find your document later on, do not type an extension. Word will then automatically add the **doc** extension to the file name.*

3 Move the mouse ⌖ over **OK** and then press the left button.

◆ Word saves your document and displays its name at the top of your screen.

◆ You should save your document every 10 to 15 minutes to store any changes made since the last time you saved the document. To save changes, move the mouse ⌖ over 🖫 and then press the left button.

SAVE A DOCUMENT TO A DISKETTE

As a precaution, you should save your document to a diskette. You can then use this copy to replace any lost data if your hard drive fails or you accidentally erase the file.

Save a Document to a Diskette

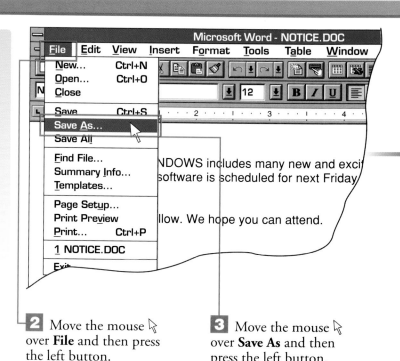

1 Insert a diskette into a floppy drive (example: **drive a:**).

2 Move the mouse ⬉ over **File** and then press the left button.

3 Move the mouse ⬉ over **Save As** and then press the left button.

INTRODUCTION TO WORD

| Getting Started | Edit Your Documents | Smart Editing | Save and Open Your Documents | Using Multiple Documents | Print Your Documents | Change Your Screen Display |

Tip

◆ After you save your document, you may want to make additional changes. You can use the **Save As** command to save your revised document with a new name. This way you still have a copy of the old version in case you regret any changes you make.

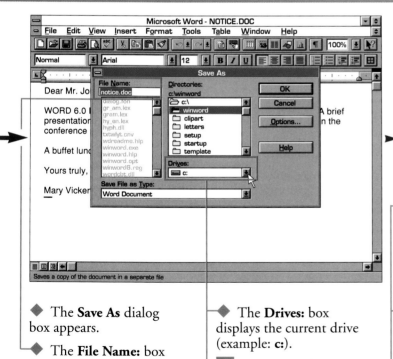

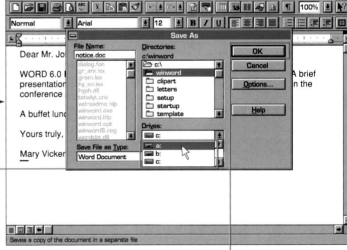

◆ The **Save As** dialog box appears.

◆ The **File Name:** box displays the current file name (example: **notice.doc**).

Note: To save your document with a different name, type a new name.

◆ The **Drives:** box displays the current drive (example: **c:**).

4 To save the file to a different drive, move the mouse ⇧ over ⬇ in the **Drives:** box and then press the left button.

◆ A list of the available drives for your computer appears.

5 Move the mouse ⇧ over the drive you want to use (example: **a:**) and then press the left button.

6 To save your document to the diskette, move the mouse ⇧ over **OK** and then press the left button.

67

PASSWORD PROTECT A DOCUMENT

You can stop other people from reading and making changes to your document by protecting it with a password.

Password Protect a Document

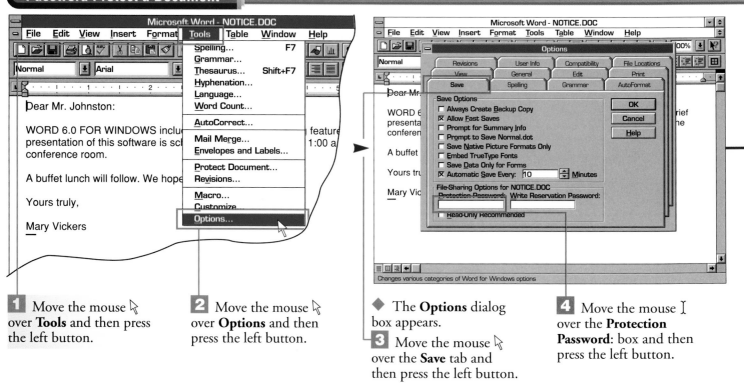

1 Move the mouse over **Tools** and then press the left button.

2 Move the mouse over **Options** and then press the left button.

◆ The **Options** dialog box appears.

3 Move the mouse over the **Save** tab and then press the left button.

4 Move the mouse over the **Protection Password:** box and then press the left button.

INTRODUCTION TO WORD

| Getting Started | Edit Your Documents | Smart Editing | **Save and Open Your Documents** | Using Multiple Documents | Print Your Documents | Change Your Screen Display |

Introduction
Save a New Document
Save a Document to a Diskette
Password Protect a Document

Exit Word
Open a Document
Find a Document

IMPORTANT!

Make sure you write down your password and store it in a safe place. You will not be able to open your document without typing the correct password.

◆ Passwords are case sensitive. For example, if your password is **Car** you cannot type **car** or **CAR** to open the file.

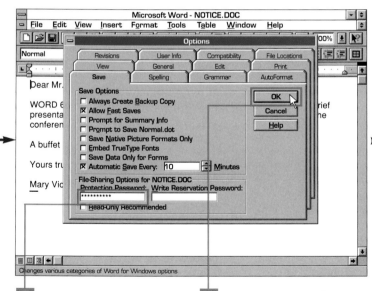

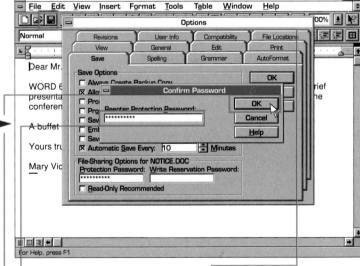

5 Type a password. Word displays an asterisk (*) for each character you type.

Note: A password can contain up to 15 characters and can include letters, numbers, symbols and spaces.

6 Move the mouse ⌖ over **OK** and then press the left button.

◆ The **Confirm Password** dialog box appears.

7 To confirm your password, retype it.

8 Move the mouse ⌖ over **OK** and then press the left button.

9 You must save your document to save the password. To do so, move the mouse ⌖ over 🖫 and then press the left button.

EXIT
WORD

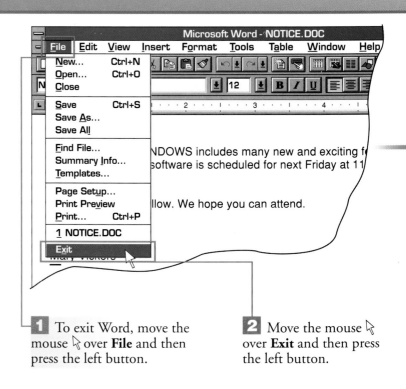

When you finish using Word, you can exit the program to return to the Windows Program Manager.

Exit Word

IMPORTANT!

You must always exit Word and Windows before turning off your computer. Failure to do so may result in damage or loss of valuable information.

Microsoft Word - NOTICE.DOC

| File | Edit | View | Insert | Format | Tools | Table | Window | Help |

New...   Ctrl+N
Open...   Ctrl+O
Close

Save   Ctrl+S
Save As...
Save All

Find File...
Summary Info...
Templates...

Page Setup...
Print Preview
Print...   Ctrl+P

1 NOTICE.DOC

Exit

...NDOWS includes many new and exciting f...
...software is scheduled for next Friday at 1...

...llow. We hope you can attend.

1 To exit Word, move the mouse over **File** and then press the left button.

2 Move the mouse over **Exit** and then press the left button.

Getting
Started

Edit
Your
Documents

Smart
Editing

**Save and
Open Your
Documents**

Using
Multiple
Documents

Print
Your
Documents

Change
Your Screen
Display

Introduction
Save a New Document
Save a Document to a Diskette
Password Protect a Document

Exit Word
Open a Document
Find a Document

This dialog box appears when exiting Word if you have not saved changes made to your document.

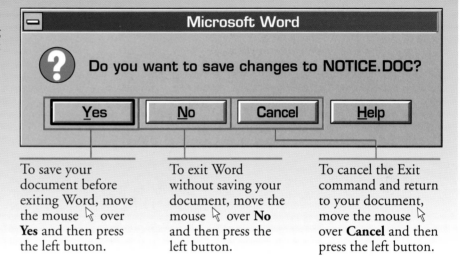

Microsoft Word

Do you want to save changes to NOTICE.DOC?

Yes   No   Cancel   Help

To save your document before exiting Word, move the mouse ⇧ over **Yes** and then press the left button.

To exit Word without saving your document, move the mouse ⇧ over **No** and then press the left button.

To cancel the Exit command and return to your document, move the mouse ⇧ over **Cancel** and then press the left button.

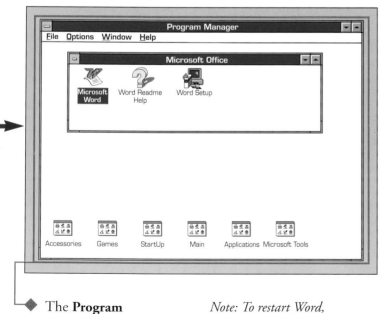

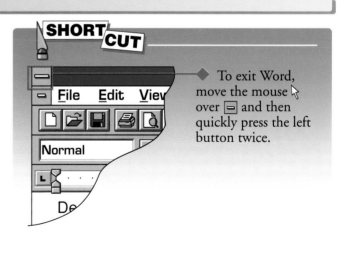

SHORT CUT

◆ To exit Word, move the mouse ⇧ over ⊟ and then quickly press the left button twice.

◆ The **Program Manager** window appears.

Note: To restart Word, refer to page 6.

OPEN A DOCUMENT

You can open a saved document and display it on your screen. This enables you to review and edit the document.

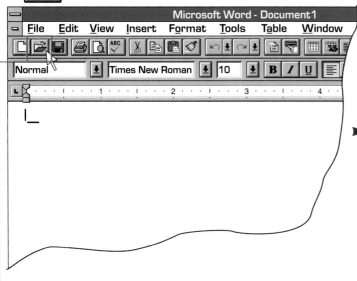

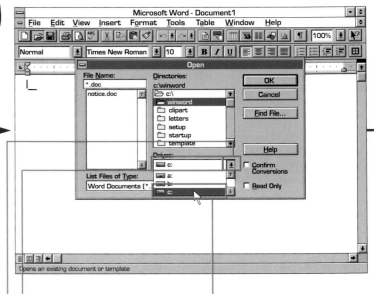

1 Move the mouse ⤢ over 📂 and then press the left button.

◆ The **Open** dialog box appears.

◆ The **Drives:** box displays the current drive (example: **c:**).

2 To open a file on another drive, move the mouse ⤢ over ⬇ in the **Drives:** box and then press the left button.

◆ A list of the available drives for your computer appears.

3 Move the mouse ⤢ over the drive containing the file you want to open and then press the left button.

Getting Started   Edit Your Documents   Smart Editing   **Save and Open Your Documents**   Using Multiple Documents   Print Your Documents   Change Your Screen Display

Introduction
Save a New Document
Save a Document to a Diskette
Password Protect a Document

Exit Word
Open a Document
Find a Document

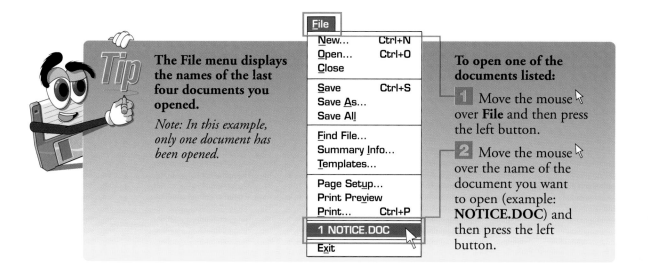

The File menu displays the names of the last four documents you opened.

Note: In this example, only one document has been opened.

To open one of the documents listed:

1 Move the mouse over **File** and then press the left button.

2 Move the mouse over the name of the document you want to open (example: **NOTICE.DOC**) and then press the left button.

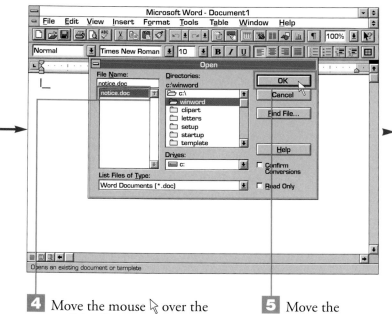

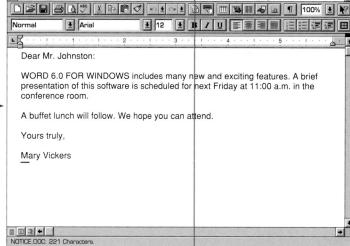

4 Move the mouse over the name of the file you want to open (example: **notice.doc**) and then press the left button.

Note: If you cannot remember the name or location of the file you want to open, refer to pages 74 to 77 to find the file.

5 Move the mouse over **OK** and then press the left button.

◆ Word opens the document and displays it on your screen. You can now make changes to the document.

◆ The name of the document appears at the top of your screen.

FIND A
DOCUMENT

If you cannot remember the location of the document you want to open, you can use the Find File feature to search for the document.

Find a Document - Search by Name

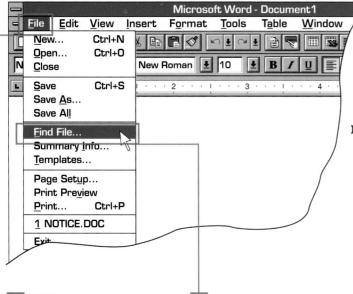

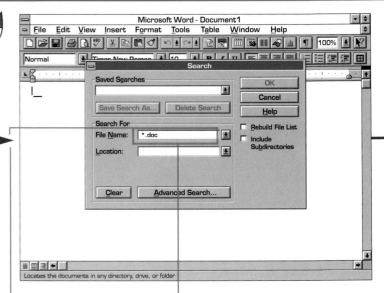

1 Move the mouse ⌖ over **File** and then press the left button.

2 Move the mouse ⌖ over **Find File** and then press the left button.

◆ The **Search** dialog box appears.

*Note: If the **Find File** dialog box appears, see IMPORTANT at the top of page 75.*

3 Move the mouse I over the box beside **File Name:** and then press the left button.

4 To search for a file with a particular extension, type *. followed by the extension. For example, type *.**doc** to find all files with the **doc** extension.

◆ To search for a file that begins with a particular sequence of letters, type the letters followed by the *.* characters. For example, type **n**.* to find all files starting with **n**.

74

| Getting Started | Edit Your Documents | Smart Editing | **Save and Open Your Documents** | Using Multiple Documents | Print Your Documents | Change Your Screen Display |

Introduction
Save a New Document
Save a Document to a Diskette
Password Protect a Document

Exit Word
Open a Document
Find a Document

IMPORTANT!

The Find File dialog box appears if you have previously used the Find File command. To display the Search dialog box and start a new search:

1 Move the mouse over **Search** and then press the left button. The **Search** dialog box appears.

| **Search...** |

2 To clear all the options you set for your last search, move the mouse over **Clear** and then press the left button.

| **Clear** |

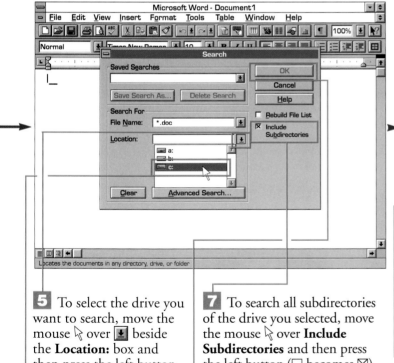

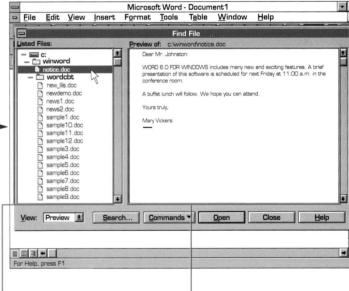

5 To select the drive you want to search, move the mouse over ⬇ beside the **Location:** box and then press the left button.

6 Move the mouse over the drive (example: **c:**) and then press the left button.

7 To search all subdirectories of the drive you selected, move the mouse over **Include Subdirectories** and then press the left button (☐ becomes ☒).

8 To start the search, move the mouse over **OK** and then press the left button.

◆ After a few moments the **Find File** dialog box appears.

◆ This area displays the names of the files Word found.

◆ This area displays the contents of the highlighted file.

9 To display the contents of another file, press ⬇ or ⬆ on your keyboard.

10 To open a file, move the mouse over its name and then quickly press the left button twice.

FIND A DOCUMENT

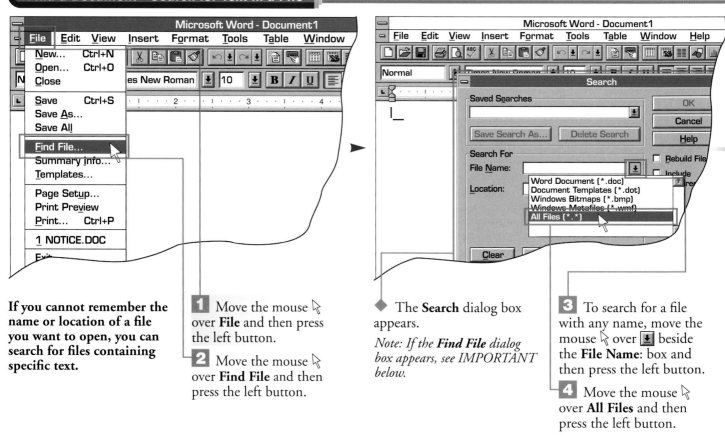

If you cannot remember the name or location of a file you want to open, you can search for files containing specific text.

1 Move the mouse ⌖ over **File** and then press the left button.

2 Move the mouse ⌖ over **Find File** and then press the left button.

◆ The **Search** dialog box appears.

*Note: If the **Find File** dialog box appears, see IMPORTANT below.*

3 To search for a file with any name, move the mouse ⌖ over ⬇ beside the **File Name:** box and then press the left button.

4 Move the mouse ⌖ over **All Files** and then press the left button.

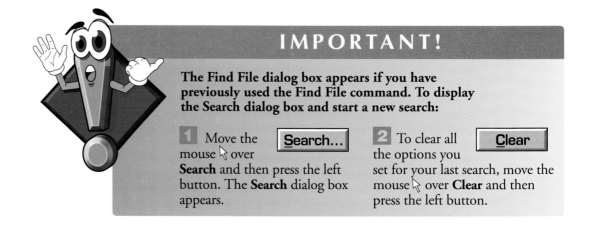

IMPORTANT!

The Find File dialog box appears if you have previously used the Find File command. To display the Search dialog box and start a new search:

1 Move the mouse ⌖ over **Search** and then press the left button. The **Search** dialog box appears.

2 To clear all the options you set for your last search, move the mouse ⌖ over **Clear** and then press the left button.

INTRODUCTION TO WORD

| Getting Started | Edit Your Documents | Smart Editing | Save and Open Your Documents | Using Multiple Documents | Print Your Documents | Change Your Screen Display |

Introduction
Save a New Document
Save a Document to a Diskette
Password Protect a Document

Exit Word
Open a Document
Find a Document

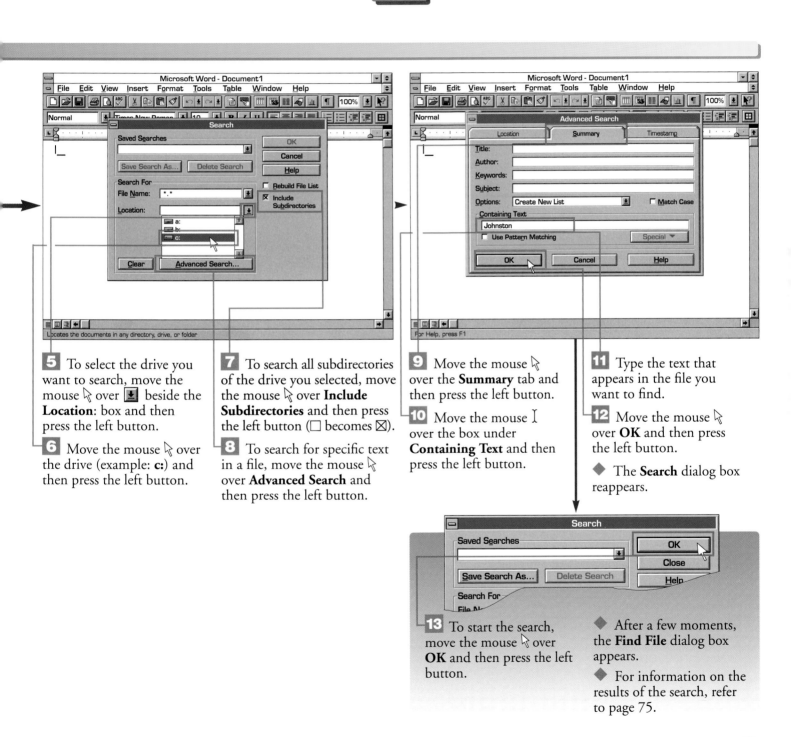

5 To select the drive you want to search, move the mouse ⬚ over ⬚ beside the **Location:** box and then press the left button.

6 Move the mouse ⬚ over the drive (example: **c:**) and then press the left button.

7 To search all subdirectories of the drive you selected, move the mouse ⬚ over **Include Subdirectories** and then press the left button (☐ becomes ☒).

8 To search for specific text in a file, move the mouse ⬚ over **Advanced Search** and then press the left button.

9 Move the mouse ⬚ over the **Summary** tab and then press the left button.

10 Move the mouse I over the box under **Containing Text** and then press the left button.

11 Type the text that appears in the file you want to find.

12 Move the mouse ⬚ over **OK** and then press the left button.

◆ The **Search** dialog box reappears.

13 To start the search, move the mouse ⬚ over **OK** and then press the left button.

◆ After a few moments, the **Find File** dialog box appears.

◆ For information on the results of the search, refer to page 75.

Overview

USING MULTIPLE DOCUMENTS

Create a New Document

Arrange Open Documents

Copy or Move Text Between Documents

Maximize a Document

Switch Between Documents

Close a Document

◆ This chapter will show you how to work with more than one document at a time. You will learn how to arrange documents on your screen and how to move between them.

You can create a document to start a new letter, report or memo. Word lets you have several documents open at the same time.

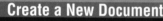

Create a New Document

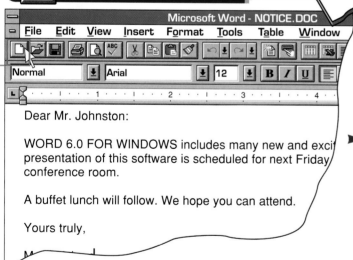

Dear Mr. Johnston:

WORD 6.0 FOR WINDOWS includes many new and excit presentation of this software is scheduled for next Friday conference room.

A buffet lunch will follow. We hope you can attend.

Yours truly,

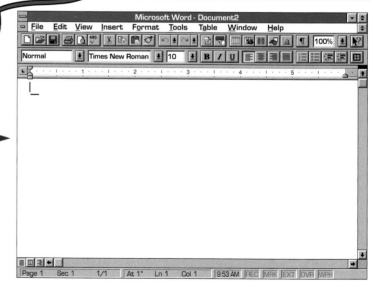

1 Move the mouse ⟨ over □ and then press the left button.

◆ A new document appears.

Note: The previous document is now hidden behind the new document.

◆ Think of each document as a separate piece of paper. When you create a document, you are placing a new piece of paper on your screen.

Getting
Started

Edit
Your
Documents

Smart
Editing

Save and
Open Your
Documents

**Using
Multiple
Documents**

Print
Your
Documents

Change
Your Screen
Display

Create a New Document
Arrange Open Documents
Copy or Move Text Between Documents
Maximize a Document
Switch Between Documents
Close a Document

If you have several documents open, some of them may be hidden from view. To view the contents of each document, you can use the Arrange All command.

Arrange Open Documents

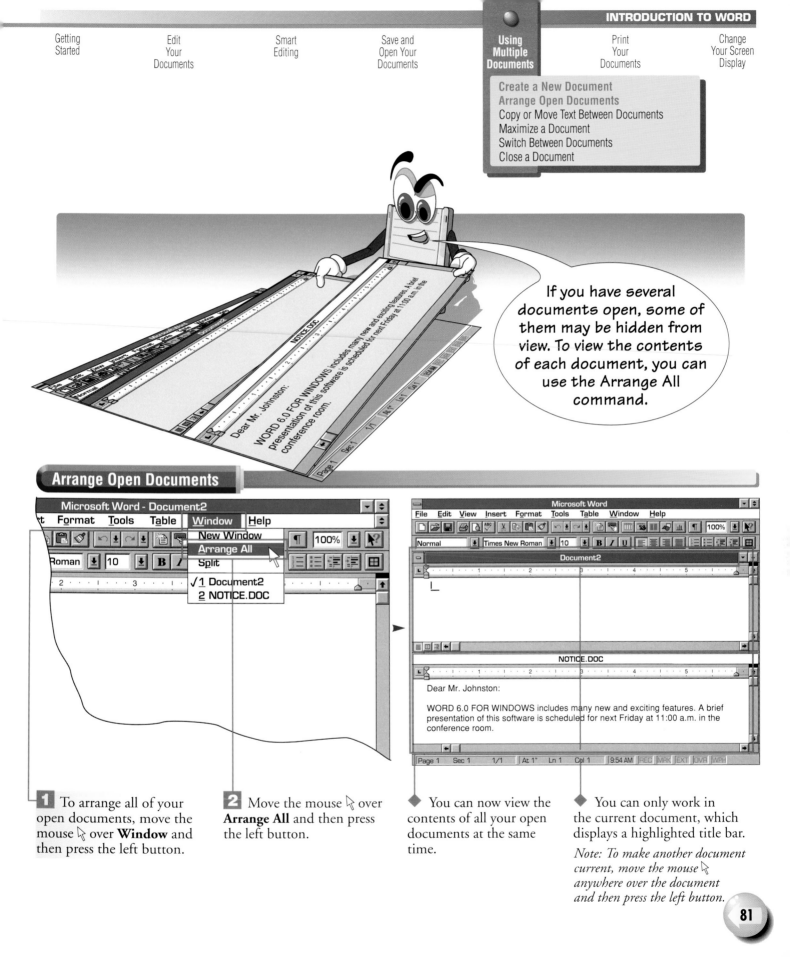

1 To arrange all of your open documents, move the mouse over **Window** and then press the left button.

2 Move the mouse over **Arrange All** and then press the left button.

◆ You can now view the contents of all your open documents at the same time.

◆ You can only work in the current document, which displays a highlighted title bar.

Note: To make another document current, move the mouse anywhere over the document and then press the left button.

81

Copying or moving text between documents saves you time when you are working in one document and want to use text from another.

Copy or Move Text Between Documents

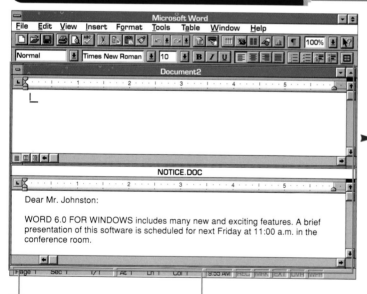

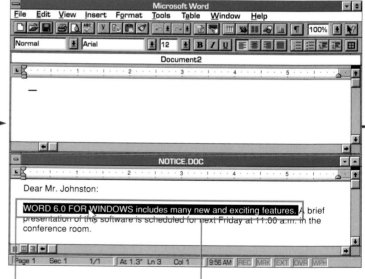

1 Open the documents you want to copy or move text between.

Note: To open a saved document, refer to page 72. To create a new document, refer to page 80.

2 Display the contents of both documents by using the **Arrange All** command.

*Note: For information on the **Arrange All** command, refer to page 81.*

3 Select the text you want to copy or move to another document.

Note: To select text, refer to page 14.

4 Move the mouse I anywhere over the selected text and I becomes ⇖.

INTRODUCTION TO WORD

Getting
Started

Edit
Your
Documents

Smart
Editing

Save and
Open Your
Documents

Using
Multiple
Documents

Print
Your
Documents

Change
Your Screen
Display

Create a New Document
Arrange Open Documents
Copy or Move Text Between Documents
Maximize a Document
Switch Between Documents
Close a Document

COPY TEXT

When you copy text, Word *copies* the text and *pastes* the copy in a new location. The original text remains in its place.

MOVE TEXT

When you move text, Word *cuts* the text and *pastes* it in a new location. The original text disappears.

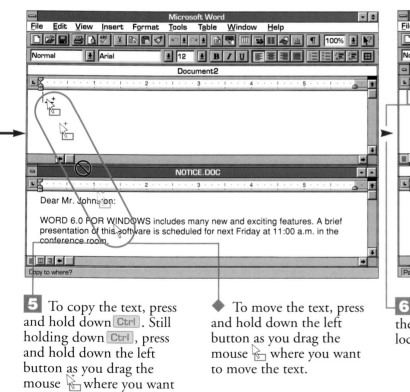

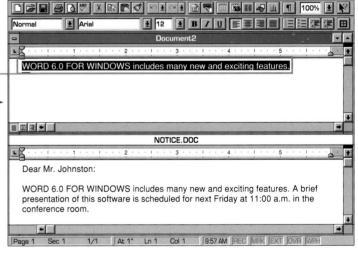

5 To copy the text, press and hold down Ctrl . Still holding down Ctrl , press and hold down the left button as you drag the mouse where you want to place the copy.

◆ To move the text, press and hold down the left button as you drag the mouse where you want to move the text.

6 Release the button and the text appears in the new location.

Note: To deselect text, move the mouse outside the selected area and then press the left button.

MAXIMIZE A DOCUMENT

SWITCH BETWEEN DOCUMENTS

You can enlarge a document to fill your entire screen. This enables you to view more of its contents.

Maximize a Document

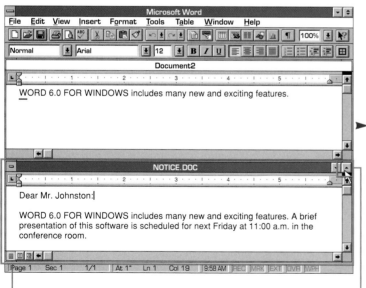

1 To select the document you want to maximize, move the mouse ⌀ anywhere over the document and then press the left button.

2 Move the mouse ⌀ over the document's **Maximize** button ▲ and then press the left button.

◆ The document enlarges to fill your entire screen.

Note: The file you maximized covers all of your open documents.

Getting
Started

Edit
Your
Documents

Smart
Editing

Save and
Open Your
Documents

Using Multiple Documents

Print
Your
Documents

Change
Your Screen
Display

INTRODUCTION TO WORD

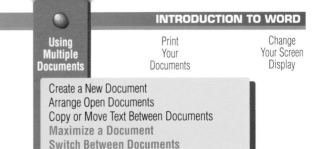

Create a New Document
Arrange Open Documents
Copy or Move Text Between Documents
Maximize a Document
Switch Between Documents
Close a Document

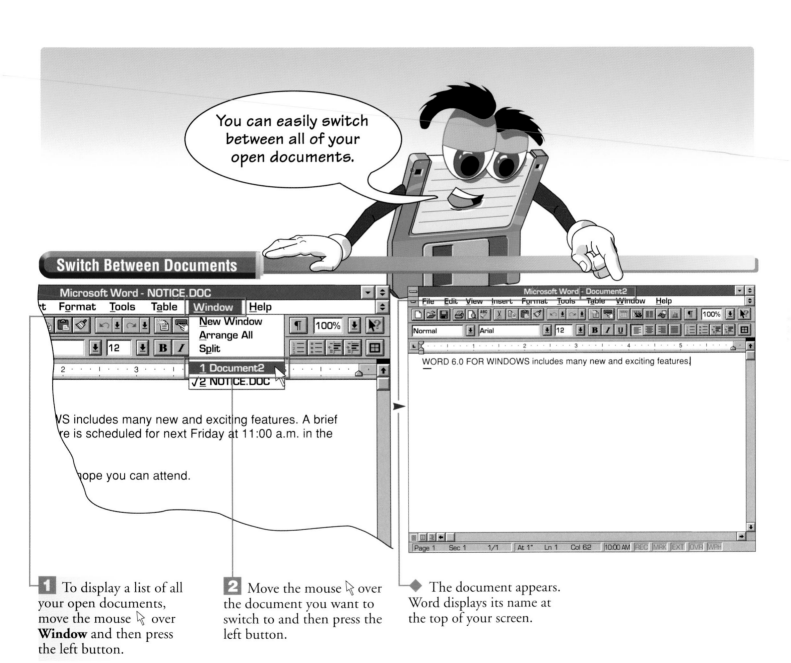

You can easily switch between all of your open documents.

Switch Between Documents

1 To display a list of all your open documents, move the mouse ⌖ over **Window** and then press the left button.

2 Move the mouse ⌖ over the document you want to switch to and then press the left button.

◆ The document appears. Word displays its name at the top of your screen.

CLOSE A DOCUMENT

When you finish working with a document, you can close it to remove the document from your screen.

Close a Document

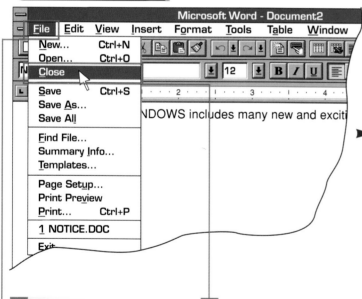

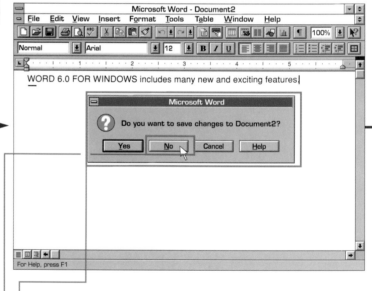

1 To close the document displayed on your screen, move the mouse ⌖ over **File** and then press the left button.

2 Move the mouse ⌖ over **Close** and then press the left button.

◆ This dialog box appears if you have not saved changes made to your document.

3 To close the document without saving the changes, move the mouse ⌖ over **No** and then press the left button.

◆ To save the changes, move the mouse ⌖ over **Yes** and then press the left button.

Note: For more information on saving a document, refer to page 64.

INTRODUCTION TO WORD

Getting
Started

Edit
Your
Documents

Smart
Editing

Save and
Open Your
Documents

Using
Multiple
Documents

Print
Your
Documents

Change
Your Screen
Display

Create a New Document
Arrange Open Documents
Copy or Move Text Between Documents
Maximize a Document
Switch Between Documents
Close a Document

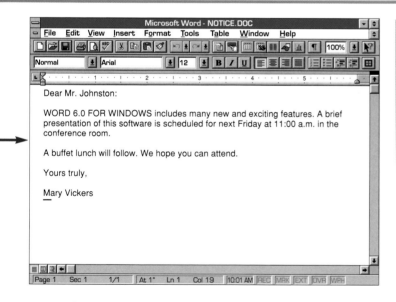

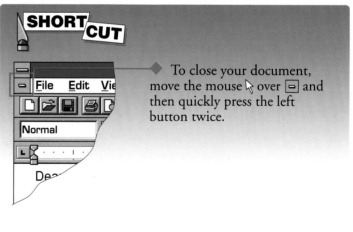

SHORTCUT

◆ To close your document, move the mouse ⌖ over ⊟ and then quickly press the left button twice.

◆ Word removes the document from your screen.

Note: If you had more than one document open, the second last document you worked on appears on your screen.

verview

PRINT YOUR DOCUMENT

Preview a Document

Print a Document

Print an Envelope

◆ This chapter will show you how to print a document and an envelope. You will also learn how to see on screen what your document will look like when printed.

The Print Preview feature lets you see on screen what your document will look like when printed.

Preview a Document

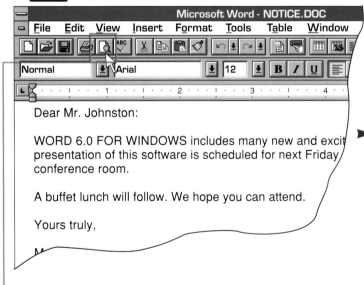

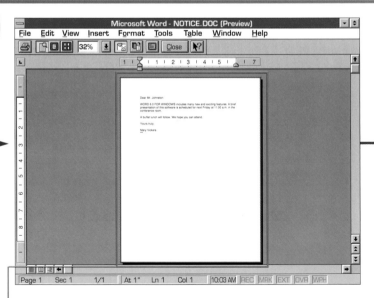

1 Move the mouse ▷ over 🔍 and then press the left button.

◆ The page you are currently working on appears in the Print Preview window.

◆ If your document contains more than one page, press **PageDown** on your keyboard to display the next page. Press **PageUp** to display the previous page.

INTRODUCTION TO WORD

| Getting Started | Edit Your Documents | Smart Editing | Save and Open Your Documents | Using Multiple Documents | **Print Your Documents** | Change Your Screen Display |

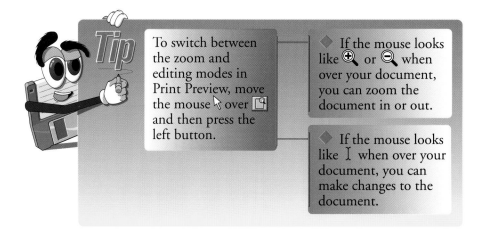

To switch between the zoom and editing modes in Print Preview, move the mouse ⬚ over ▣ and then press the left button.

◆ If the mouse looks like ⊕ or ⊖ when over your document, you can zoom the document in or out.

◆ If the mouse looks like Ɪ when over your document, you can make changes to the document.

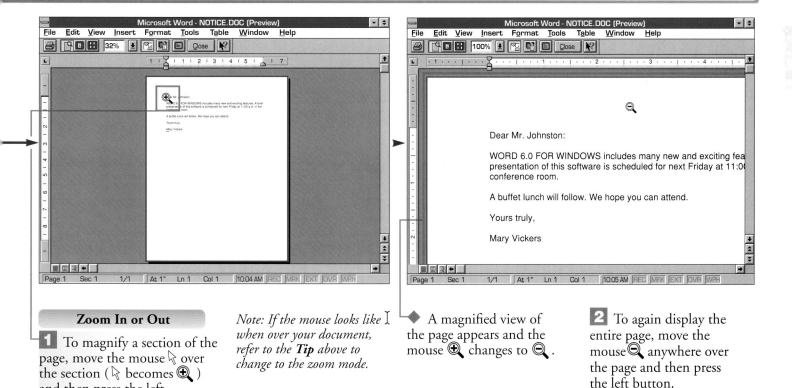

Zoom In or Out

1 To magnify a section of the page, move the mouse ⬚ over the section (⬚ becomes ⊕) and then press the left button.

*Note: If the mouse looks like Ɪ when over your document, refer to the **Tip** above to change to the zoom mode.*

◆ A magnified view of the page appears and the mouse ⊕ changes to ⊖ .

2 To again display the entire page, move the mouse ⊖ anywhere over the page and then press the left button.

PREVIEW A DOCUMENT

In Print Preview, Word can display more than one page at a time. This lets you view the overall style of multiple pages at once.

Display Multiple Pages

1 Move the mouse ⬚ over ▦ and then press and hold down the left button.

2 Still holding down the button, move the mouse ⬚ over the number of pages you want to display at once.

Note: If you drag the mouse ⬚ down or to the right, more choices appear.

INTRODUCTION TO WORD

| Getting Started | Edit Your Documents | Smart Editing | Save and Open Your Documents | Using Multiple Documents | **Print Your Documents** | Change Your Screen Display |

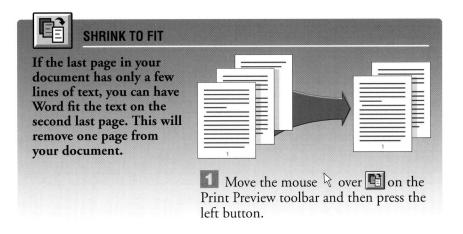

SHRINK TO FIT

If the last page in your document has only a few lines of text, you can have Word fit the text on the second last page. This will remove one page from your document.

1 Move the mouse ⌖ over 🖹 on the Print Preview toolbar and then press the left button.

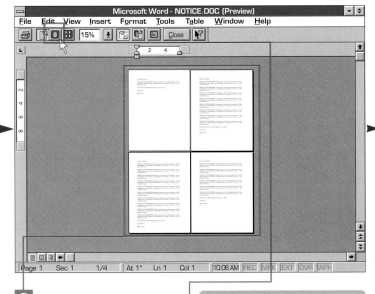

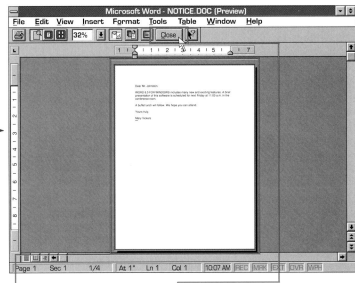

3 Release the button and the number of pages you specified appears on your screen.

Note: In this example, the document contains four pages.

Display One Page

1 To display a single page, move the mouse ⌖ over 🖹 and then press the left button.

◆ A single page appears on your screen.

◆ Press **PageDown** on your keyboard to display the next page. Press **PageUp** to display the previous page.

Close Print Preview

1 To close Print Preview and return to your document, move the mouse ⌖ over **Close** and then press the left button.

PRINT A DOCUMENT

You can print a single page, specific pages or your entire document. Before printing your document, make sure your printer is on and it contains paper.

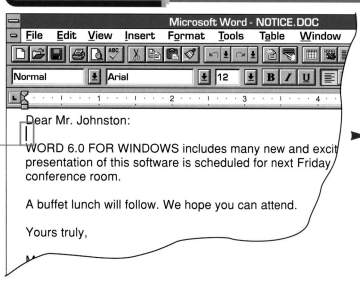

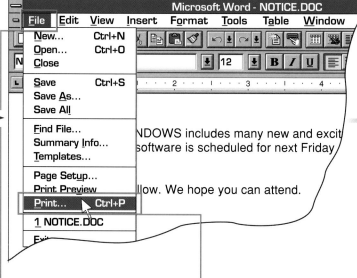

1 To print a single page, position the insertion point anywhere on the page you want to print.

◆ To print your entire document or specific pages, position the insertion point anywhere in the document.

◆ To print a small section of text, select the text.

Note: To select text, refer to page 14.

2 Move the mouse ⌖ over **File** and then press the left button.

3 Move the mouse ⌖ over **Print** and then press the left button.

| Getting Started | Edit Your Documents | Smart Editing | Save and Open Your Documents | Using Multiple Documents | Print Your Documents | Change Your Screen Display |

Preview a Document
Print a Document
Print an Envelope

SHORTCUT

PRINT YOUR ENTIRE DOCUMENT

◆ To quickly print your entire document, move the mouse over and then press the left button.

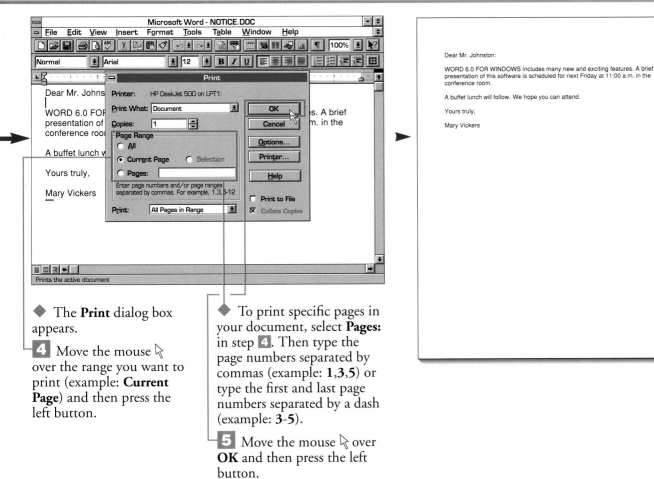

◆ The **Print** dialog box appears.

4 Move the mouse over the range you want to print (example: **Current Page**) and then press the left button.

◆ To print specific pages in your document, select **Pages:** in step **4**. Then type the page numbers separated by commas (example: **1,3,5**) or type the first and last page numbers separated by a dash (example: **3-5**).

5 Move the mouse over **OK** and then press the left button.

95

You can use the Envelope feature to create and then print an envelope.

Print an Envelope

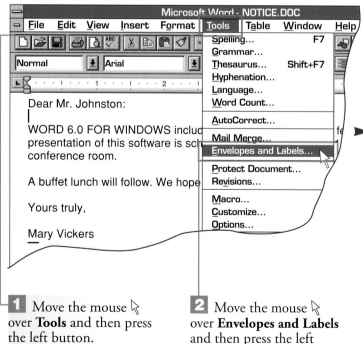

1 Move the mouse ⟍ over **Tools** and then press the left button.

2 Move the mouse ⟍ over **Envelopes and Labels** and then press the left button.

◆ The **Envelopes and Labels** dialog box appears.

3 Move the mouse ⟍ over the **Envelopes** tab and then press the left button.

◆ A delivery address appears in this area if Word found one in your document.

4 If a delivery address did not appear, move the mouse I over this area and then press the left button. Then type the address.

INTRODUCTION TO WORD

| Getting Started | Edit Your Documents | Smart Editing | Save and Open Your Documents | Using Multiple Documents | **Print Your Documents** | Change Your Screen Display |

Preview a Document
Print a Document
Print an Envelope

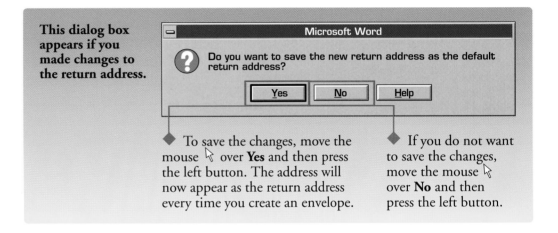

This dialog box appears if you made changes to the return address.

◆ To save the changes, move the mouse ↖ over **Yes** and then press the left button. The address will now appear as the return address every time you create an envelope.

◆ If you do not want to save the changes, move the mouse ↖ over **No** and then press the left button.

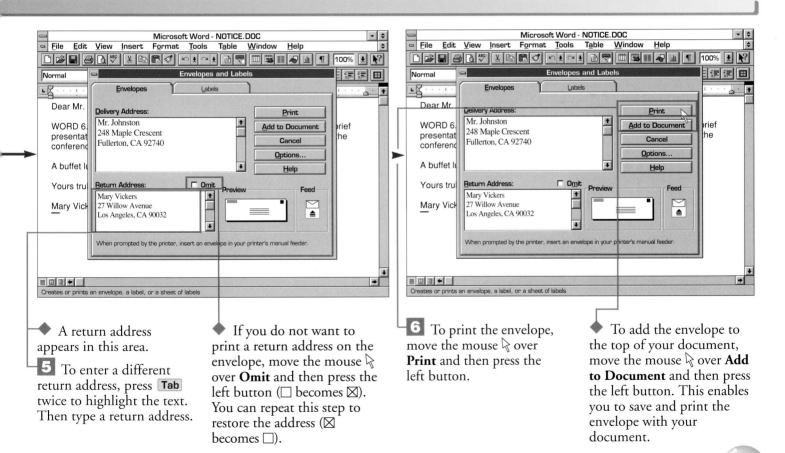

◆ A return address appears in this area.

5 To enter a different return address, press `Tab` twice to highlight the text. Then type a return address.

◆ If you do not want to print a return address on the envelope, move the mouse ↖ over **Omit** and then press the left button (□ becomes ⊠). You can repeat this step to restore the address (⊠ becomes □).

6 To print the envelope, move the mouse ↖ over **Print** and then press the left button.

◆ To add the envelope to the top of your document, move the mouse ↖ over **Add to Document** and then press the left button. This enables you to save and print the envelope with your document.

97

Overview

CHANGE YOUR SCREEN DISPLAY

Change Views

Zoom In or Out

Display or Hide Toolbars

Display or Hide the Ruler

Using Full Screen View

◆ This chapter will show you how to change your screen display to best suit your needs. You will learn how to zoom your document in and out and display the largest working area.

CHANGE VIEWS

Word offers three basic views you can use to display your document. You can choose the view that best suits your needs.

Change Views

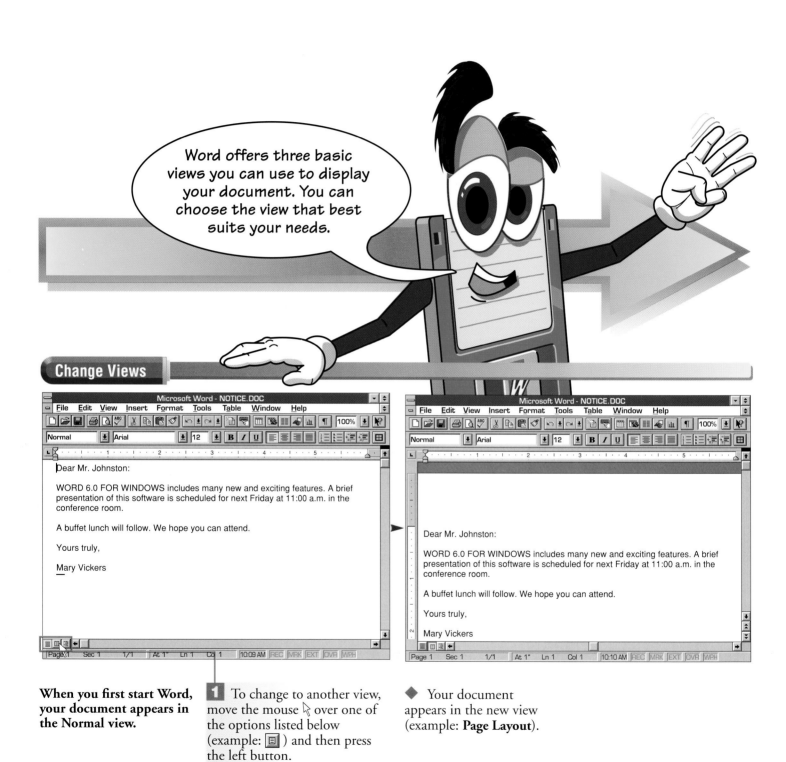

When you first start Word, your document appears in the Normal view.

1 To change to another view, move the mouse ↖ over one of the options listed below (example: ▤) and then press the left button.

▤ Normal view

▥ Page Layout view

▤ Outline view

◆ Your document appears in the new view (example: **Page Layout**).

INTRODUCTION TO WORD

Getting Started | Edit Your Documents | Smart Editing | Save and Open Your Documents | Using Multiple Documents | Print Your Documents | **Change Your Screen Display**

Three Basic Ways to View Your Document

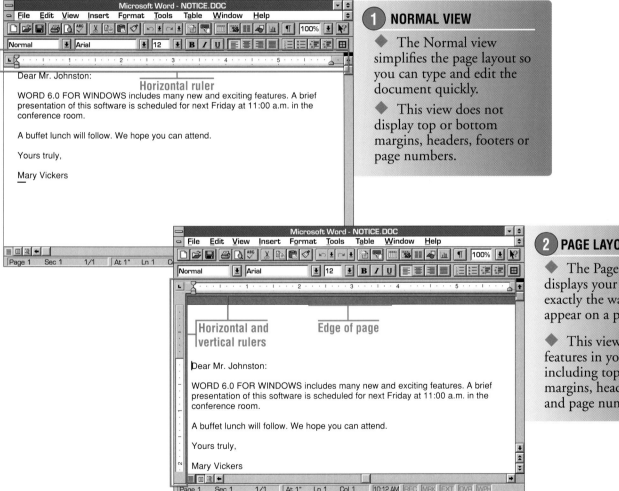

1 NORMAL VIEW

◆ The Normal view simplifies the page layout so you can type and edit the document quickly.

◆ This view does not display top or bottom margins, headers, footers or page numbers.

2 PAGE LAYOUT VIEW

◆ The Page Layout view displays your document exactly the way it will appear on a printed page.

◆ This view displays all features in your document including top and bottom margins, headers, footers and page numbers.

3 OUTLINE VIEW

◆ The Outline view lets you create an outline of your document, similar to a Table of Contents. You can display the headings and subheadings and hide the body text. This view helps you work more efficiently with longer documents.

ZOOM IN OR OUT

Word lets you enlarge or reduce the display of text on your screen. You can magnify the document to read small text or shrink the document to view all the text on one page.

Zoom Your Document In or Out

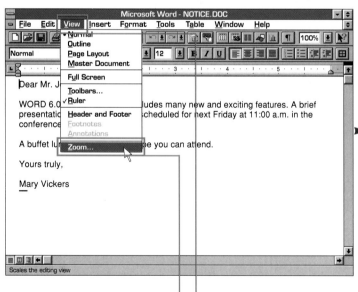

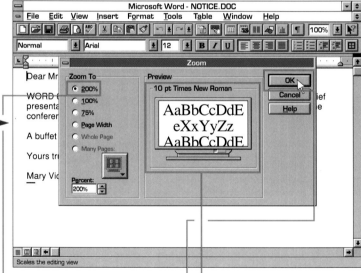

When you first start Word, your document appears in the 100% zoom setting.

■1 To display your document using a different setting, move the mouse ⟍ over **View** and then press the left button.

■2 Move the mouse ⟍ over **Zoom** and then press the left button.

◆ The **Zoom** dialog box appears.

■3 Move the mouse ⟍ over the zoom setting you want to use (example: **200%**) and then press the left button.

◆ A sample of the zoom setting you selected appears.

■4 Move the mouse ⟍ over **OK** and then press the left button.

INTRODUCTION TO WORD

| Getting Started | Edit Your Documents | Smart Editing | Save and Open Your Documents | Using Multiple Documents | Print Your Documents | **Change Your Screen Display** |

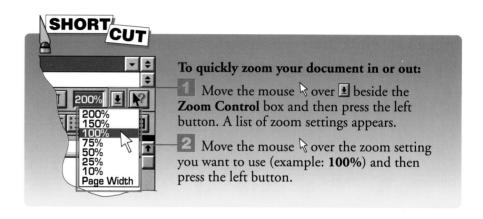

SHORTCUT

To quickly zoom your document in or out:

1 Move the mouse ⇖ over ⬇ beside the **Zoom Control** box and then press the left button. A list of zoom settings appears.

2 Move the mouse ⇖ over the zoom setting you want to use (example: **100%**) and then press the left button.

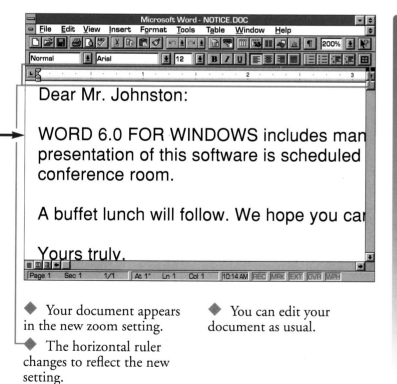

Dear Mr. Johnston:

WORD 6.0 FOR WINDOWS includes man presentation of this software is scheduled conference room.

A buffet lunch will follow. We hope you ca

Yours truly,

♦ Your document appears in the new zoom setting.

♦ The horizontal ruler changes to reflect the new setting.

♦ You can edit your document as usual.

ZOOM SETTINGS

Setting	Description
200%	Twice the normal size
100%	The normal size
75%	Three-quarters the normal size
Page Width	Displays the entire width of your document
Whole Page	Displays the entire page
Many Pages	Displays multiple pages at the same time

To use the **Many Pages** zoom setting, you must specify the number of pages you want to display.

♦ In the **Zoom** dialog box, move the mouse ⇖ over ▦ and then press and hold down the left button as you move the mouse ⇖ over the number of pages you want to display. Then release the button.

*Note: The **Whole Page** and **Many Pages** settings are only available if you are in the Page Layout view. To change to the Page Layout view, refer to page 100.*

DISPLAY OR HIDE TOOLBARS

Word offers eight different toolbars that you can display or hide at any time. Each toolbar contains a series of buttons that let you quickly choose commands.

Display or Hide Toolbars

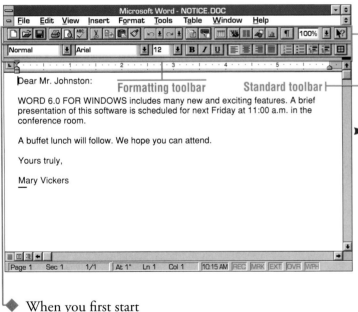

Formatting toolbar   Standard toolbar

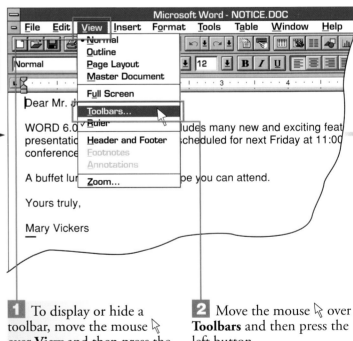

◆ When you first start Word, the Standard and Formatting toolbars appear on your screen.

1 To display or hide a toolbar, move the mouse ⌖ over **View** and then press the left button.

2 Move the mouse ⌖ over **Toolbars** and then press the left button.

◆ The **Toolbars** dialog box appears.

INTRODUCTION TO WORD

| Getting Started | Edit Your Documents | Smart Editing | Save and Open Your Documents | Using Multiple Documents | Print Your Documents | **Change Your Screen Display** |

Change Views
Zoom In or Out
Display or Hide Toolbars
Display or Hide the Ruler
Using Full Screen View

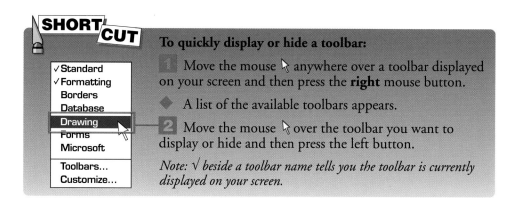

SHORT CUT

√ Standard
√ Formatting
  Borders
  Database
  Drawing
  Forms
  Microsoft

  Toolbars...
  Customize...

To quickly display or hide a toolbar:

1 Move the mouse ⟍ anywhere over a toolbar displayed on your screen and then press the **right** mouse button.

◆ A list of the available toolbars appears.

2 Move the mouse ⟍ over the toolbar you want to display or hide and then press the left button.

Note: √ beside a toolbar name tells you the toolbar is currently displayed on your screen.

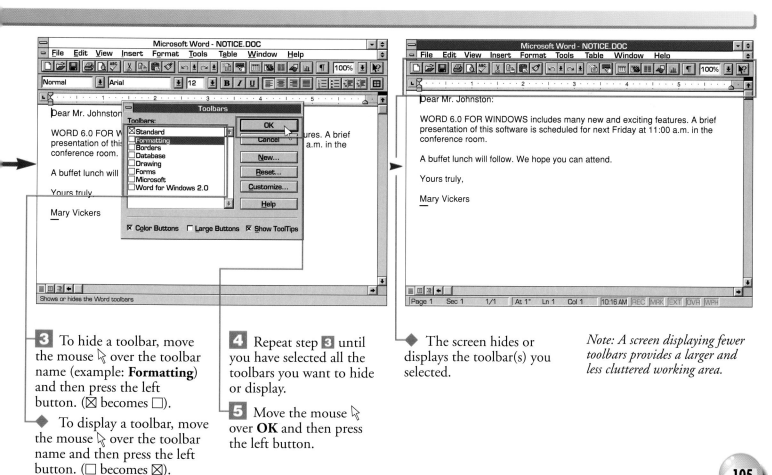

3 To hide a toolbar, move the mouse ⟍ over the toolbar name (example: **Formatting**) and then press the left button. (⊠ becomes ☐).

◆ To display a toolbar, move the mouse ⟍ over the toolbar name and then press the left button. (☐ becomes ⊠).

4 Repeat step **3** until you have selected all the toolbars you want to hide or display.

5 Move the mouse ⟍ over **OK** and then press the left button.

◆ The screen hides or displays the toolbar(s) you selected.

Note: A screen displaying fewer toolbars provides a larger and less cluttered working area.

105

The Ruler lets you indent paragraphs and change margin and tab settings. If you are not using the ruler, you can hide it to provide a larger and less cluttered working area.

Display or Hide the Ruler

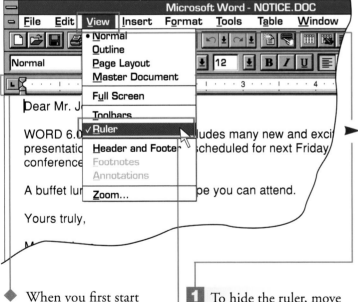

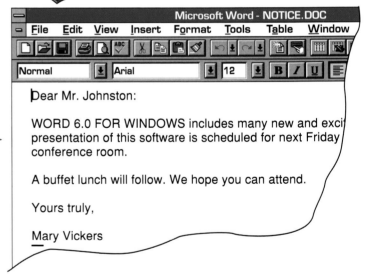

◆ When you first start Word, the ruler appears on your screen.

1 To hide the ruler, move the mouse ⟍ over **View** and then press the left button.

2 Move the mouse ⟍ over **Ruler** and then press the left button.

◆ The **Ruler** disappears from your screen.

To again display the ruler, repeat steps **1** and **2**.

| Getting Started | Edit Your Documents | Smart Editing | Save and Open Your Documents | Using Multiple Documents | Print Your Documents | **Change Your Screen Display** |

Change Views
Zoom In or Out
Display or Hide Toolbars
Display or Hide the Ruler
Using Full Screen View

You can use the Full Screen view to display more of your document. This will hide all screen elements such as the ruler, menu and toolbars to provide you with more working area.

Using Full Screen View

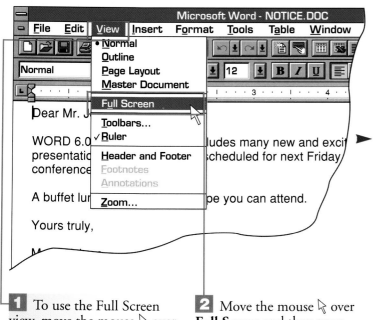

Dear Mr. Johnston:

WORD 6.0 FOR WINDOWS includes many new and exciting features. A brief presentation of this software is scheduled for next Friday at 11:00 a.m. in the conference room.

A buffet lunch will follow. We hope you can attend.

Yours truly,

Mary Vickers

1 To use the Full Screen view, move the mouse ⟍ over **View** and then press the left button.

2 Move the mouse ⟍ over **Full Screen** and then press the left button.

◆ Word uses the entire screen to display the text in your document.

3 To return to the previous view, move the mouse ⟍ over and then press the left button **or** press Alt, V, U.

Overview

FORMAT CHARACTERS

Bold, Underline and Italics

Change Fonts

Insert a Symbol

◆ This chapter will show you how to emphasize important information and make text easier to read. You will learn how to change the design and size of text and insert symbols into your document.

BOLD, UNDERLINE AND ITALICS

You can use the Bold, Underline and Italic features to emphasize important information. This will improve the overall appearance of your document.

B Bold Text

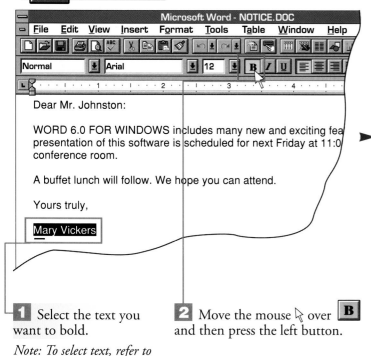

1 Select the text you want to bold.

Note: To select text, refer to page 14.

2 Move the mouse ⌖ over **B** and then press the left button.

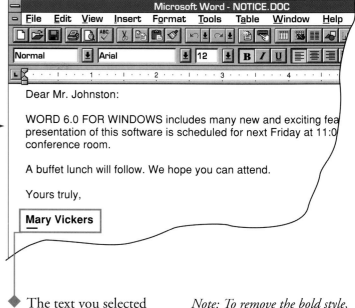

◆ The text you selected appears in the bold style.

Note: To deselect text, move the mouse I outside the selected area and then press the left button.

*Note: To remove the bold style, repeat steps **1** and **2**.*

Bold, Underline and Italics
Change Fonts
Insert a Symbol

I ITALICIZE TEXT

You can *italicize text* → You can *italicize text*

1 Select the text you want to italicize.

Note: To select text, refer to page 14.

2 Move the mouse over *I* and then press the left button.

◆ The text you selected appears in italics.

Note: To remove the italic style, repeat steps 1 and 2.

U Underline Text

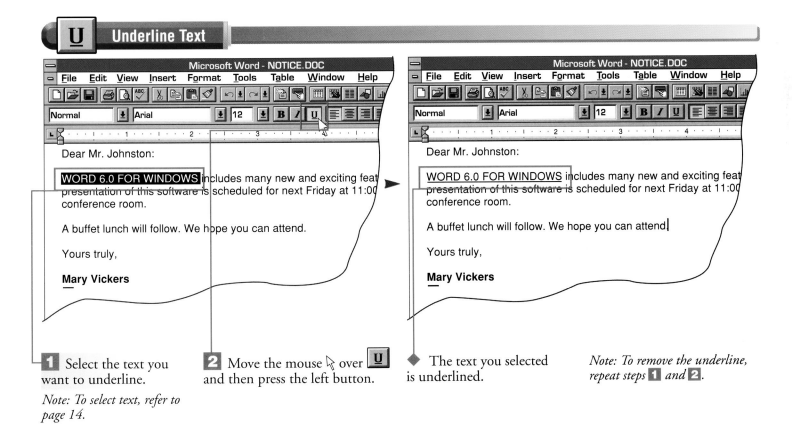

1 Select the text you want to underline.

Note: To select text, refer to page 14.

2 Move the mouse over **U** and then press the left button.

◆ The text you selected is underlined.

Note: To remove the underline, repeat steps 1 and 2.

CHANGE FONTS

You can change the design and size of characters in your document to emphasize headings and make text easier to read.

Change Fonts

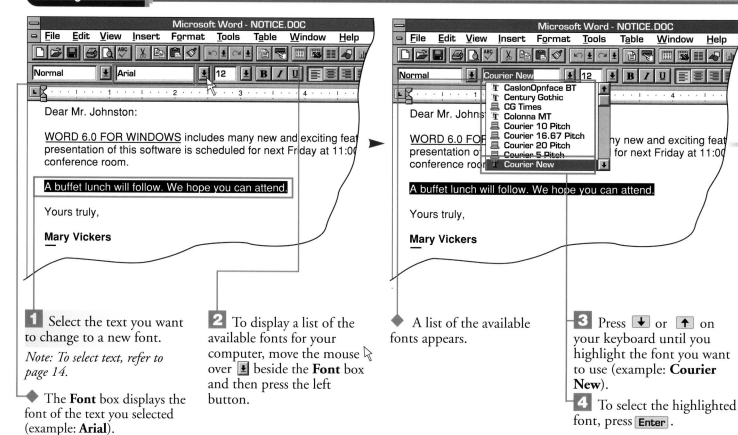

1 Select the text you want to change to a new font.

Note: To select text, refer to page 14.

◆ The **Font** box displays the font of the text you selected (example: **Arial**).

2 To display a list of the available fonts for your computer, move the mouse over ⬇ beside the **Font** box and then press the left button.

◆ A list of the available fonts appears.

3 Press ⬇ or ⬆ on your keyboard until you highlight the font you want to use (example: **Courier New**).

4 To select the highlighted font, press **Enter**.

Format Characters	Format Paragraphs	Format Pages	Smart Formatting	Working With Tables	Using Graphics	Using Templates and Wizards	Customize Word	Merge Documents	Sharing Data

Bold, Underline and Italics
Change Fonts
Insert a Symbol

REMOVE ALL CHARACTER FORMATTING

You can instantly remove all character formatting from text in your document.

1 Select the text that displays the character formatting you want to remove.

2 Press `Ctrl` + **Spacebar** on your keyboard.

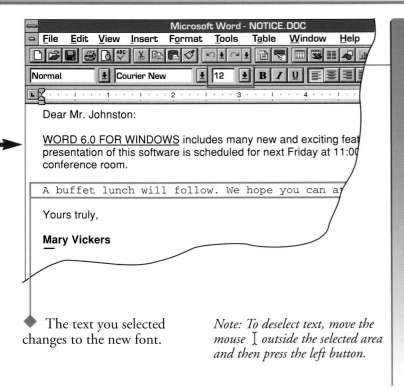

♦ The text you selected changes to the new font.

Note: To deselect text, move the mouse ⌶ outside the selected area and then press the left button.

CHANGE FONT SIZE

You can increase or decrease the size of text in your document.

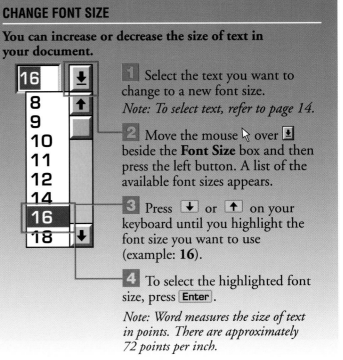

1 Select the text you want to change to a new font size.
Note: To select text, refer to page 14.

2 Move the mouse �ksover ▼ beside the **Font Size** box and then press the left button. A list of the available font sizes appears.

3 Press ▼ or ▲ on your keyboard until you highlight the font size you want to use (example: **16**).

4 To select the highlighted font size, press `Enter`.

Note: Word measures the size of text in points. There are approximately 72 points per inch.

CHANGE FONTS

You can change the design and size of characters in your document at the same time by using the Font dialog box. This lets you turn a dull, lifeless letter into an interesting, attractive document.

Change Fonts

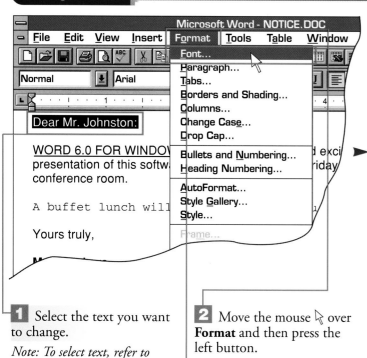

1 Select the text you want to change.

Note: To select text, refer to page 14.

2 Move the mouse ⍾ over **Format** and then press the left button.

3 Move the mouse ⍾ over **Font** and then press the left button.

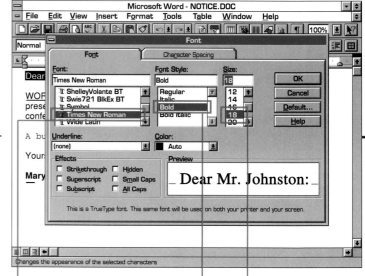

4 Move the mouse ⍾ over the font you want to use (example: **Times New Roman**) and then press the left button.

Note: To view all of the available font options, use the scroll bar. To use the scroll bar, refer to page 13.

5 Move the mouse ⍾ over the font style you want to use (example: **Bold**) and then press the left button.

6 Move the mouse ⍾ over the font size you want to use (example: **18**) and then press the left button.

Bold, Underline and Italics
Change Fonts
Insert a Symbol

TEXT EFFECTS

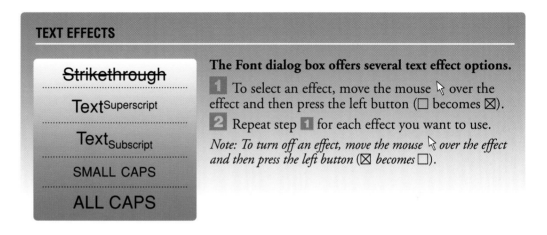

~~Strikethrough~~

Text^{Superscript}

Text_{Subscript}

SMALL CAPS

ALL CAPS

The Font dialog box offers several text effect options.

1 To select an effect, move the mouse ⬚ over the effect and then press the left button (□ becomes ☒).

2 Repeat step **1** for each effect you want to use.

Note: To turn off an effect, move the mouse ⬚ over the effect and then press the left button (☒ becomes □).

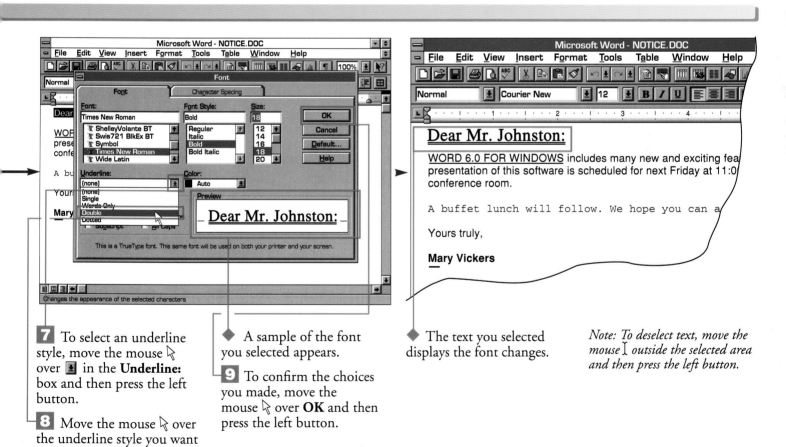

7 To select an underline style, move the mouse ⬚ over ⬇ in the **Underline:** box and then press the left button.

8 Move the mouse ⬚ over the underline style you want to use (example: **Double**) and then press the left button.

♦ A sample of the font you selected appears.

9 To confirm the choices you made, move the mouse ⬚ over **OK** and then press the left button.

♦ The text you selected displays the font changes.

Note: To deselect text, move the mouse I outside the selected area and then press the left button.

INSERT A SYMBOL

Word lets you insert symbols into your document that are not displayed on your keyboard.

Insert a Symbol

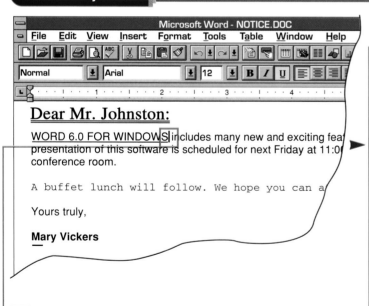

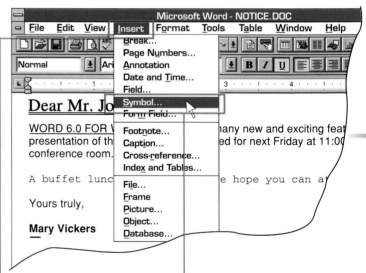

1 Position the insertion point where you want a symbol to appear in your document.

2 Move the mouse ⌖ over **Insert** and then press the left button.

3 Move the mouse ⌖ over **Symbol** and then press the left button.

WORKING WITH WORD

| Format Characters | Format Paragraphs | Format Pages | Smart Formatting | Working With Tables | Using Graphics | Using Templates and Wizards | Customize Word | Merge Documents | Sharing Data |

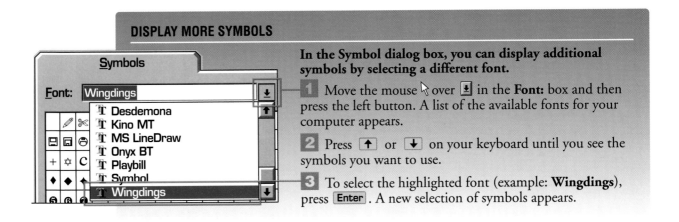

DISPLAY MORE SYMBOLS

In the Symbol dialog box, you can display additional symbols by selecting a different font.

1 Move the mouse ↖ over ⬇ in the **Font:** box and then press the left button. A list of the available fonts for your computer appears.

2 Press ⬆ or ⬇ on your keyboard until you see the symbols you want to use.

3 To select the highlighted font (example: **Wingdings**), press **Enter**. A new selection of symbols appears.

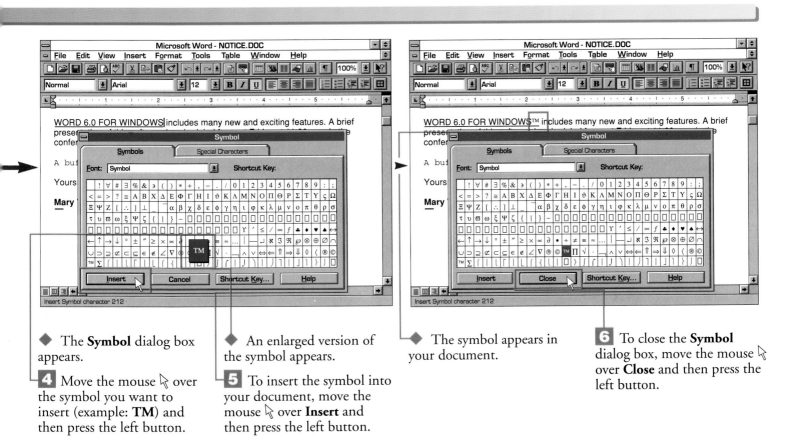

◆ The **Symbol** dialog box appears.

4 Move the mouse ↖ over the symbol you want to insert (example: **TM**) and then press the left button.

◆ An enlarged version of the symbol appears.

5 To insert the symbol into your document, move the mouse ↖ over **Insert** and then press the left button.

◆ The symbol appears in your document.

6 To close the **Symbol** dialog box, move the mouse ↖ over **Close** and then press the left button.

117

verview

FORMAT PARAGRAPHS

Change Paragraph Alignment

Change Line Spacing

Change Tab Settings

Indent Paragraphs

Create Numbered and Bulleted Lists

Add Borders

Add Shading

◆ This chapter will show you how to present information more attractively by changing the appearance of paragraphs in your document. You will learn how to set tabs, indent paragraphs and add borders and shading.

CHANGE PARAGRAPH ALIGNMENT

You can enhance the appearance of your document by aligning text in different ways. Word offers four alignment options.

Right

Center

Left

Full

Center Text

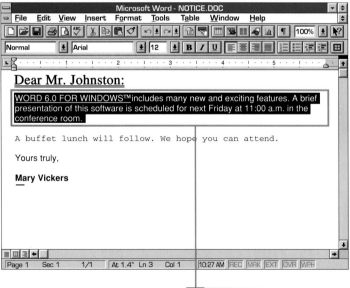

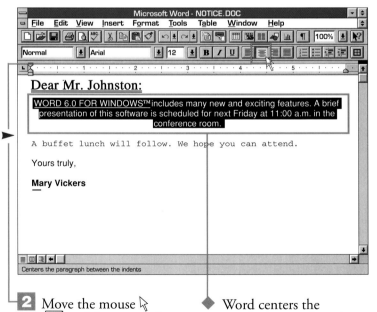

Word automatically left aligns any text you type in your document.

1 To center text, select the paragraph(s) you want to center.

Note: To select text, refer to page 14.

2 Move the mouse ♔ over  and then press the left button.

◆ Word centers the paragraph(s) you selected.

| Format Characters | **Format Paragraphs** | Format Pages | Smart Formatting | Working With Tables | Using Graphics | Using Templates and Wizards | Customize Word | Merge Documents | Sharing Data |

Change Paragraph Alignment   Create Numbered and Bulleted Lists
Change Line Spacing   Add Borders
Change Tab Settings   Add Shading
Indent Paragraphs

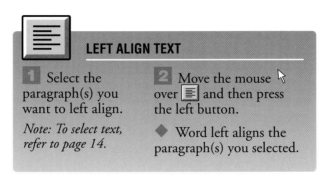

LEFT ALIGN TEXT

1 Select the paragraph(s) you want to left align.

Note: To select text, refer to page 14.

2 Move the mouse over ☰ and then press the left button.

◆ Word left aligns the paragraph(s) you selected.

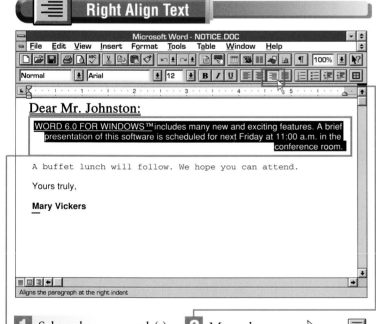

Right Align Text

1 Select the paragraph(s) you want to right align.

Note: To select text, refer to page 14.

2 Move the mouse � over ☰ and then press the left button.

◆ Word right aligns the paragraph(s) you selected.

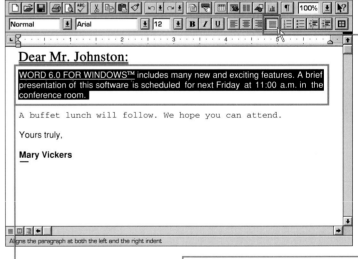

Fully Align Text

1 Select the paragraph(s) you want to fully align.

Note: To select text, refer to page 14.

2 Move the mouse � over ☰ and then press the left button.

◆ Word fully aligns the paragraph(s) you selected.

CHANGE LINE SPACING

You can make your document easier to read by changing the amount of space between the lines of text.

Single line spacing
This is the initial (or default) setting.

1.5 line spacing

Double line spacing

Change Line Spacing

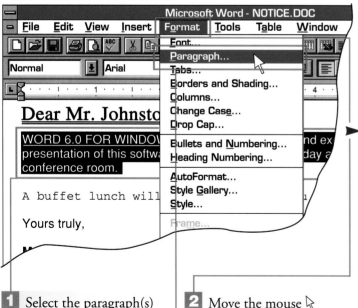

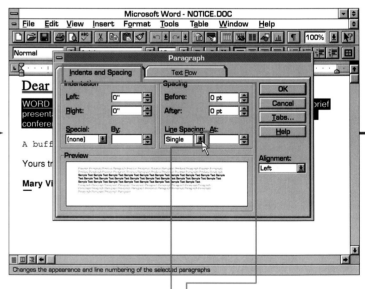

1 Select the paragraph(s) you want to change to a new line spacing.

Note: To select text, refer to page 14.

2 Move the mouse ⬚ over **Format** and then press the left button.

3 Move the mouse ⬚ over **Paragraph** and then press the left button.

◆ The **Paragraph** dialog box appears.

4 Move the mouse ⬚ over the **Indents and Spacing** tab and then press the left button.

5 Move the mouse ⬚ over ⬚ in the **Line Spacing:** box and then press the left button.

122

Format Characters	**Format Paragraphs**	Format Pages	Smart Formatting	Working With Tables	Using Graphics	Using Templates and Wizards	Customize Word	Merge Documents	Sharing Data

Change Paragraph Alignment   Create Numbered and Bulleted Lists
Change Line Spacing   Add Borders
Change Tab Settings   Add Shading
Indent Paragraphs

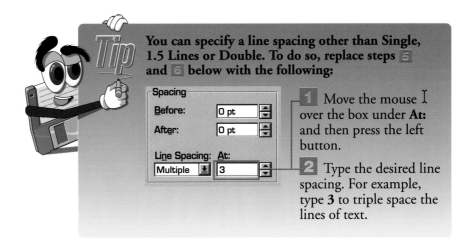

Tip

You can specify a line spacing other than Single, 1.5 Lines or Double. To do so, replace steps **5** and **6** below with the following:

1 Move the mouse I over the box under **At:** and then press the left button.

2 Type the desired line spacing. For example, type **3** to triple space the lines of text.

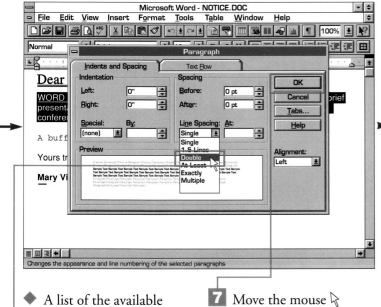

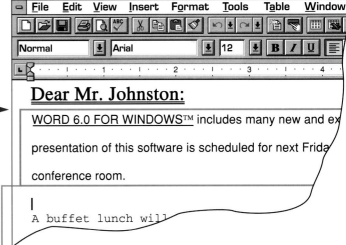

◆ A list of the available line spacing options appears.

6 Move the mouse ⌖ over the line spacing you want to use (example: **Double**) and then press the left button.

7 Move the mouse ⌖ over **OK** and then press the left button.

◆ Word changes the line spacing of the paragraph(s) you selected.

Note: To deselect text, move the mouse I outside the selected area and then press the left button.

CHANGE TAB SETTINGS

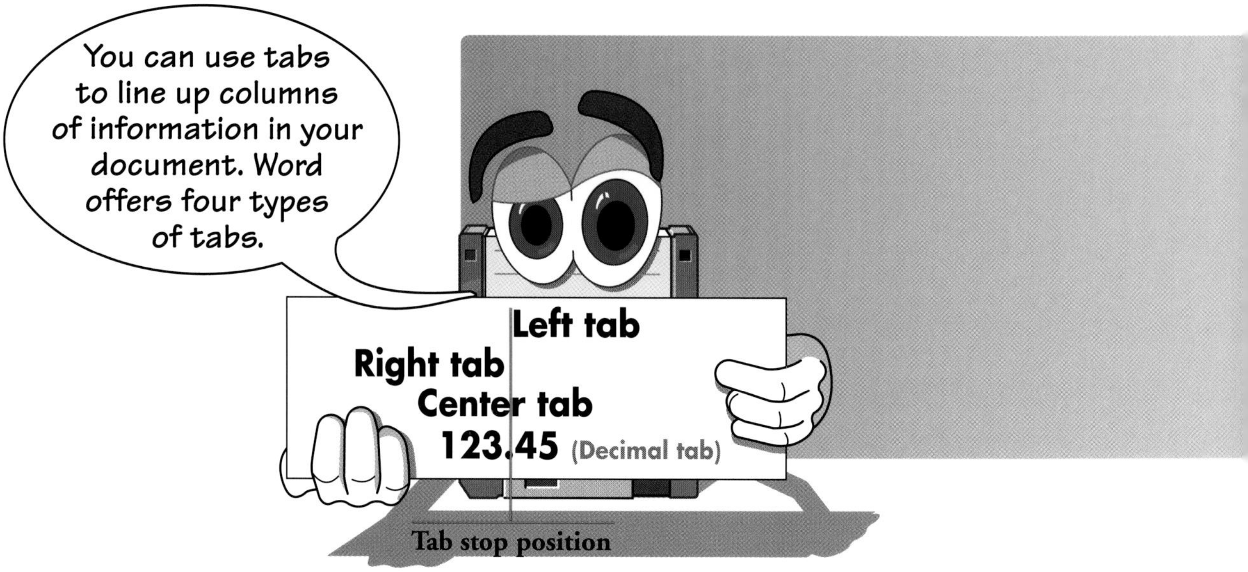

You can use tabs to line up columns of information in your document. Word offers four types of tabs.
Left tab
Right tab
Center tab
123.45 (Decimal tab)
Tab stop position

Add a Tab Stop

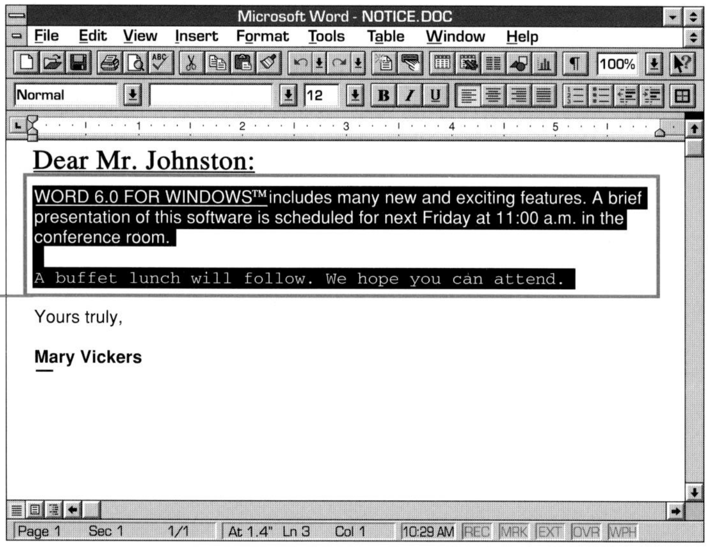

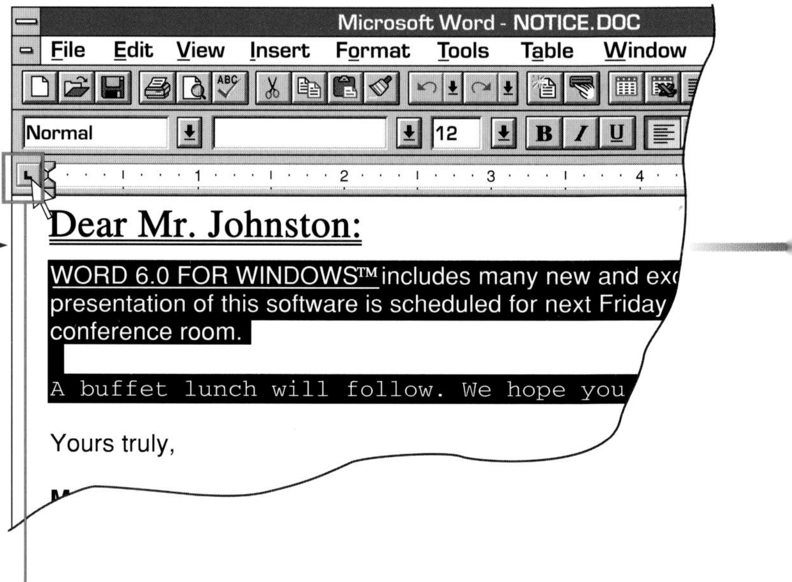

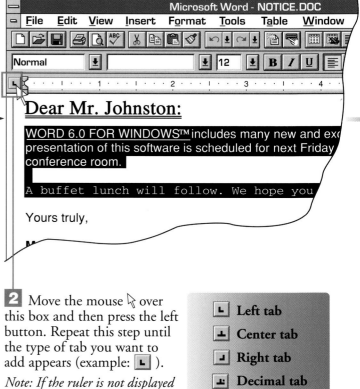

1 Select the paragraph(s) you want to contain the new tab stops.

Note: To select text, refer to page 14.

◆ To add tab stops to text you are about to type, position the insertion point where you want to begin typing the text.

2 Move the mouse over this box and then press the left button. Repeat this step until the type of tab you want to add appears (example: L).

Note: If the ruler is not displayed on your screen, refer to page 106.

- **Left tab**
- **Center tab**
- **Right tab**
- **Decimal tab**

| Format Characters | **Format Paragraphs** | Format Pages | Smart Formatting | Working With Tables | Using Graphics | Using Templates and Wizards | Customize Word | Merge Documents | Sharing Data |

Change Paragraph Alignment
Change Line Spacing
Change Tab Settings
Indent Paragraphs

Create Numbered and Bulleted Lists
Add Borders
Add Shading

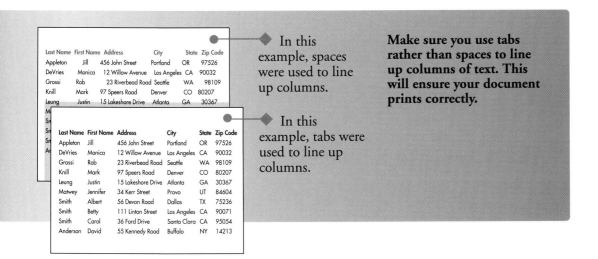

◆ In this example, spaces were used to line up columns.

Make sure you use tabs rather than spaces to line up columns of text. This will ensure your document prints correctly.

◆ In this example, tabs were used to line up columns.

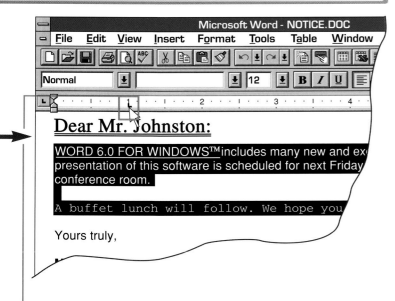

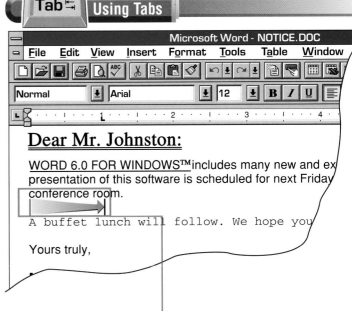
Using Tabs

3 Move the mouse Ⓢ over the position on the ruler where you want to add a tab stop and then press the left button.

Note: Make sure you position the mouse Ⓢ over the lower half of the ruler.

◆ The new tab stop appears on the ruler.

After you have set the tabs, you can use them to quickly move the insertion point across your screen.

1 Position the insertion point at the beginning of the line you want to move across.

2 Press **Tab**. The insertion point and any text that follows moves to the first tab stop.

CHANGE TAB SETTINGS

You can have Word insert a line or row of dots before a tab stop to help lead the eye from one column of information to another.

Chapter No.	Page		Name	Phone No.
Chapter 1	10		Allen, David	- - - - - - 890-8888
Chapter 2	36		Bell, Alex	- - - - - - - 842-3434
Chapter 3	42		Johnston, Mary	- - - 890-2222
Chapter 4	72		Knight, Joanne	- - - 845-1111
Chapter 5	96		Smith, John	- - - - - - 845-1234

Please Enter Information in the Area Provided:
Last Name _____
Address _____ First Name _____
City/State _____ Apt. No. _____
Zip Code _____

Add a Tab Stop With Leader Characters

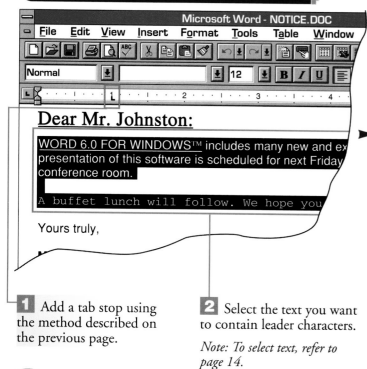

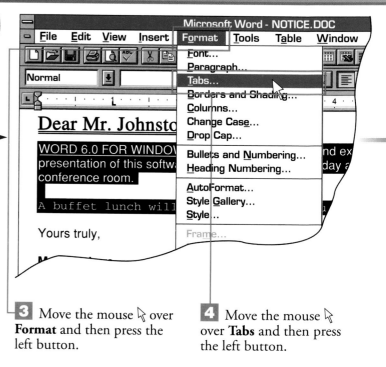

1 Add a tab stop using the method described on the previous page.

2 Select the text you want to contain leader characters.

Note: To select text, refer to page 14.

3 Move the mouse ⇗ over **Format** and then press the left button.

4 Move the mouse ⇗ over **Tabs** and then press the left button.

| Format Characters | Format Paragraphs | Format Pages | Smart Formatting | Working With Tables | Using Graphics | Using Templates and Wizards | Customize Word | Merge Documents | Sharing Data |

Change Paragraph Alignment
Change Line Spacing
Change Tab Settings
Indent Paragraphs

Create Numbered and Bulleted Lists
Add Borders
Add Shading

Tab without leader characters

Text ⟶|

When you press **Tab**, the insertion point and any text that follows moves to the first tab stop.

Tab with leader characters

Text········⟶|

When you press **Tab**, the insertion point and any text that follows moves to the first tab stop. Word also inserts a line or row of dots before the tab stop.

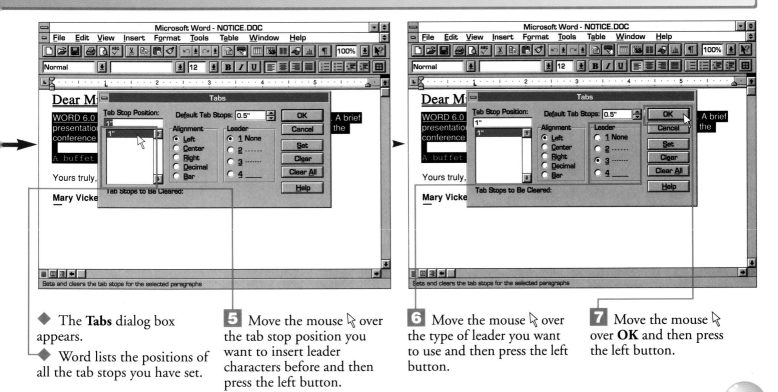

◆ The **Tabs** dialog box appears.

◆ Word lists the positions of all the tab stops you have set.

5 Move the mouse ⬚ over the tab stop position you want to insert leader characters before and then press the left button.

6 Move the mouse ⬚ over the type of leader you want to use and then press the left button.

7 Move the mouse ⬚ over **OK** and then press the left button.

127

You can easily move a tab stop to a different location on the ruler.

Move a Tab Stop

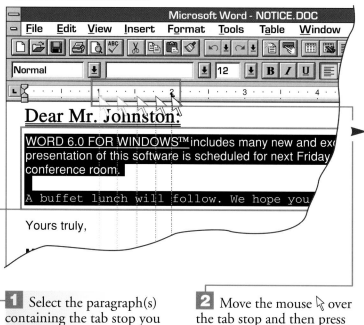

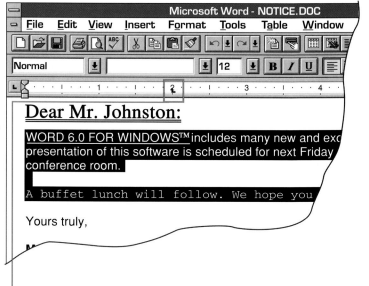

1 Select the paragraph(s) containing the tab stop you want to move.

2 Move the mouse over the tab stop and then press and hold down the left button as you drag the tab stop to a new position.

◆ A dotted line indicates the new tab stop position.

3 Release the button and the tab stop moves to the new position.

| Format Characters | **Format Paragraphs** | Format Pages | Smart Formatting | Working With Tables | Using Graphics | Using Templates and Wizards | Customize Word | Merge Documents | Sharing Data |

Change Paragraph Alignment
Change Line Spacing
Change Tab Settings
Indent Paragraphs

Create Numbered and Bulleted Lists
Add Borders
Add Shading

Word lets you remove a tab stop from the ruler.

Dear Mr. Johnston:

WORD 6.0 FOR WINDOWS™ includes many new and exciting features. A brief presentation of this software is scheduled for next Friday at 11:00 a.m. in the conference room.

Remove a Tab Stop

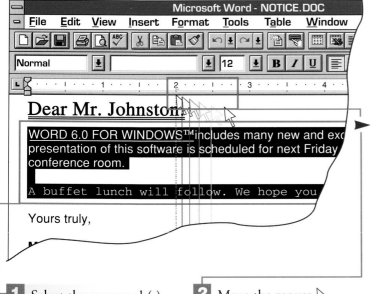

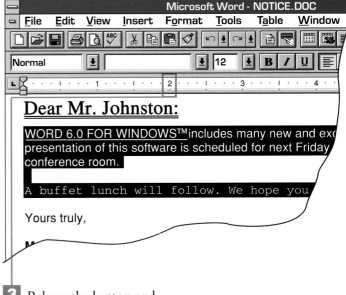

1 Select the paragraph(s) containing the tab stop you want to remove.

2 Move the mouse over the tab stop and then press and hold down the left button as you drag the tab stop downward off the ruler.

3 Release the button and the tab stop disappears.

INDENT PARAGRAPHS

Indent first line of paragraph

Indent left edge of paragraph

Indent right edge of paragraph

You can use the indent feature to emphasize paragraphs in your document. Word offers several indent options.

Indent Paragraphs

You can move these symbols on the ruler to indent paragraphs in your document.

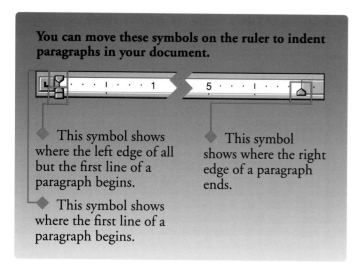

◆ This symbol shows where the left edge of all but the first line of a paragraph begins.

◆ This symbol shows where the first line of a paragraph begins.

◆ This symbol shows where the right edge of a paragraph ends.

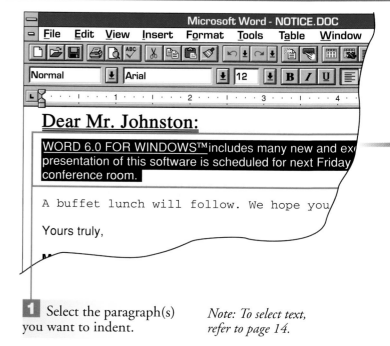

Microsoft Word - NOTICE.DOC

File   Edit   View   Insert   Format   Tools   Table   Window

Normal   Arial   12   B   I   U

Dear Mr. Johnston:

WORD 6.0 FOR WINDOWS™ includes many new and ex presentation of this software is scheduled for next Friday conference room.

A buffet lunch will follow. We hope you

Yours truly,

1 Select the paragraph(s) you want to indent.

Note: To select text, refer to page 14.

Format Characters	**Format Paragraphs**	Format Pages	Smart Formatting	Working With Tables	Using Graphics	Using Templates and Wizards	Customize Word	Merge Documents	Sharing Data

Change Paragraph Alignment
Change Line Spacing
Change Tab Settings
Indent Paragraphs

Create Numbered and Bulleted Lists
Add Borders
Add Shading

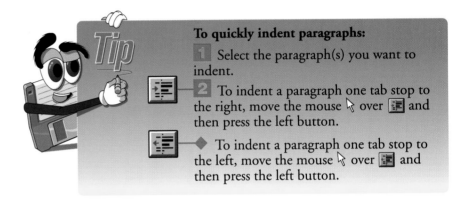

To quickly indent paragraphs:

■1 Select the paragraph(s) you want to indent.

■2 To indent a paragraph one tab stop to the right, move the mouse ⇗ over 📄 and then press the left button.

◆ To indent a paragraph one tab stop to the left, move the mouse ⇗ over 📄 and then press the left button.

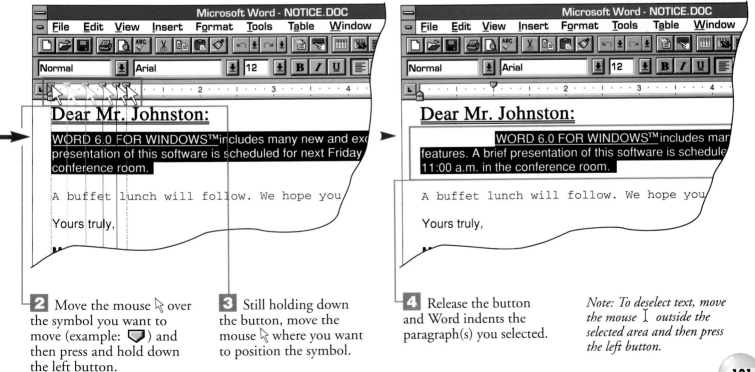

2 Move the mouse ⇗ over the symbol you want to move (example: ▽) and then press and hold down the left button.

3 Still holding down the button, move the mouse ⇗ where you want to position the symbol.

4 Release the button and Word indents the paragraph(s) you selected.

Note: To deselect text, move the mouse I outside the selected area and then press the left button.

CREATE NUMBERED AND BULLETED LISTS

You can emphasize text in a list by beginning each item with a bullet or number. Word offers several bullet and number styles to choose from.

Create Numbered and Bulleted Lists

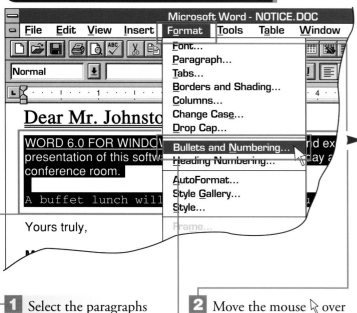

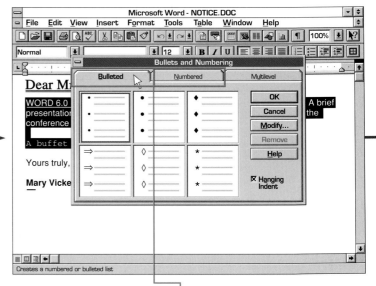

1 Select the paragraphs you want to display bullets or numbers.

Note: To select text, refer to page 14.

2 Move the mouse ⃗ over **Format** and then press the left button.

3 Move the mouse ⃗ over **Bullets and Numbering** and then press the left button.

◆ The **Bullets and Numbering** dialog box appears.

4 To create a bulleted list, move the mouse ⃗ over the **Bulleted** tab and then press the left button.

◆ To create a numbered list, move the mouse ⃗ over the **Numbered** tab and then press the left button.

| Format Characters | **Format Paragraphs** | Format Pages | Smart Formatting | Working With Tables | Using Graphics | Using Templates and Wizards | Customize Word | Merge Documents | Sharing Data |

Change Paragraph Alignment
Change Line Spacing
Change Tab Settings
Indent Paragraphs

Create Numbered and Bulleted Lists
Add Borders
Add Shading

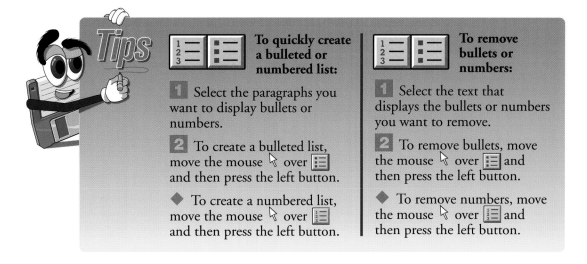

To quickly create a bulleted or numbered list:

1 Select the paragraphs you want to display bullets or numbers.

2 To create a bulleted list, move the mouse ⟍ over 🗎 and then press the left button.

◆ To create a numbered list, move the mouse ⟍ over 🗎 and then press the left button.

To remove bullets or numbers:

1 Select the text that displays the bullets or numbers you want to remove.

2 To remove bullets, move the mouse ⟍ over 🗎 and then press the left button.

◆ To remove numbers, move the mouse ⟍ over 🗎 and then press the left button.

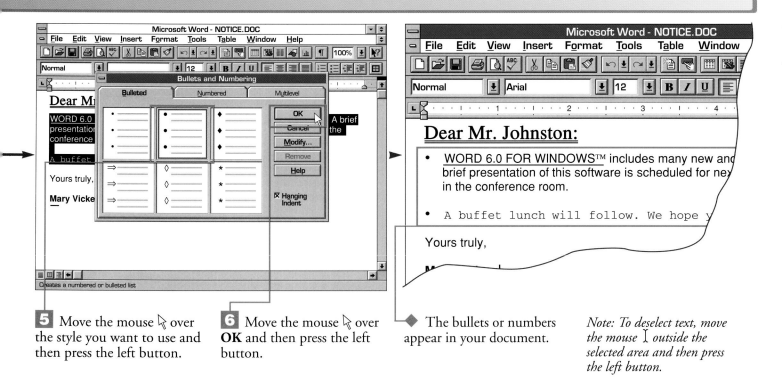

5 Move the mouse ⟍ over the style you want to use and then press the left button.

6 Move the mouse ⟍ over **OK** and then press the left button.

◆ The bullets or numbers appear in your document.

Note: To deselect text, move the mouse I outside the selected area and then press the left button.

ADD BORDERS

You can add borders to draw attention to important information and improve the overall appearance of your document.

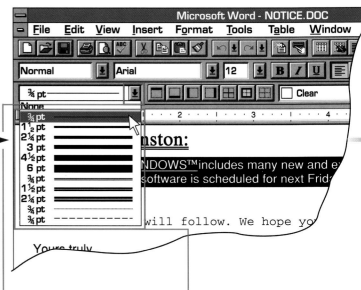

Add Borders

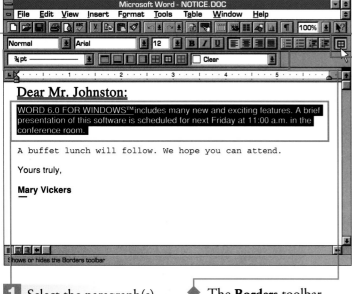

1 Select the paragraph(s) you want to display borders.

2 Move the mouse ⬚ over ⬚ and then press the left button.

◆ The **Borders** toolbar appears.

*Note: To hide the **Borders** toolbar, repeat step **2**.*

3 To select a line style, move the mouse ⬚ over ⬚ in the **Line Style** box and then press the left button.

◆ A list of the available line styles appears.

4 Move the mouse ⬚ over the line style you want to use and then press the left button.

Format Characters	Format Paragraphs	Format Pages	Smart Formatting	Working With Tables	Using Graphics	Using Templates and Wizards	Customize Word	Merge Documents	Sharing Data

Change Paragraph Alignment
Change Line Spacing
Change Tab Settings
Indent Paragraphs

Create Numbered and Bulleted Lists
Add Borders
Add Shading

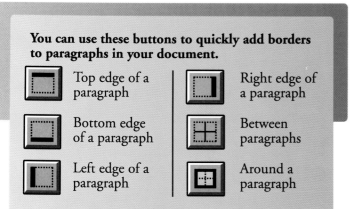

You can use these buttons to quickly add borders to paragraphs in your document.

Top edge of a paragraph

Right edge of a paragraph

Bottom edge of a paragraph

Between paragraphs

Left edge of a paragraph

Around a paragraph

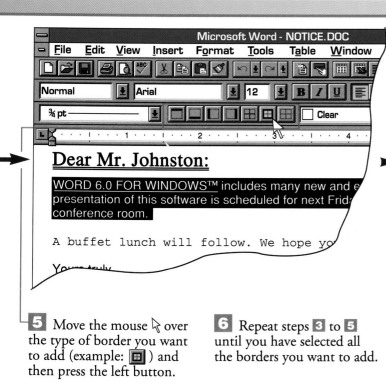

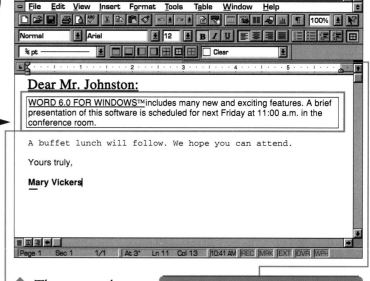

5 Move the mouse ⌖ over the type of border you want to add (example: ▣) and then press the left button.

6 Repeat steps **3** to **5** until you have selected all the borders you want to add.

◆ The paragraph displays the border(s) you selected.

Note: To deselect a paragraph, move the mouse I outside the selected area and then press the left button.

To remove borders:

1 Select the paragraph(s) displaying the borders you want to remove.

2 Move the mouse ⌖ over ▦ and then press the left button.

ADD SHADING

> You can add shading to paragraphs in your document to highlight them.

Add Shading

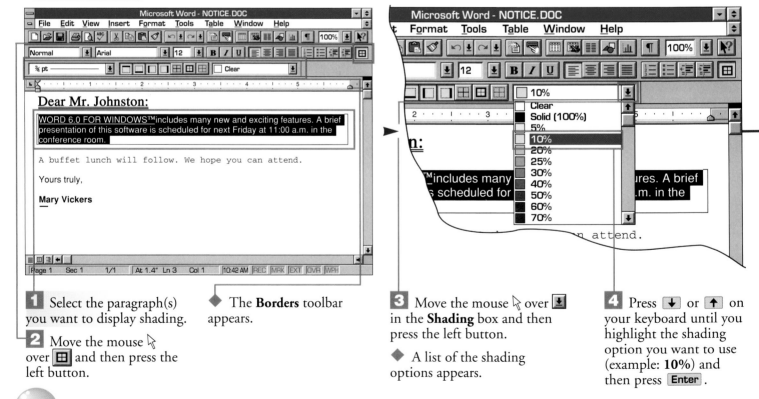

1 Select the paragraph(s) you want to display shading.

2 Move the mouse ⇧ over 田 and then press the left button.

◆ The **Borders** toolbar appears.

3 Move the mouse ⇧ over ⬇ in the **Shading** box and then press the left button.

◆ A list of the shading options appears.

4 Press ⬇ or ⬆ on your keyboard until you highlight the shading option you want to use (example: **10%**) and then press **Enter**.

136

| Format Characters | **Format Paragraphs** | Format Pages | Smart Formatting | Working With Tables | Using Graphics | Using Templates and Wizards | Customize Word | Merge Documents | Sharing Data |

Change Paragraph Alignment
Change Line Spacing
Change Tab Settings
Indent Paragraphs

Create Numbered and Bulleted Lists
Add Borders
Add Shading

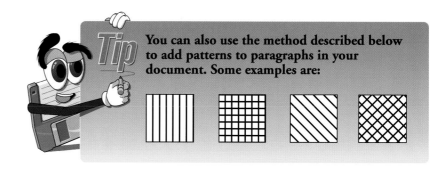

Tip

You can also use the method described below to add patterns to paragraphs in your document. Some examples are:

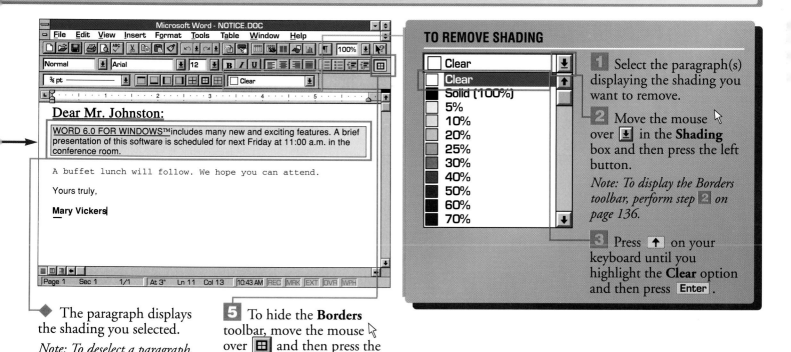

◆ The paragraph displays the shading you selected.

Note: To deselect a paragraph, move the mouse I outside the selected area and then press the left button.

5 To hide the **Borders** toolbar, move the mouse ▷ over ⊞ and then press the left button.

TO REMOVE SHADING

Clear
Clear
Solid (100%)
5%
10%
20%
25%
30%
40%
50%
60%
70%

1 Select the paragraph(s) displaying the shading you want to remove.

2 Move the mouse ▷ over ⊞ in the **Shading** box and then press the left button.

Note: To display the Borders toolbar, perform step 2 on page 136.

3 Press ↑ on your keyboard until you highlight the **Clear** option and then press **Enter**.

137

FORMAT PAGES

Insert a Page Break

Create a New Section

Change Paper Size

Change Margins

Add Headers or Footers

Add Footnotes

Add Page Numbers

Center a Page

Create Columns

◆ This chapter will show you how to change the look of entire pages in your document. You will learn how to change margins, add page numbers and display information in columns.

INSERT A PAGE BREAK

> If you want to start a new page at a specific place in your document, you can insert a page break. A page break defines where one page ends and another begins.

A page break you inserted.

When you fill an entire page with text, Word automatically starts a new one by inserting a page break.

A page break Word inserted.

Insert a Page Break

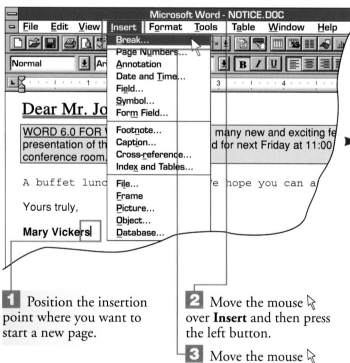

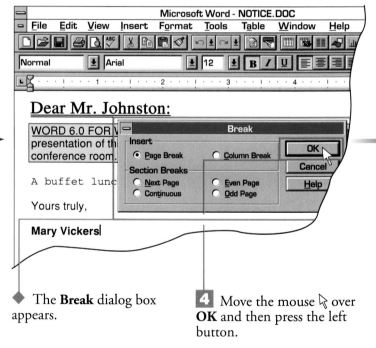

1 Position the insertion point where you want to start a new page.

2 Move the mouse ⟍ over **Insert** and then press the left button.

3 Move the mouse ⟍ over **Break** and then press the left button.

◆ The **Break** dialog box appears.

4 Move the mouse ⟍ over **OK** and then press the left button.

140

Format Characters	Format Paragraphs	**Format Pages**	Smart Formatting	Working With Tables	Using Graphics	Using Templates and Wizards	Customize Word	Merge Documents	Sharing Data

Insert a Page Break   Add Footnotes
Create a New Section   Add Page Numbers
Change Paper Size   Center a Page
Change Margins   Create Columns
Add Headers or Footers

To quickly insert a page break:

1 Position the insertion point where you want to start a new page.

2 Press Ctrl + Enter.

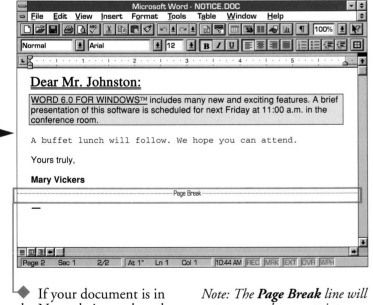

Delete a Page Break

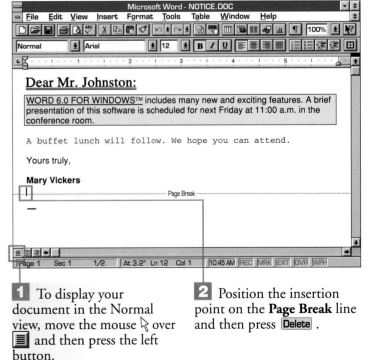

◆ If your document is in the Normal view, a dotted line with the words **Page Break** appears across your screen. This line defines where one page ends and another begins.

Note: The **Page Break** *line will not appear when you print your document.*

1 To display your document in the Normal view, move the mouse ⬍ over ▤ and then press the left button.

2 Position the insertion point on the **Page Break** line and then press Delete.

141

CREATE A NEW SECTION

> If you want to change the page formatting of a part of your document, you must divide the document into separate sections. Otherwise, the changes will affect your entire document.

Create a New Section

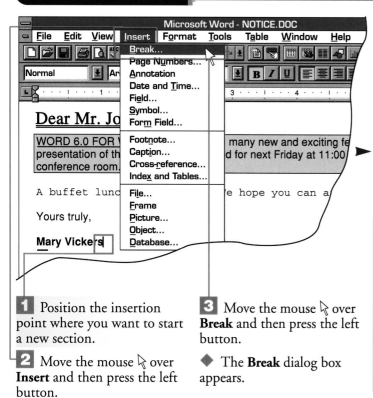

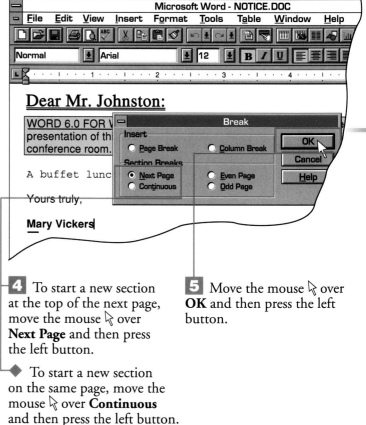

1 Position the insertion point where you want to start a new section.

2 Move the mouse ⟍ over **Insert** and then press the left button.

3 Move the mouse ⟍ over **Break** and then press the left button.

◆ The **Break** dialog box appears.

4 To start a new section at the top of the next page, move the mouse ⟍ over **Next Page** and then press the left button.

◆ To start a new section on the same page, move the mouse ⟍ over **Continuous** and then press the left button.

5 Move the mouse ⟍ over **OK** and then press the left button.

| Format Characters | Format Paragraphs | **Format Pages** | Smart Formatting | Working With Tables | Using Graphics | Using Templates and Wizards | Customize Word | Merge Documents | Sharing Data |

Insert a Page Break
Create a New Section
Change Paper Size
Change Margins
Add Headers or Footers

Add Footnotes
Add Page Numbers
Center a Page
Create Columns

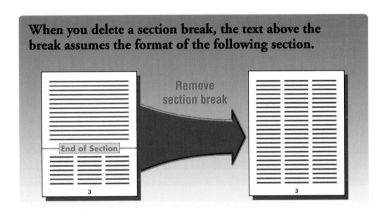

When you delete a section break, the text above the break assumes the format of the following section.

End of Section

Remove section break

3   3

Delete a Section Break

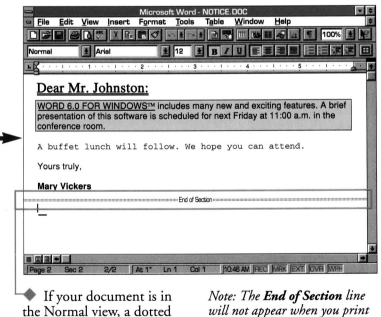

Microsoft Word - NOTICE.DOC

Dear Mr. Johnston:

WORD 6.0 FOR WINDOWS™ includes many new and exciting features. A brief presentation of this software is scheduled for next Friday at 11:00 a.m. in the conference room.

A buffet lunch will follow. We hope you can attend.

Yours truly,

Mary Vickers

End of Section

Page 2   Sec 2   2/2   At 1"   Ln 1   Col 1   10:46 AM   REC   MRK   EXT   OVR   WPH

◆ If your document is in the Normal view, a dotted line with the words **End of Section** appears across your screen. This line defines where one section ends and another begins.

*Note: The **End of Section** line will not appear when you print your document.*

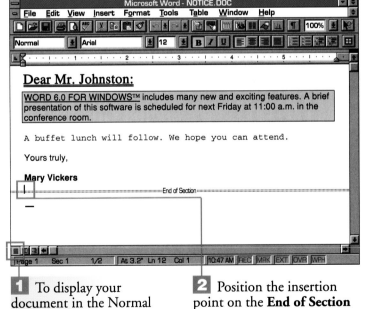

Microsoft Word - NOTICE.DOC

Dear Mr. Johnston:

WORD 6.0 FOR WINDOWS™ includes many new and exciting features. A brief presentation of this software is scheduled for next Friday at 11:00 a.m. in the conference room.

A buffet lunch will follow. We hope you can attend.

Yours truly,

Mary Vickers

End of Section

Page 1   Sec 1   1/2   At 3.2"   Ln 12   Col 1   10:47 AM   REC   MRK   EXT   OVR   WPH

1 To display your document in the Normal view, move the mouse ⟍ over 📄 and then press the left button.

2 Position the insertion point on the **End of Section** line and then press Delete .

143

CHANGE PAPER SIZE

Word automatically sets each page in your document to print on 8.5 by 11 inch paper. If you want to use a different paper size, you can change this setting.

Change Paper Size

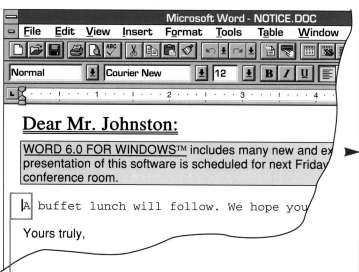

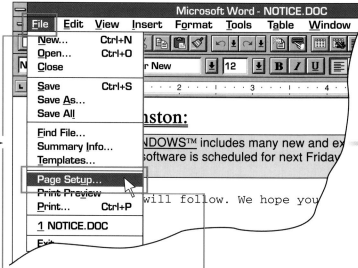

1 To change the paper size for your entire document, position the insertion point anywhere in the document.

◆ To change the paper size for a part of your document, position the insertion point in the section you want to change.

Note: For information on sections, refer to page 142.

2 Move the mouse ⬚ over **File** and then press the left button.

3 Move the mouse ⬚ over **Page Setup** and then press the left button.

◆ The **Page Setup** dialog box appears.

| Format Characters | Format Paragraphs | **Format Pages** | Smart Formatting | Working With Tables | Using Graphics | Using Templates and Wizards | Customize Word | Merge Documents | Sharing Data |

Insert a Page Break
Create a New Section
Change Paper Size
Change Margins
Add Headers or Footers

Add Footnotes
Add Page Numbers
Center a Page
Create Columns

CHANGE PAGE ORIENTATION

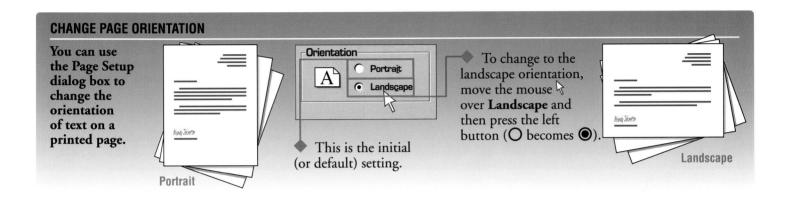

You can use the Page Setup dialog box to change the orientation of text on a printed page.

Portrait

◆ This is the initial (or default) setting.

◆ To change to the landscape orientation, move the mouse over **Landscape** and then press the left button (○ becomes ◉).

Landscape

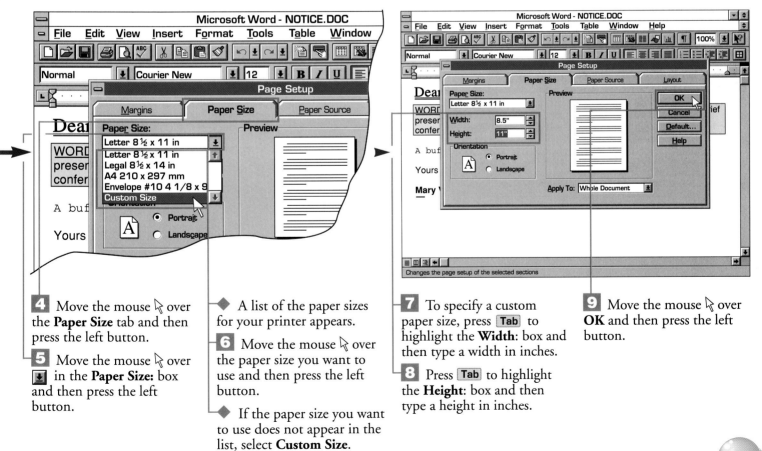

4 Move the mouse over the **Paper Size** tab and then press the left button.

5 Move the mouse over ▼ in the **Paper Size:** box and then press the left button.

◆ A list of the paper sizes for your printer appears.

6 Move the mouse over the paper size you want to use and then press the left button.

◆ If the paper size you want to use does not appear in the list, select **Custom Size**.

7 To specify a custom paper size, press **Tab** to highlight the **Width:** box and then type a width in inches.

8 Press **Tab** to highlight the **Height:** box and then type a height in inches.

9 Move the mouse over **OK** and then press the left button.

CHANGE MARGINS

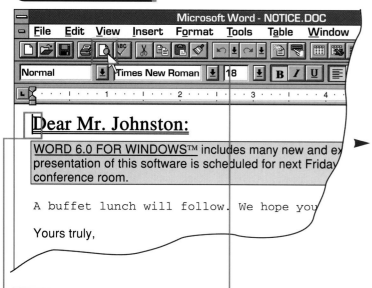

A margin is the amount of space between the text and the edges of your paper.

When you create a document, the top and bottom margins are set at 1 inch. You can change these settings to accommodate letterhead or other specialty papers.

The left and right margins are set at 1.25 inches. You can change these settings to increase or decrease the amount of text on a page.

Change Margins

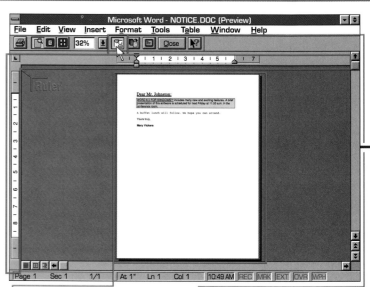

1 To change the margins for your entire document, position the insertion point anywhere in the document.

To change the margins for a part of your document, position the insertion point in the section you want to change.

Note: For information on sections, refer to page 142.

2 To change the margins, move the mouse ⌖ over 🔍 and then press the left button.

The page you were working on appears in the Print Preview window.

Note: For more information on using Print Preview, refer to pages 90 to 93.

3 If the ruler is not displayed, move the mouse ⌖ over 🖼 and then press the left button.

| Format Characters | Format Paragraphs | **Format Pages** | Smart Formatting | Working With Tables | Using Graphics | Using Templates and Wizards | Customize Word | Merge Documents | Sharing Data |

Insert a Page Break
Create a New Section
Change Paper Size
Change Margins
Add Headers or Footers

Add Footnotes
Add Page Numbers
Center a Page
Create Columns

If you want to change the left and right margins for a part of your document, it is much easier to change the indentation.

Note: To indent paragraphs, refer to page 130.

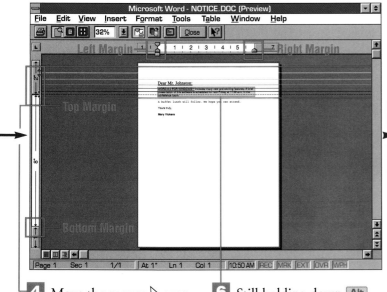

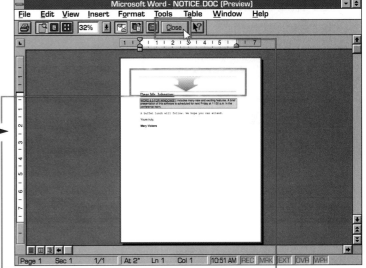

4 Move the mouse ⟍ over the margin boundary you want to move and ⟍ changes to ↕ or ↔.

5 To display the page measurements as you drag the margin boundary, press and hold down Alt .

6 Still holding down Alt , press and hold down the left button as you drag the margin boundary to a new location. A dotted line shows the location of the new margin.

7 Release the button and then Alt to display the margin changes.

8 Repeat steps **4** to **7** for each margin you want to change.

9 To close Print Preview and return to your document, move the mouse ⟍ over **Close** and then press the left button.

Note: The top and bottom margins are not visible on your screen when in the Normal view.

147

ADD HEADERS OR FOOTERS

Headers display information at the top of each page. Footers display information at the bottom of each page. They may include the title of your document, the date or your company name.

Header ◆ **GLOBAL REPORT**

Seventy-five percent of the World's people live in the Third World. These nations supply the developed nations with a multitude of raw materials and natural resources, and also buy many of our exports, (40% of U.S. exports are bought by the Third World). Clearly the lives of the people in the developed and underdeveloped worlds are unavoidably interrelated. It is for this reason that it is important for the rich nations to study the problems in other countries and help them to overcome them.

One major problem in most underdeveloped countries (UDC), is that since the Colonial period, exploitation of their arable land has rapidly increased. Companies from the developed countries (DC) are blamed for abusing the land, but the farmers and locals are often guilty as well. 75% of the energy supplied in the UDC's is produced by wood burning. To get this wood they must tear down trees, and eventually whole forests disappear. The land then no longer has anything holding it together. This results in soil erosion and loss of water retaining abilities.

Development in the Western sense is to industrialize your economy. It is essential for the Third World to develop their production techniques, especially in agriculture, in order to compete effectively on the World Markets. This kind of development, however, requires not only costly machinery, but expensive fossil fuels for operation. For countries already billions in debt this is obviously not economically possible.

CHAPTER 1

◆ Footer

Add Headers or Footers (to every page)

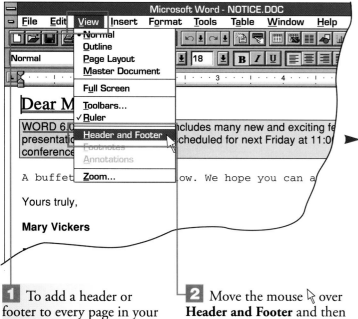

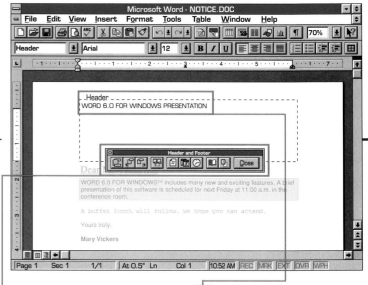

1 To add a header or footer to every page in your document, move the mouse ⌖ over **View** and then press the left button.

2 Move the mouse ⌖ over **Header and Footer** and then press the left button.

◆ The text in your document appears dimmed.

◆ The **Header and Footer** toolbar appears.

3 To create a header, type the header text. You can format the header text as you would any text in your document.

| Format Characters | Format Paragraphs | **Format Pages** | Smart Formatting | Working With Tables | Using Graphics | Using Templates and Wizards | Customize Word | Merge Documents | Sharing Data |

Insert a Page Break
Create a New Section
Change Paper Size
Change Margins
Add Headers or Footers

Add Footnotes
Add Page Numbers
Center a Page
Create Columns

Headers or footers will not appear on your screen if you are in the Normal view.

1 To view headers or footers, move the mouse over and then press the left button.

Note: For more information on Print Preview, refer to pages 90 to 93.

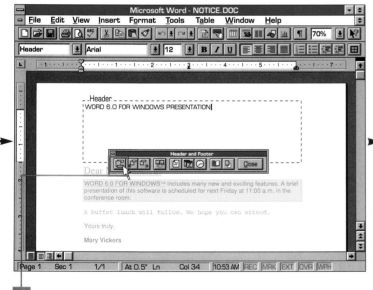

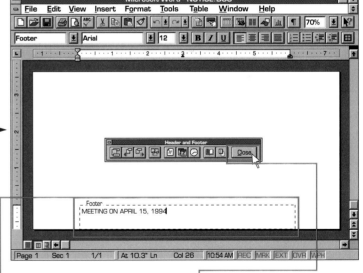

4 To create a footer, move the mouse over and then press the left button.

Note: You can return to the header area at any time by repeating step **4***.*

◆ The **Footer** area appears.

5 Type the footer text. You can format the footer text as you would any text in your document.

6 To return to your document, move the mouse over **Close** and then press the left button.

ADD HEADERS
OR FOOTERS

You can have different headers and footers on different pages in your document.

WORD OFFERS TWO OPTIONS:

Different Odd and Even
This option lets you display one header or footer on odd-numbered pages and a different header or footer on even-numbered pages.

Different First Page
This option lets you display one header or footer on the first page of your document and a different header or footer on all pages that follow.

Add Headers or Footers (vary within a document)

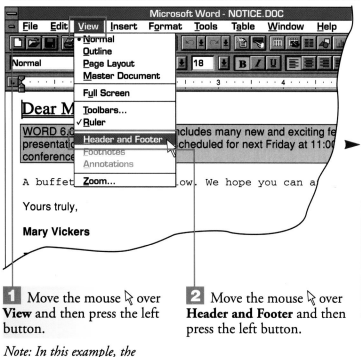

1 Move the mouse ⌖ over **View** and then press the left button.

Note: In this example, the document contains three pages.

2 Move the mouse ⌖ over **Header and Footer** and then press the left button.

◆ A Header area appears.

◆ To display the Footer area, move the mouse ⌖ over 🗎 and then press the left button. You can repeat this step to return to the Header area.

3 To display the **Page Setup** dialog box, move the mouse ⌖ over 🖼 and then press the left button.

| Format Characters | Format Paragraphs | **Format Pages** | Smart Formatting | Working With Tables | Using Graphics | Using Templates and Wizards | Customize Word | Merge Documents | Sharing Data |

Insert a Page Break   Add Footnotes
Create a New Section   Add Page Numbers
Change Paper Size   Center a Page
Change Margins   Create Columns
Add Headers or Footers

You type header or footer text in two or three of the following sections.

Note: The number of sections depends on the options you selected in step [ ] below.

First Page Header/Footer

The text you type in this section will only appear on the first page of your document.

Note: If you do not want a header or footer to appear on the first page, leave this section blank.

Header/Footer

The text you type in this section will appear on all but the first page of your document.

Odd Page Header/Footer

The text you type in this section will appear on each odd-numbered page in your document.

Even Page Header/Footer

The text you type in this section will appear on each even-numbered page in your document.

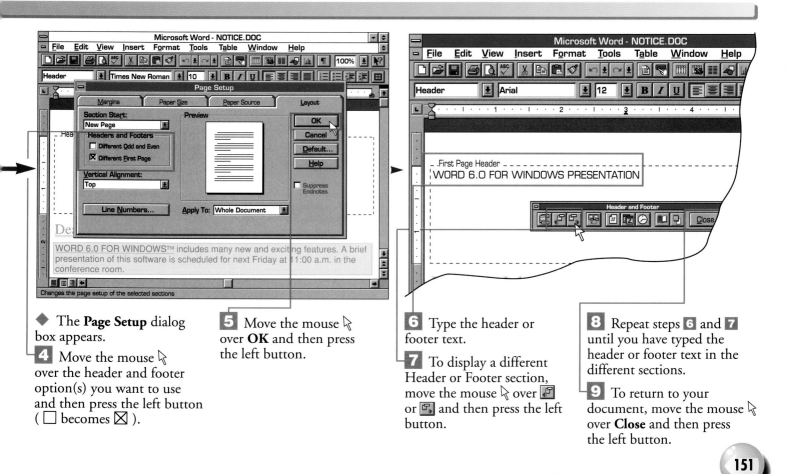

◆ The **Page Setup** dialog box appears.

4 Move the mouse over the header and footer option(s) you want to use and then press the left button (☐ becomes ☒).

5 Move the mouse over **OK** and then press the left button.

6 Type the header or footer text.

7 To display a different Header or Footer section, move the mouse over 🔳 or 🔳 and then press the left button.

8 Repeat steps **6** and **7** until you have typed the header or footer text in the different sections.

9 To return to your document, move the mouse over **Close** and then press the left button.

151

A footnote appears at the bottom of a page to provide extra information on an item in your document. Word automatically numbers a footnote and places it on the same page as the item it refers to.

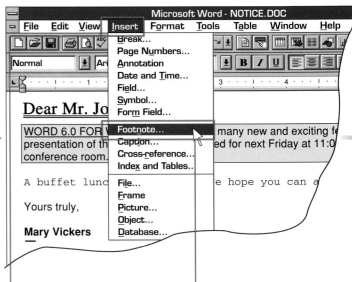

Add Footnotes

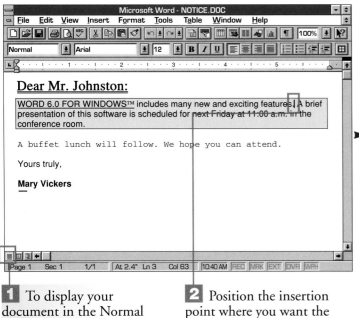

1 To display your document in the Normal view, move the mouse ⌖ over ▤ and then press the left button.

2 Position the insertion point where you want the number for the footnote to appear in your document.

3 Move the mouse ⌖ over **Insert** and then press the left button.

4 Move the mouse ⌖ over **Footnote** and then press the left button.

Format Characters	Format Paragraphs	**Format Pages**	Smart Formatting	Working With Tables	Using Graphics	Using Templates and Wizards	Customize Word	Merge Documents	Sharing Data

Insert a Page Break	**Add Footnotes**
Create a New Section	Add Page Numbers
Change Paper Size	Center a Page
Change Margins	Create Columns
Add Headers or Footers	

EDIT A FOOTNOTE

1 To edit a footnote, move the mouse I over the footnote number in your document and then quickly press the left button twice. The footnote appears.

2 Edit the text as you would any text in your document.

3 When you finish editing the footnote, move the mouse ⍦ over **Close** and then press the left button.

DELETE A FOOTNOTE

1 To delete a footnote, select the footnote number in your document and then press Delete .

Note: To select text, refer to page 14.

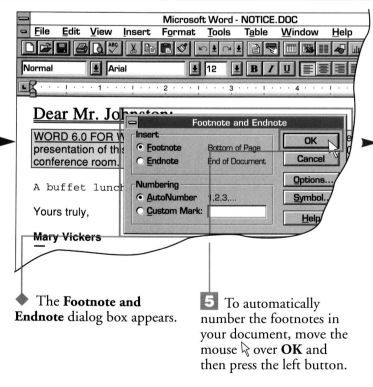

◆ The **Footnote and Endnote** dialog box appears.

5 To automatically number the footnotes in your document, move the mouse ⍦ over **OK** and then press the left button.

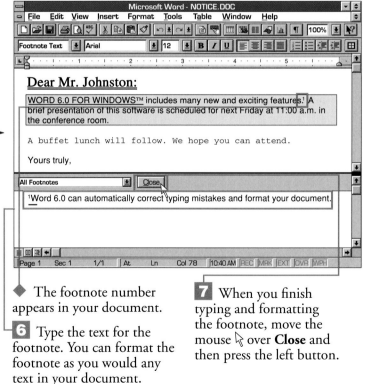

◆ The footnote number appears in your document.

6 Type the text for the footnote. You can format the footnote as you would any text in your document.

7 When you finish typing and formatting the footnote, move the mouse ⍦ over **Close** and then press the left button.

ADD PAGE NUMBERS

You can use Word's page number feature to automatically number the pages in your document.

Add Page Numbers

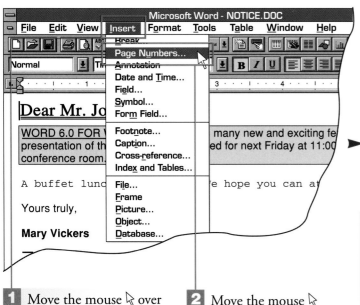

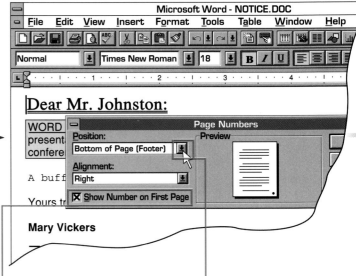

1 Move the mouse ⟨ over **Insert** and then press the left button.

2 Move the mouse ⟨ over **Page Numbers** and then press the left button.

◆ The **Page Numbers** dialog box appears.

◆ To hide the page number on the first page of your document, move the mouse ⟨ over **Show Number on First Page** and then press the left button (☒ becomes ☐).

3 To select a position for the page numbers, move the mouse ⟨ over ⬇ in the **Position:** box and then press the left button.

| Format Characters | Format Paragraphs | Format Pages | Smart Formatting | Working With Tables | Using Graphics | Using Templates and Wizards | Customize Word | Merge Documents | Sharing Data |

Insert a Page Break
Create a New Section
Change Paper Size
Change Margins
Add Headers or Footers

Add Footnotes
Add Page Numbers
Center a Page
Create Columns

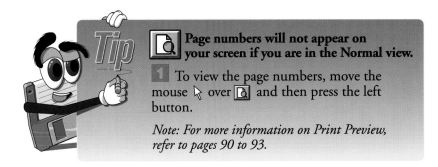

Page numbers will not appear on your screen if you are in the Normal view.

1 To view the page numbers, move the mouse ⅄ over 🔍 and then press the left button.

Note: For more information on Print Preview, refer to pages 90 to 93.

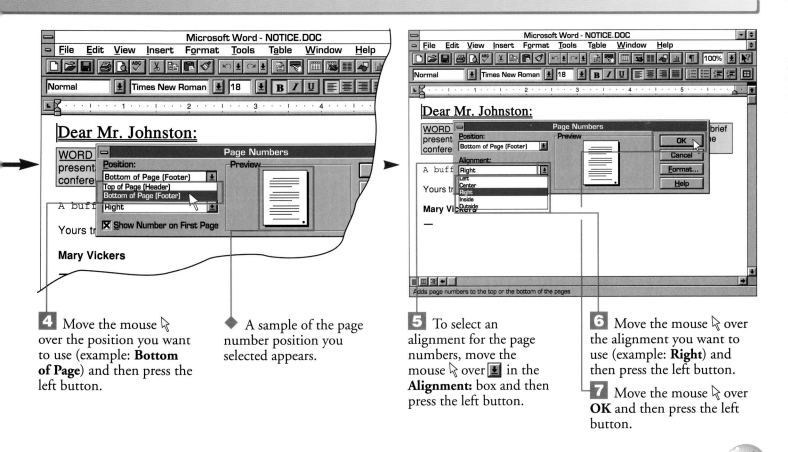

4 Move the mouse ⅄ over the position you want to use (example: **Bottom of Page**) and then press the left button.

◆ A sample of the page number position you selected appears.

5 To select an alignment for the page numbers, move the mouse ⅄ over ▼ in the **Alignment:** box and then press the left button.

6 Move the mouse ⅄ over the alignment you want to use (example: **Right**) and then press the left button.

7 Move the mouse ⅄ over **OK** and then press the left button.

155

CENTER A PAGE

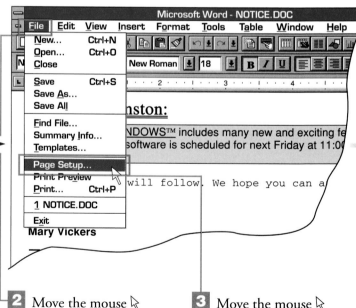

You can vertically center text on a page. This is useful when creating title pages or short memos.

Center a Page

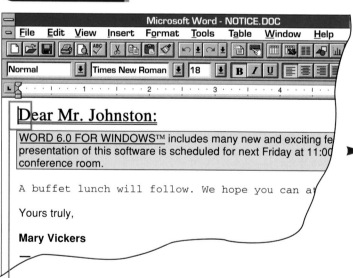

1 To center the text on all pages in your document, position the insertion point anywhere in the document.

◆ To center the text for a part of your document, position the insertion point in the section you want to change.

Note: For information on sections, refer to page 142.

2 Move the mouse ⌕ over **File** and then press the left button.

3 Move the mouse ⌕ over **Page Setup** and then press the left button.

WORKING WITH WORD

| Format Characters | Format Paragraphs | **Format Pages** | Smart Formatting | Working With Tables | Using Graphics | Using Templates and Wizards | Customize Word | Merge Documents | Sharing Data |

Insert a Page Break | Add Footnotes
Create a New Section | Add Page Numbers
Change Paper Size | **Center a Page**
Change Margins | Create Columns
Add Headers or Footers

Text will not appear centered on your screen if you are in the Normal view.

1 To view the text centered on a page, move the mouse ↓ over 🔍 and then press the left button.

Note: For more information on Print Preview, refer to pages 90 to 93.

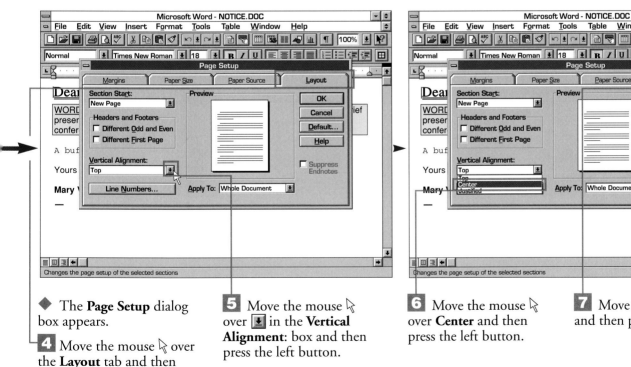

◆ The **Page Setup** dialog box appears.

4 Move the mouse ↓ over the **Layout** tab and then press the left button.

5 Move the mouse ↓ over ⬇ in the **Vertical Alignment**: box and then press the left button.

6 Move the mouse ↓ over **Center** and then press the left button.

7 Move the mouse ↓ over **OK** and then press the left button.

CREATE COLUMNS

You can quickly and easily display your text in columns like those found in a newspaper. This feature is useful for creating documents such as newsletters and brochures.

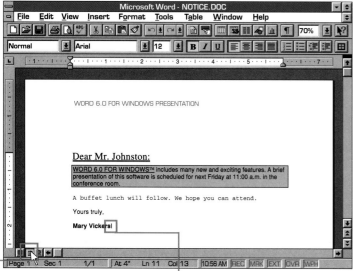

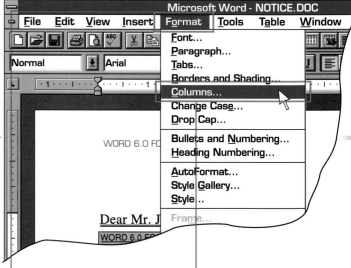

In the Normal view, Word cannot display columns side-by-side.

1 To display your document in the Page Layout view, move the mouse ⍺ over 📄 and then press the left button.

2 To display all the text in your document in columns, position the insertion point anywhere in the document.

◆ To display the text in part of your document in columns, position the insertion point in the section you want to change.

Note: For information on sections, refer to page 142.

3 Move the mouse ⍺ over **Format** and then press the left button.

4 Move the mouse ⍺ over **Columns** and then press the left button.

158

Format Characters	Format Paragraphs	**Format Pages**	Smart Formatting	Working With Tables	Using Graphics	Using Templates and Wizards	Customize Word	Merge Documents	Sharing Data

Insert a Page Break   Add Footnotes
Create a New Section   Add Page Numbers
Change Paper Size   Center a Page
Change Margins   **Create Columns**
Add Headers or Footers

INSERT A COLUMN BREAK

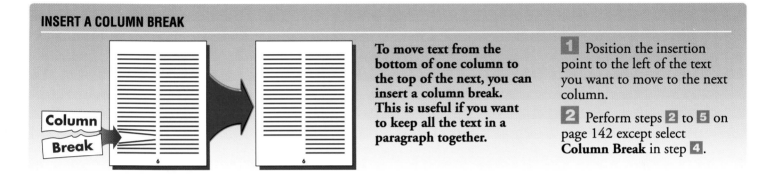

To move text from the bottom of one column to the top of the next, you can insert a column break. This is useful if you want to keep all the text in a paragraph together.

1 Position the insertion point to the left of the text you want to move to the next column.

2 Perform steps **2** to **5** on page 142 except select **Column Break** in step **4**.

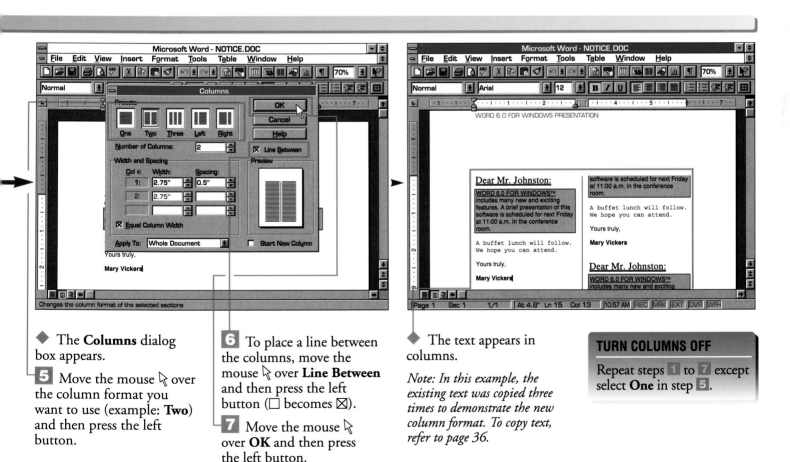

◆ The **Columns** dialog box appears.

5 Move the mouse ⌖ over the column format you want to use (example: **Two**) and then press the left button.

6 To place a line between the columns, move the mouse ⌖ over **Line Between** and then press the left button (□ becomes ⊠).

7 Move the mouse ⌖ over **OK** and then press the left button.

◆ The text appears in columns.

Note: In this example, the existing text was copied three times to demonstrate the new column format. To copy text, refer to page 36.

TURN COLUMNS OFF

Repeat steps **1** to **7** except select **One** in step **5**.

verview

SMART FORMATTING

Format a Document Automatically

Create a Paragraph Style

Apply a Style

Create a Character Style

Change an Existing Style

◆ This chapter will show you Word's powerful formatting features. You will learn how to instantly change the appearance of your entire document and format your document using styles.

FORMAT A DOCUMENT AUTOMATICALLY

> The AutoFormat feature will select and then apply the best formats to your document.

Format a Document Automatically

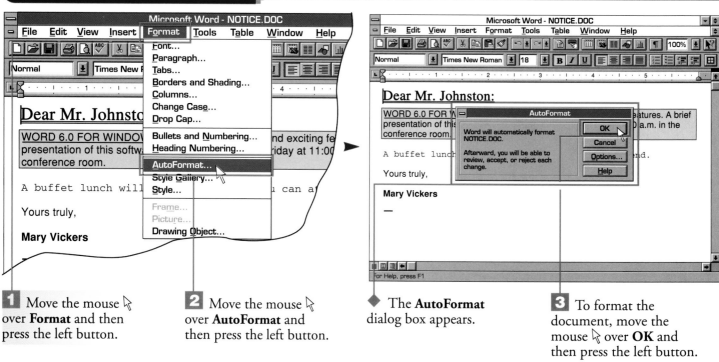

1 Move the mouse ᐟ over **Format** and then press the left button.

2 Move the mouse ᐟ over **AutoFormat** and then press the left button.

◆ The **AutoFormat** dialog box appears.

3 To format the document, move the mouse ᐟ over **OK** and then press the left button.

WORKING WITH WORD

Format Characters | Format Paragraphs | Format Pages | **Smart Formatting** | Working With Tables | Using Graphics | Using Templates and Wizards | Customize Word | Merge Documents | Sharing Data

Format a Document Automatically
Create a Paragraph Style
Apply a Style

Create a Character Style
Change an Existing Style

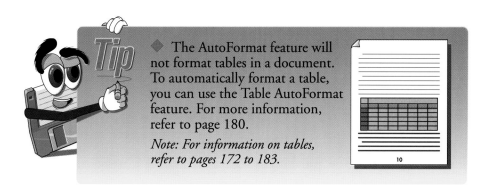

◆ The AutoFormat feature will not format tables in a document. To automatically format a table, you can use the Table AutoFormat feature. For more information, refer to page 180.

Note: For information on tables, refer to pages 172 to 183.

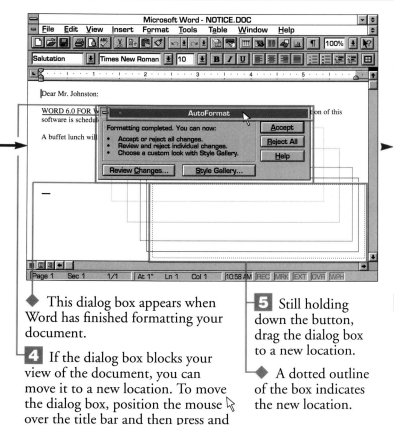

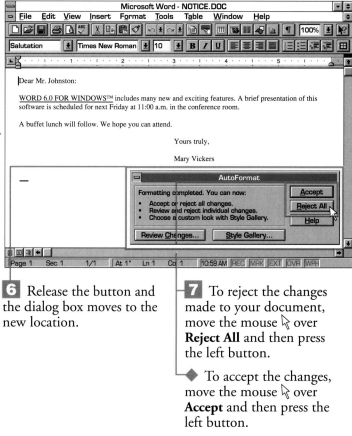

◆ This dialog box appears when Word has finished formatting your document.

4 If the dialog box blocks your view of the document, you can move it to a new location. To move the dialog box, position the mouse ⇖ over the title bar and then press and hold down the left button.

5 Still holding down the button, drag the dialog box to a new location.

◆ A dotted outline of the box indicates the new location.

6 Release the button and the dialog box moves to the new location.

7 To reject the changes made to your document, move the mouse ⇖ over **Reject All** and then press the left button.

◆ To accept the changes, move the mouse ⇖ over **Accept** and then press the left button.

163

A paragraph style is a set of commands that change the appearance of entire paragraphs. You can apply these styles to parts of your document to save time and keep the appearance of text consistent.

Create a Paragraph Style

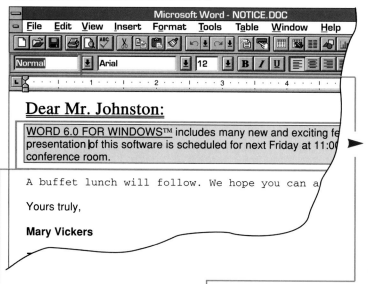

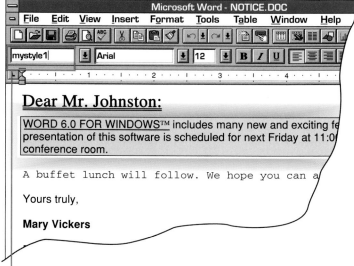

1 Format a paragraph with the characteristics you want to copy to other paragraphs in your document (example: shading and borders).

2 Position the insertion point anywhere in the paragraph.

3 Move the mouse I over the **Style** box and then press the left button.

4 Type a name for the style (example: **mystyle 1**).

5 Press **Enter** on your keyboard to create the style.

Note: To create a character style, refer to page 166.

WORKING WITH WORD

| Format Characters | Format Paragraphs | Format Pages | **Smart Formatting** | Working With Tables | Using Graphics | Using Templates and Wizards | Customize Word | Merge Documents | Sharing Data |

Format a Document Automatically
Create a Paragraph Style
Apply a Style

Create a Character Style
Change an Existing Style

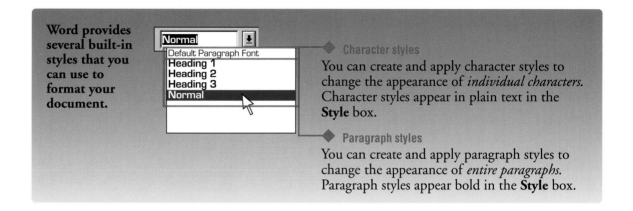

Word provides several built-in styles that you can use to format your document.

◆ **Character styles**

You can create and apply character styles to change the appearance of *individual characters*. Character styles appear in plain text in the **Style** box.

◆ **Paragraph styles**

You can create and apply paragraph styles to change the appearance of *entire paragraphs*. Paragraph styles appear bold in the **Style** box.

Apply a Style

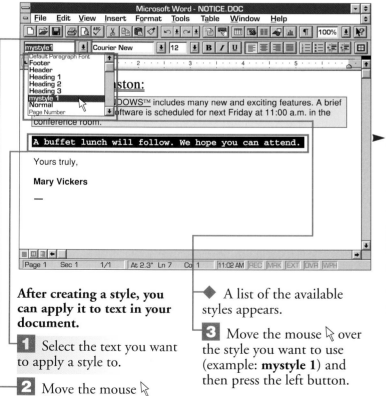

After creating a style, you can apply it to text in your document.

1 Select the text you want to apply a style to.

2 Move the mouse ↳ over ⬇ beside the **Style** box and then press the left button.

◆ A list of the available styles appears.

3 Move the mouse ↳ over the style you want to use (example: **mystyle 1**) and then press the left button.

◆ Word applies the style to the text you selected.

Note: To deselect text, move the mouse I outside the selected area and then press the left button.

CREATE A CHARACTER STYLE

A character style is a set of commands that change the appearance of individual characters. You can apply these styles to parts of your document to save time and keep the appearance of text consistent.

Create a Character Style

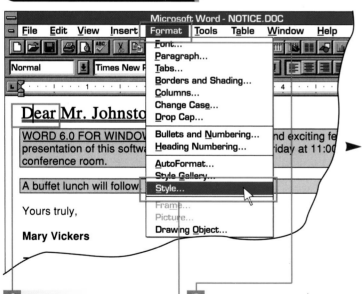

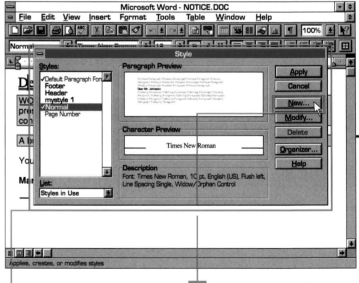

1 Position the insertion point anywhere in a word that displays the formats you want the new style to contain.

2 Move the mouse over **Format** and then press the left button.

3 Move the mouse over **Style** and then press the left button.

◆ The **Style** dialog box appears.

4 Move the mouse over **New** and then press the left button.

◆ The **New Style** dialog box appears.

Format Characters | Format Paragraphs | Format Pages | **Smart Formatting** | Working With Tables | Using Graphics | Using Templates and Wizards | Customize Word | Merge Documents | Sharing Data

Format a Document Automatically
Create a Paragraph Style
Apply a Style

Create a Character Style
Change an Existing Style

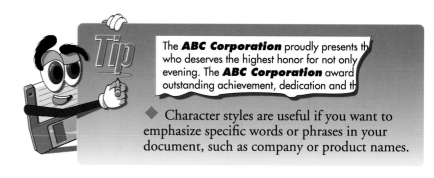

◆ Character styles are useful if you want to emphasize specific words or phrases in your document, such as company or product names.

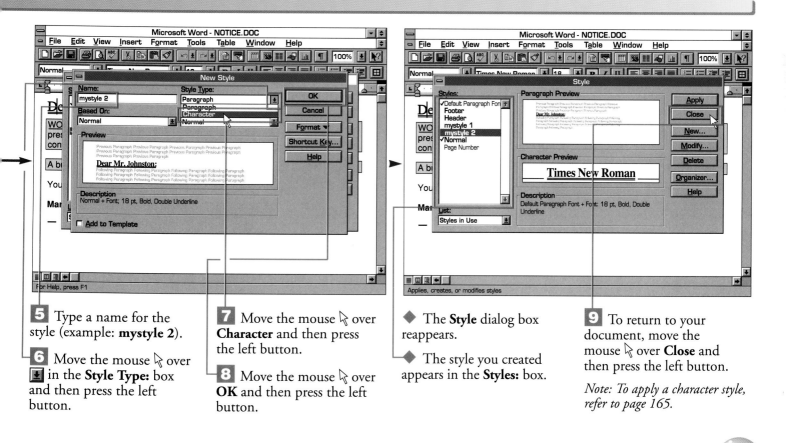

5 Type a name for the style (example: **mystyle 2**).

6 Move the mouse ⬇ over ⬇ in the **Style Type:** box and then press the left button.

7 Move the mouse ⬇ over **Character** and then press the left button.

8 Move the mouse ⬇ over **OK** and then press the left button.

◆ The **Style** dialog box reappears.

◆ The style you created appears in the **Styles:** box.

9 To return to your document, move the mouse ⬇ over **Close** and then press the left button.

Note: To apply a character style, refer to page 165.

CHANGE AN EXISTING STYLE

You can easily make changes to an existing style. All text assigned to the original style will automatically display the new formats.

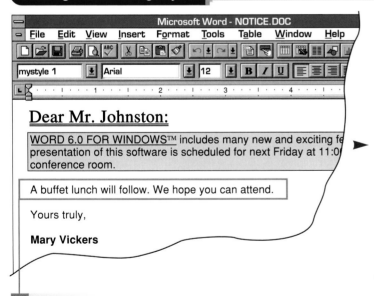

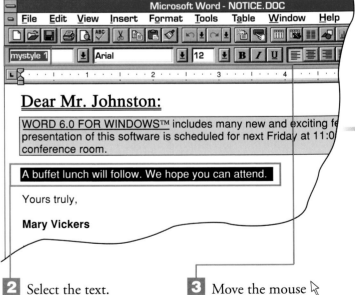

1 Make the desired formatting changes to text assigned to the style you want to change.

Note: In this example, the borders and shading were removed from the paragraph.

2 Select the text.

Note: To select text, refer to page 14.

3 Move the mouse ⟋ over the **Style** box and then press the left button.

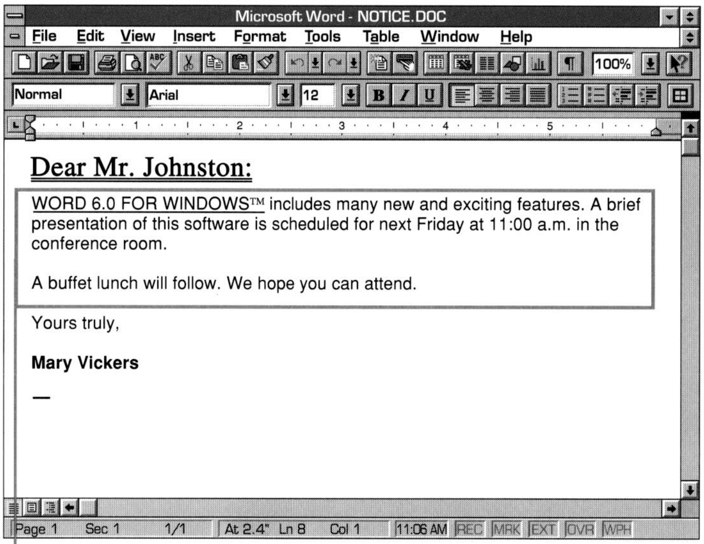

WORKING WITH WORD

| Format Characters | Format Paragraphs | Format Pages | **Smart Formatting** | Working With Tables | Using Graphics | Using Templates and Wizards | Customize Word | Merge Documents | Sharing Data |

Format a Document Automatically
Create a Paragraph Style
Apply a Style

Create a Character Style
Change an Existing Style

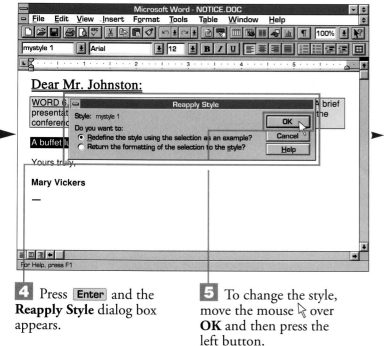

4 Press **Enter** and the **Reapply Style** dialog box appears.

5 To change the style, move the mouse �}︎ over **OK** and then press the left button.

◆ All text assigned to the style reflects the change.

Note: To deselect text, move the mouse I outside the selected area and then press the left button.

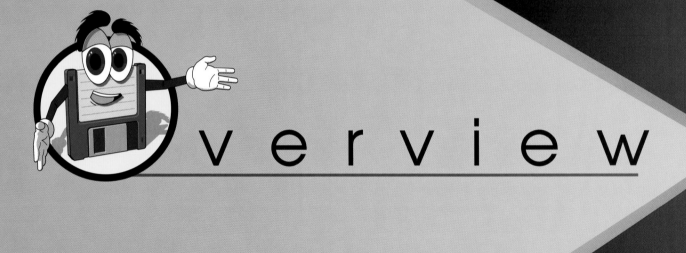

Overview

WORKING WITH TABLES

Create a Table

Type Text

Add a Row or Column

Delete a Row or Column

Change Column Width

Format a Table

Merge Cells

◆ This chapter will show you how to use tables to organize information in your document. You will learn how to create a table and change its appearance to best suit your needs.

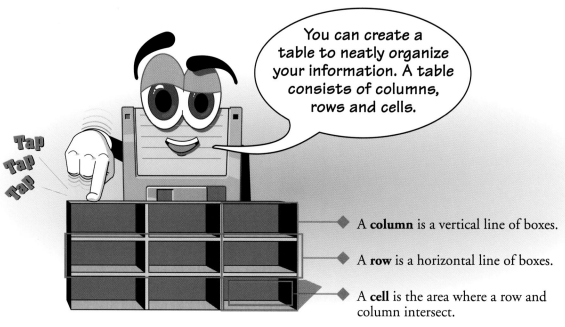

You can create a table to neatly organize your information. A table consists of columns, rows and cells.

◆ A **column** is a vertical line of boxes.

◆ A **row** is a horizontal line of boxes.

◆ A **cell** is the area where a row and column intersect.

Create a Table

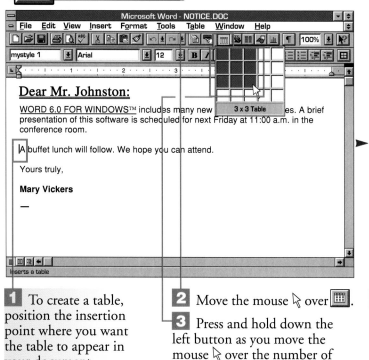

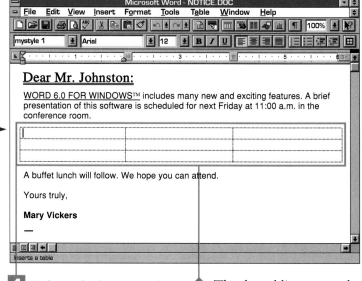

1 To create a table, position the insertion point where you want the table to appear in your document.

2 Move the mouse ⓀΚ over 📅.

3 Press and hold down the left button as you move the mouse Ⓚ over the number of rows and columns you want in your table (example: **3 x 3**).

4 Release the button and the table appears.

◆ The dotted lines around the cells in the table will not appear when you print your document. To print table lines, you can add borders using the **Table AutoFormat** feature. Refer to page 180 for more information.

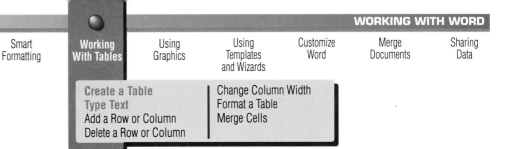

| Format Characters | Format Paragraphs | Format Pages | Smart Formatting | Working With Tables | Using Graphics | Using Templates and Wizards | Customize Word | Merge Documents | Sharing Data |

Create a Table
Type Text
Add a Row or Column
Delete a Row or Column

Change Column Width
Format a Table
Merge Cells

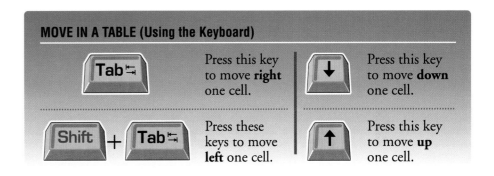

MOVE IN A TABLE (Using the Keyboard)

Tab — Press this key to move **right** one cell.

↓ — Press this key to move **down** one cell.

Shift + **Tab** — Press these keys to move **left** one cell.

↑ — Press this key to move **up** one cell.

Type Text in a Table

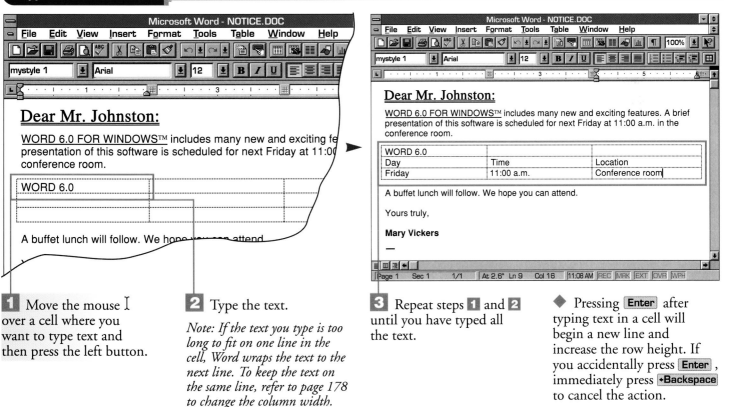

1 Move the mouse I over a cell where you want to type text and then press the left button.

2 Type the text.

Note: If the text you type is too long to fit on one line in the cell, Word wraps the text to the next line. To keep the text on the same line, refer to page 178 to change the column width.

3 Repeat steps **1** and **2** until you have typed all the text.

◆ Pressing **Enter** after typing text in a cell will begin a new line and increase the row height. If you accidentally press **Enter**, immediately press **←Backspace** to cancel the action.

ADD A ROW
OR COLUMN

You can add a row or column to your table if you want to insert new information.

Add a Row

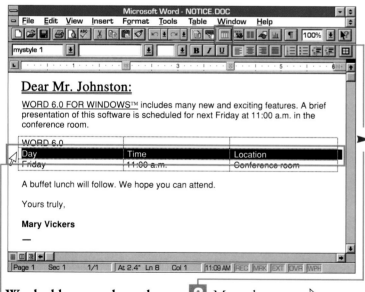

Word adds a row above the row you select.

1 To select a row, move the mouse I to the left edge of the row (I changes to ⇗) and then press the left button.

2 Move the mouse ⇗ over 🏢 and then press the left button.

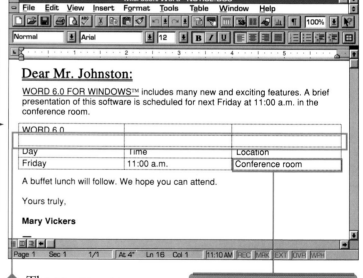

◆ The new row appears.

Note: To deselect a row, move the mouse I outside the table and then press the left button.

To add a row to the bottom of your table:

1 Position the insertion point in the bottom right cell of your table.

2 Press **Tab** and the new row appears.

Format Characters	Format Paragraphs	Format Pages	Smart Formatting	Working With Tables	Using Graphics	Using Templates and Wizards	Customize Word	Merge Documents	Sharing Data

Create a Table   Change Column Width
Type Text   Format a Table
Add a Row or Column   Merge Cells
Delete a Row or Column

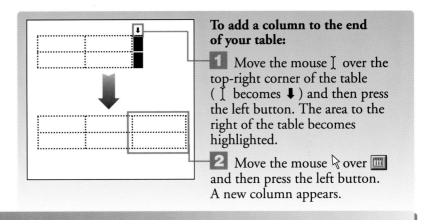

To add a column to the end of your table:

1 Move the mouse I over the top-right corner of the table (I becomes ↓) and then press the left button. The area to the right of the table becomes highlighted.

2 Move the mouse ⇘ over ▦ and then press the left button. A new column appears.

Add a Column

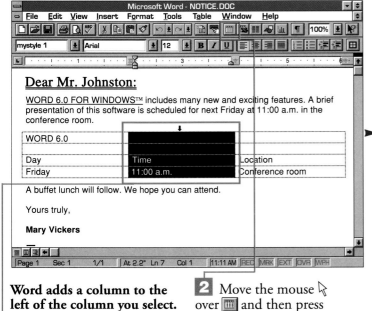

Word adds a column to the left of the column you select.

1 To select a column, move the mouse I to the top edge of the column (I changes to ↓) and then press the left button.

2 Move the mouse ⇘ over ▦ and then press the left button.

◆ The new column appears.

Note: To deselect a column, move the mouse I outside the table and then press the left button.

175

DELETE A ROW OR COLUMN

You can delete a row or column from your table. This lets you remove information or extra cells you no longer need.

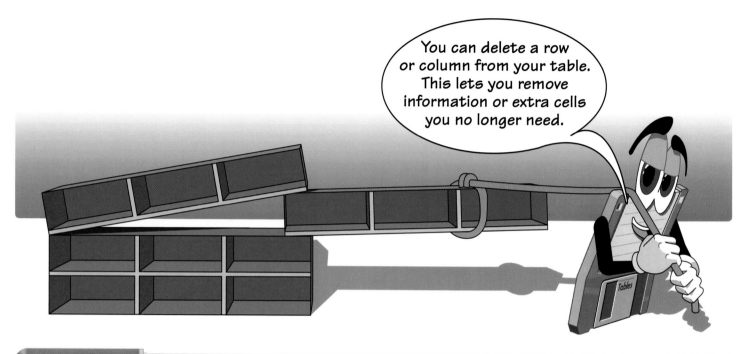

Delete a Row

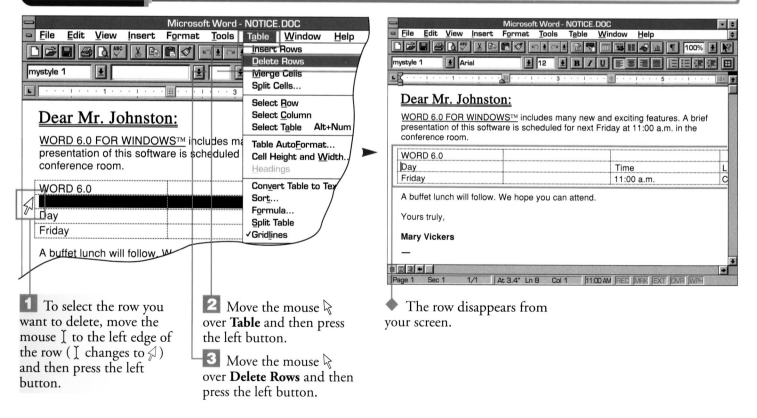

1 To select the row you want to delete, move the mouse I to the left edge of the row (I changes to ⇗) and then press the left button.

2 Move the mouse ⇗ over **Table** and then press the left button.

3 Move the mouse ⇗ over **Delete Rows** and then press the left button.

◆ The row disappears from your screen.

WORKING WITH WORD

| Format Characters | Format Paragraphs | Format Pages | Smart Formatting | Working With Tables | Using Graphics | Using Templates and Wizards | Customize Word | Merge Documents | Sharing Data |

Create a Table
Type Text
Add a Row or Column
Delete a Row or Column

Change Column Width
Format a Table
Merge Cells

DELETE A TABLE

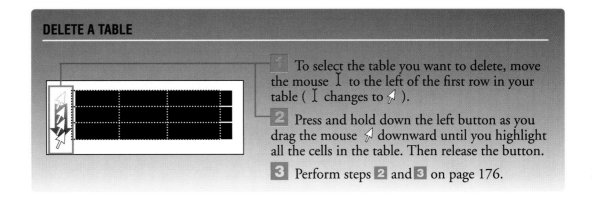

1 To select the table you want to delete, move the mouse I to the left of the first row in your table (I changes to ↗).

2 Press and hold down the left button as you drag the mouse ↗ downward until you highlight all the cells in the table. Then release the button.

3 Perform steps **2** and **3** on page 176.

Delete a Column

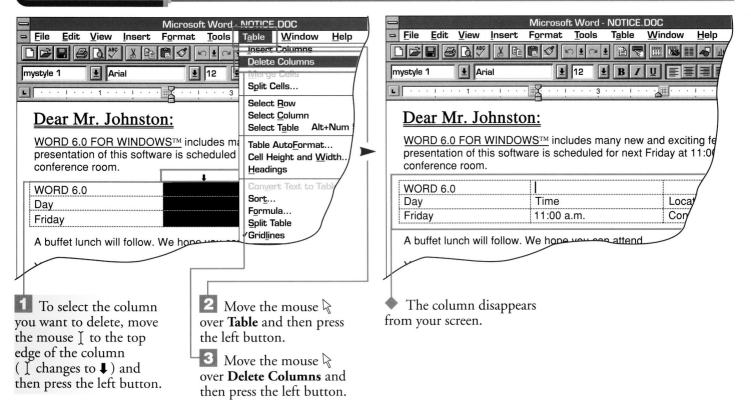

1 To select the column you want to delete, move the mouse I to the top edge of the column (I changes to ↓) and then press the left button.

2 Move the mouse ↖ over **Table** and then press the left button.

3 Move the mouse ↖ over **Delete Columns** and then press the left button.

◆ The column disappears from your screen.

CHANGE
COLUMN WIDTH

You can adjust the columns in your table to make them wider or narrower.

Change Column Width

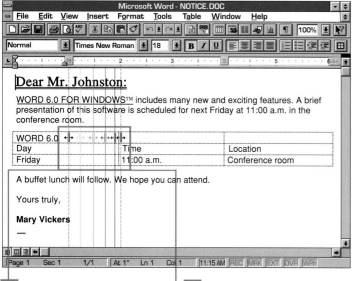

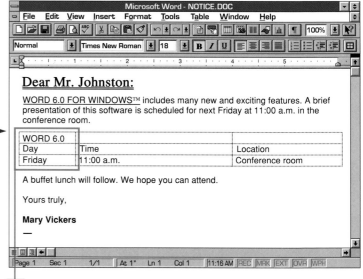

1 Move the mouse I over the right edge of the column you want to change (I becomes ←‖→).

2 Press and hold down the left button as you drag the edge of the column to a new position.

◆ The dotted line indicates the new position.

3 Release the button and the new column width appears.

Note: The width of the entire table remains the same.

| Format Characters | Format Paragraphs | Format Pages | Smart Formatting | **Working With Tables** | Using Graphics | Using Templates and Wizards | Customize Word | Merge Documents | Sharing Data |

Create a Table
Type Text
Add a Row or Column
Delete a Row or Column

Change Column Width
Format a Table
Merge Cells

You can have Word adjust a column width to best fit the longest item in the column.

Change Column Width Automatically

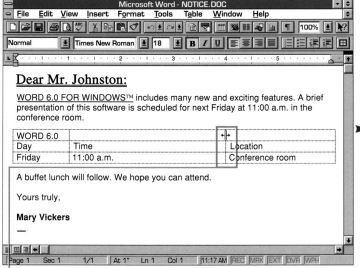

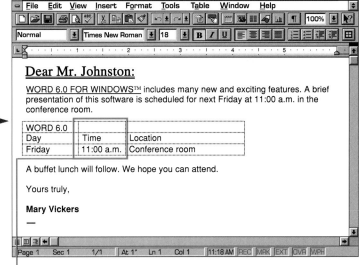

1 Move the mouse I over the right edge of the column you want to change (I becomes ↔).

2 Quickly press the left button twice.

◆ The column width changes to best fit the longest item in the column.

Note: The width of the entire table changes.

You can use the Table AutoFormat feature to emphasize information and enhance the appearance of your table.

Format a Table

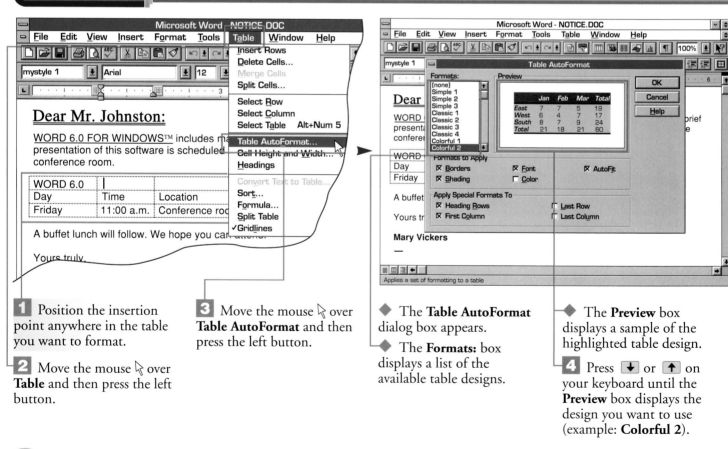

1 Position the insertion point anywhere in the table you want to format.

2 Move the mouse ⇧ over **Table** and then press the left button.

3 Move the mouse ⇧ over **Table AutoFormat** and then press the left button.

◆ The **Table AutoFormat** dialog box appears.

◆ The **Formats:** box displays a list of the available table designs.

◆ The **Preview** box displays a sample of the highlighted table design.

4 Press ⬇ or ⬆ on your keyboard until the **Preview** box displays the design you want to use (example: **Colorful 2**).

WORKING WITH WORD

| Format Characters | Format Paragraphs | Format Pages | Smart Formatting | **Working With Tables** | Using Graphics | Using Templates and Wizards | Customize Word | Merge Documents | Sharing Data |

Create a Table
Type Text
Add a Row or Column
Delete a Row or Column

Change Column Width
Format a Table
Merge Cells

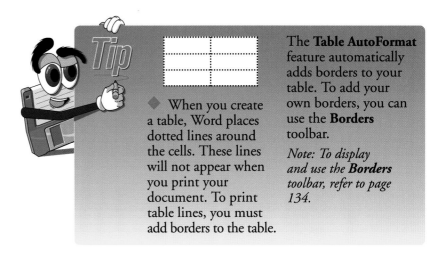

When you create a table, Word places dotted lines around the cells. These lines will not appear when you print your document. To print table lines, you must add borders to the table.

The **Table AutoFormat** feature automatically adds borders to your table. To add your own borders, you can use the **Borders** toolbar.

*Note: To display and use the **Borders** toolbar, refer to page 134.*

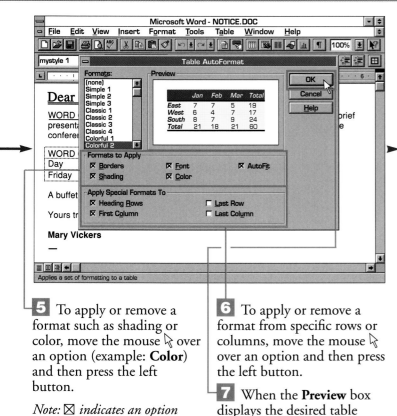

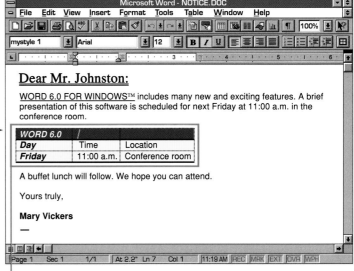

5 To apply or remove a format such as shading or color, move the mouse over an option (example: **Color**) and then press the left button.

Note: ⊠ indicates an option is on. □ indicates an option is off.

6 To apply or remove a format from specific rows or columns, move the mouse over an option and then press the left button.

7 When the **Preview** box displays the desired table appearance, move the mouse over **OK** and then press the left button.

◆ Word applies the formats you selected to the table.

REMOVE FORMATS

To remove the formats from the table, perform steps **1** to **3**, select **(none)** in step **4** and then perform step **7**.

You can combine two or more cells in your table to create one large cell. This is useful if you want to display a title at the top of your table.

Merge Cells

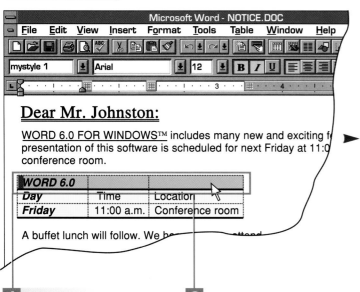

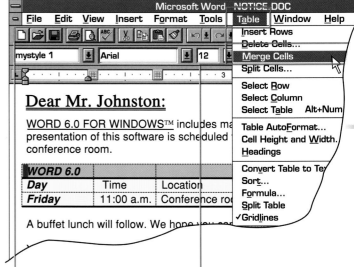

1 Move the mouse I over the first cell you want to join with other cells.

Note: You can only join cells in the same row. You cannot join cells in the same column.

2 Press and hold down the left button as you move the mouse I to highlight the cells you want to join. Then release the button.

3 Move the mouse ⌖ over **Table** and then press the left button.

4 Move the mouse ⌖ over **Merge Cells** and then press the left button.

WORKING WITH WORD

| Format Characters | Format Paragraphs | Format Pages | Smart Formatting | **Working With Tables** | Using Graphics | Using Templates and Wizards | Customize Word | Merge Documents | Sharing Data |

Create a Table
Type Text
Add a Row or Column
Delete a Row or Column

Change Column Width
Format a Table
Merge Cells

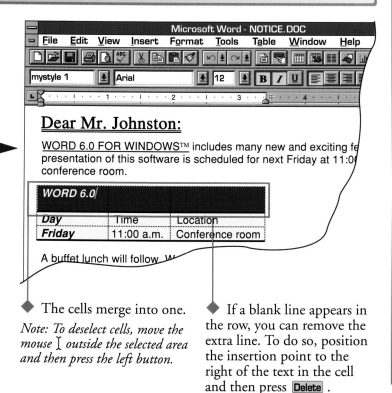

Dear Mr. Johnston:

WORD 6.0 FOR WINDOWS™ includes many new and exciting fe
presentation of this software is scheduled for next Friday at 11:0
conference room.

WORD 6.0		
Day	Time	Location
Friday	11:00 a.m.	Conference room

A buffet lunch will follow. W

◆ The cells merge into one.

Note: To deselect cells, move the mouse ⌶ outside the selected area and then press the left button.

◆ If a blank line appears in the row, you can remove the extra line. To do so, position the insertion point to the right of the text in the cell and then press Delete .

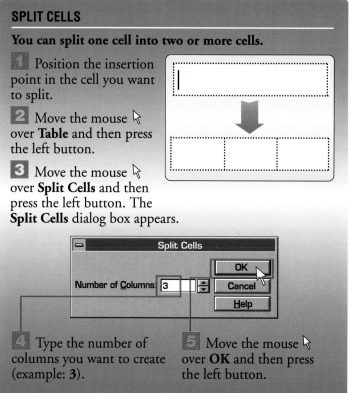

SPLIT CELLS

You can split one cell into two or more cells.

1 Position the insertion point in the cell you want to split.

2 Move the mouse ⌖ over **Table** and then press the left button.

3 Move the mouse ⌖ over **Split Cells** and then press the left button. The **Split Cells** dialog box appears.

Split Cells

Number of Columns: 3

OK
Cancel
Help

4 Type the number of columns you want to create (example: **3**).

5 Move the mouse ⌖ over **OK** and then press the left button.

Overview

USING GRAPHICS

Insert a Graphic

Insert a Frame

Size a Graphic

Move a Graphic

◆ This chapter will show you how to use graphics to make your document more attractive. You will learn how to insert, size and move a graphic to obtain the look you want.

INSERT A GRAPHIC

Word lets you insert many different graphics into your document.

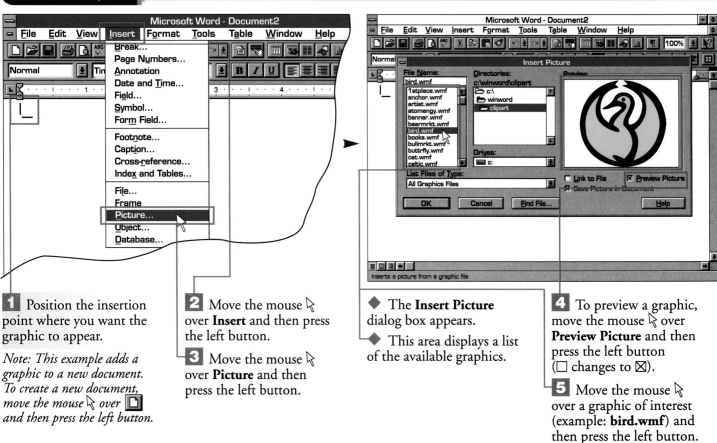

1 Position the insertion point where you want the graphic to appear.

Note: This example adds a graphic to a new document. To create a new document, move the mouse ⬚ over ⬚ and then press the left button.

2 Move the mouse ⬚ over **Insert** and then press the left button.

3 Move the mouse ⬚ over **Picture** and then press the left button.

◆ The **Insert Picture** dialog box appears.

◆ This area displays a list of the available graphics.

4 To preview a graphic, move the mouse ⬚ over **Preview Picture** and then press the left button (□ changes to ☒).

5 Move the mouse ⬚ over a graphic of interest (example: **bird.wmf**) and then press the left button. A preview of the graphic appears.

WORKING WITH WORD

| Format Characters | Format Paragraphs | Format Pages | Smart Formatting | Working With Tables | **Using Graphics** | Using Templates and Wizards | Customize Word | Merge Documents | Sharing Data |

Insert a Graphic
Insert a Frame
Size a Graphic
Move a Graphic

To make your document more attractive and interesting, Word provides close to 100 graphics. You can also buy additional graphics (clip art images) at most computer stores.

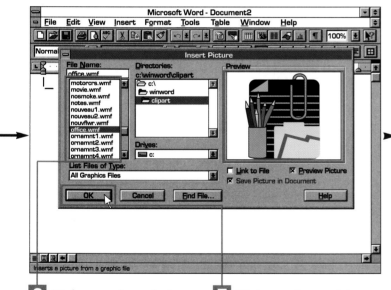

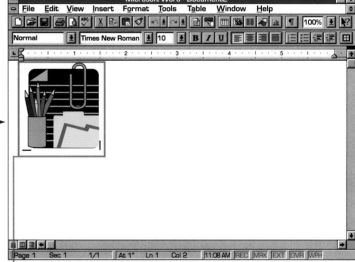

6 To browse through the available graphics, press ↑ or ↓ on your keyboard until the graphic you want to use appears (example: **office.wmf**).

7 To insert the graphic, move the mouse ⋈ over **OK** and then press the left button.

◆ The graphic appears in your document.

INSERT A FRAME

If you want to place a graphic in a specific location on a page or wrap text around a graphic, you must enclose the graphic in a frame.

Insert a Frame

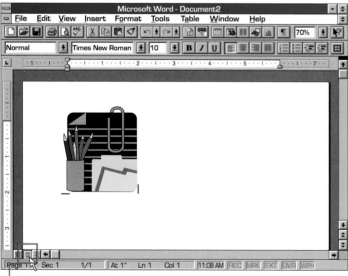

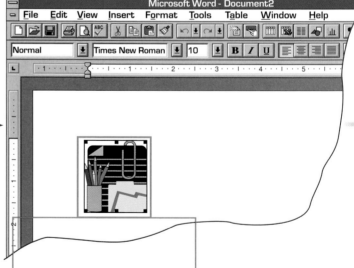

1 To display the actual location of a graphic on your page, move the mouse ⬚ over ▣ and then press the left button.

◆ The document appears in the Page Layout view.

2 To select the graphic, move the mouse Ⲓ anywhere over the graphic and then press the left button.

◆ A border appears around the graphic. The squares (■) on the border let you change the size of the graphic.

Note: To change the size of the graphic, refer to page 190.

WORKING WITH WORD

| Format Characters | Format Paragraphs | Format Pages | Smart Formatting | Working With Tables | **Using Graphics** | Using Templates and Wizards | Customize Word | Merge Documents | Sharing Data |

Insert a Graphic
Insert a Frame
Size a Graphic
Move a Graphic

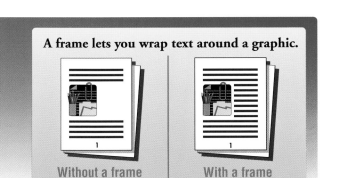

A frame lets you wrap text around a graphic.

Without a frame | With a frame

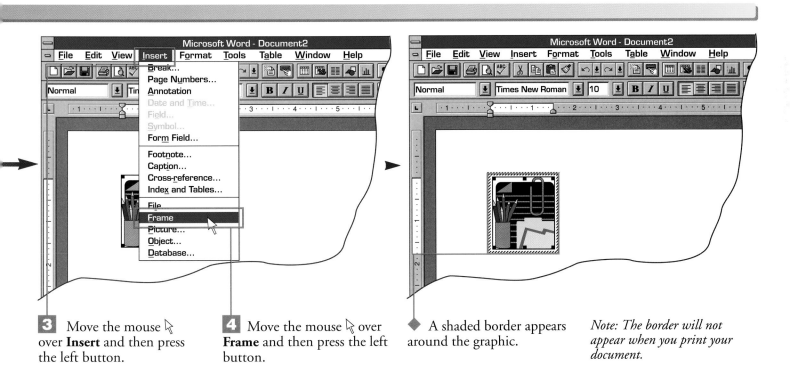

3 Move the mouse ⬚ over **Insert** and then press the left button.

4 Move the mouse ⬚ over **Frame** and then press the left button.

◆ A shaded border appears around the graphic.

Note: The border will not appear when you print your document.

SIZE A GRAPHIC

MOVE A GRAPHIC

You can change the size of a graphic or move a graphic to another location in your document.

Size a Graphic

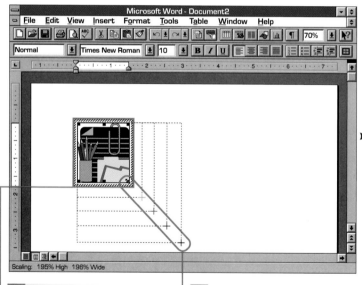

Scaling: 195% High 196% Wide

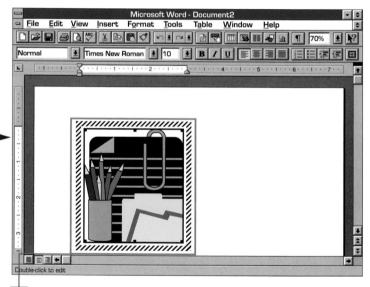

Double-click to edit

1 To select the graphic you want to size, move the mouse anywhere over the graphic and then press the left button.

◆ A box with sizing handles (■) appears around the graphic.

2 Move the mouse over one of the sizing handles (■) and changes to ↘.

3 Press and hold down the left button as you drag the graphic to the desired size.

4 Release the button to display the graphic at the new size.

Note: You can change the size of a graphic by dragging any sizing handle (■) around the graphic.

190

| Format
Characters | Format
Paragraphs | Format
Pages | Smart
Formatting | Working
With Tables | **Using
Graphics** | Using
Templates
and Wizards | Customize
Word | Merge
Documents | Sharing
Data |

Insert a Graphic
Insert a Frame
Size a Graphic
Move a Graphic

DELETE A GRAPHIC

1 To select the graphic you want to delete, move the mouse anywhere over the graphic and then press the left button.

2 Press `Delete`.

Move a Graphic

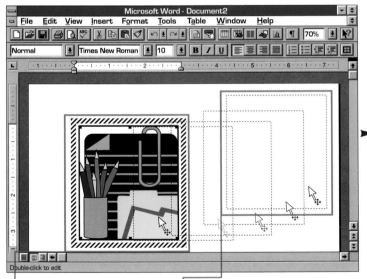

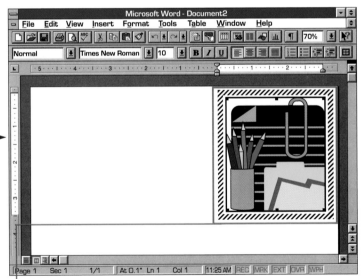

1 Position the mouse anywhere over the graphic you want to move.

2 Press and hold down the left button as you drag the graphic to a new location.

◆ A dotted box indicates the new location.

3 Release the button and the graphic appears in the new location.

Overview

USING TEMPLATES AND WIZARDS

Using a Template

Using a Wizard

◆ This chapter will show you how to create a document using a template or a wizard. These features save you time by automatically setting up many commonly used documents.

USING A TEMPLATE

Templates save you time by providing the basic framework for many commonly used documents.

Using a Template to Create a Document

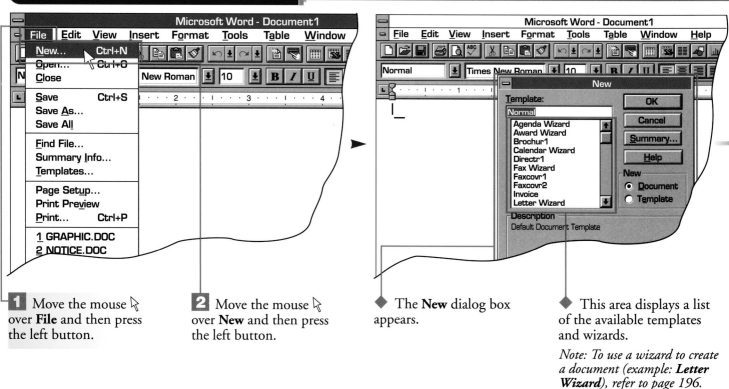

1 Move the mouse ⌖ over **File** and then press the left button.

2 Move the mouse ⌖ over **New** and then press the left button.

◆ The **New** dialog box appears.

◆ This area displays a list of the available templates and wizards.

*Note: To use a wizard to create a document (example: **Letter Wizard**), refer to page 196.*

WORKING WITH WORD

| Format Characters | Format Paragraphs | Format Pages | Smart Formatting | Working With Tables | Using Graphics | **Using Templates and Wizards** | Customize Word | Merge Documents | Sharing Data |

Using a Template
Using a Wizard

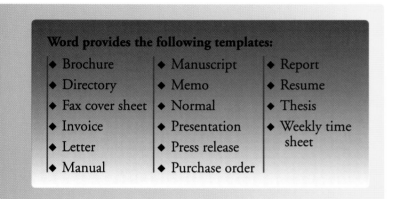

Word provides the following templates:

- ◆ Brochure
- ◆ Directory
- ◆ Fax cover sheet
- ◆ Invoice
- ◆ Letter
- ◆ Manual

- ◆ Manuscript
- ◆ Memo
- ◆ Normal
- ◆ Presentation
- ◆ Press release
- ◆ Purchase order

- ◆ Report
- ◆ Resume
- ◆ Thesis
- ◆ Weekly time sheet

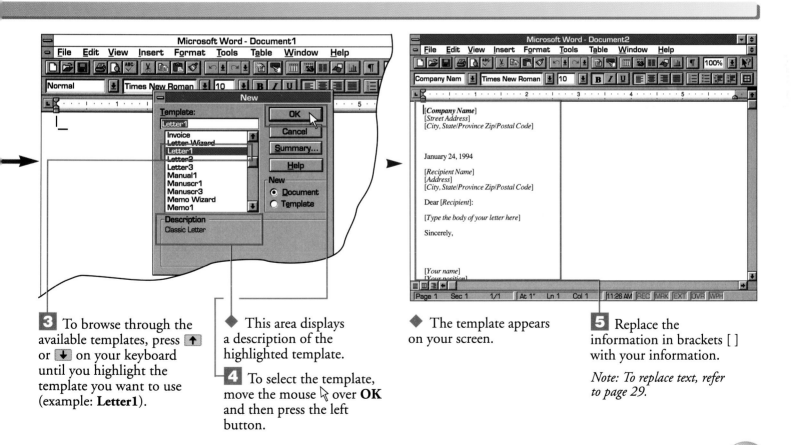

3 To browse through the available templates, press ↑ or ↓ on your keyboard until you highlight the template you want to use (example: **Letter1**).

◆ This area displays a description of the highlighted template.

4 To select the template, move the mouse � over **OK** and then press the left button.

◆ The template appears on your screen.

5 Replace the information in brackets [ ] with your information.

Note: To replace text, refer to page 29.

195

USING A WIZARD

A wizard asks questions and uses your responses to automatically set up a document.

Using a Wizard to Create a Document

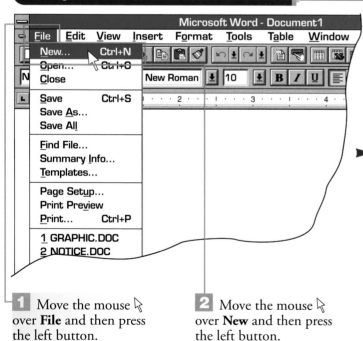

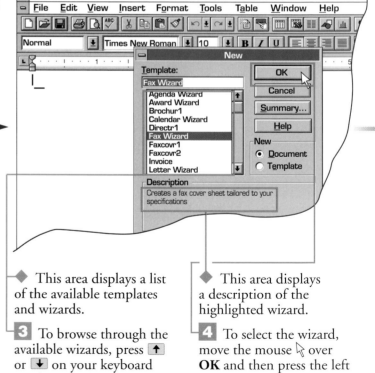

1 Move the mouse ⌖ over **File** and then press the left button.

2 Move the mouse ⌖ over **New** and then press the left button.

◆ The **New** dialog box appears.

◆ This area displays a list of the available templates and wizards.

3 To browse through the available wizards, press ⬆ or ⬇ on your keyboard until you highlight the wizard you want to use (example: **Fax Wizard**).

◆ This area displays a description of the highlighted wizard.

4 To select the wizard, move the mouse ⌖ over **OK** and then press the left button.

WORKING WITH WORD

| Format Characters | Format Paragraphs | Format Pages | Smart Formatting | Working With Tables | Using Graphics | **Using Templates and Wizards** | Customize Word | Merge Documents | Sharing Data |

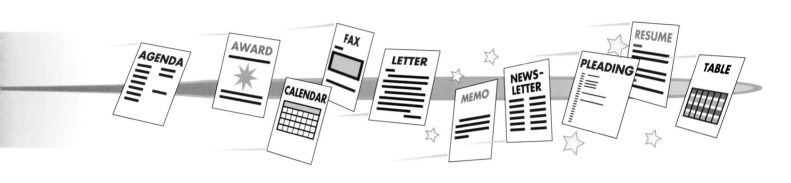

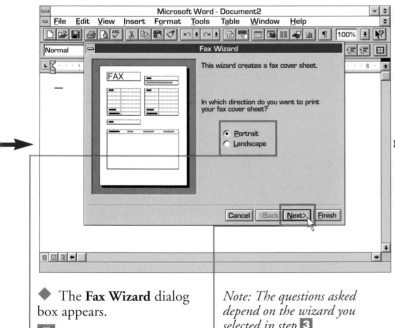

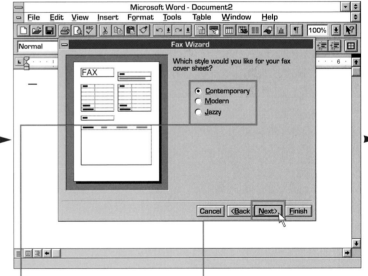

◆ The **Fax Wizard** dialog box appears.

5 Move the mouse ☐ over the direction you want to print your fax cover sheet (example: **Portrait**) and then press the left button.

Note: The questions asked depend on the wizard you selected in step **3**.

6 To display the next question, move the mouse ☐ over **Next** and then press the left button.

7 Move the mouse ☐ over the style you want for your fax cover sheet (example: **Contemporary**) and then press the left button.

8 To display the next question, move the mouse ☐ over **Next** and then press the left button.

Note: To continue creating the fax cover sheet, refer to the next page.

Using a Wizard to Create a Document (Continued)

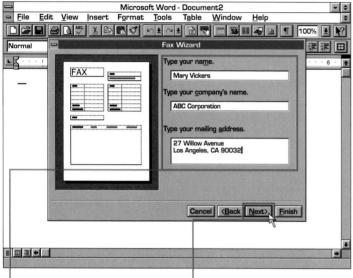

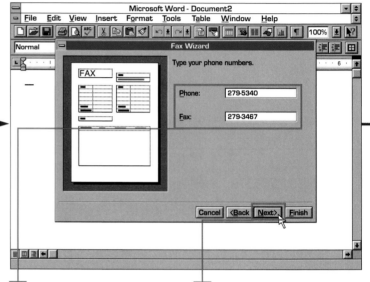

9 Press **Tab** twice to move to the first box and then type your name.

Press **Tab** to move to the second box and then type your company's name.

Press **Tab** to move to the third box and then type your mailing address.

10 To display the next question, move the mouse ⊾ over **Next** and then press the left button.

11 Press **Tab** twice to move to the first box and then type your phone number.

Press **Tab** to move to the second box and then type your fax number.

12 To display the next question, move the mouse ⊾ over **Next** and then press the left button.

> If you want to change your response to a question, move the mouse ⊾ over ‹Back and then press the left button. This returns you to the previous screen.

WORKING WITH WORD

| Format Characters | Format Paragraphs | Format Pages | Smart Formatting | Working With Tables | Using Graphics | **Using Templates and Wizards** | Customize Word | Merge Documents | Sharing Data |

Using a Template
Using a Wizard

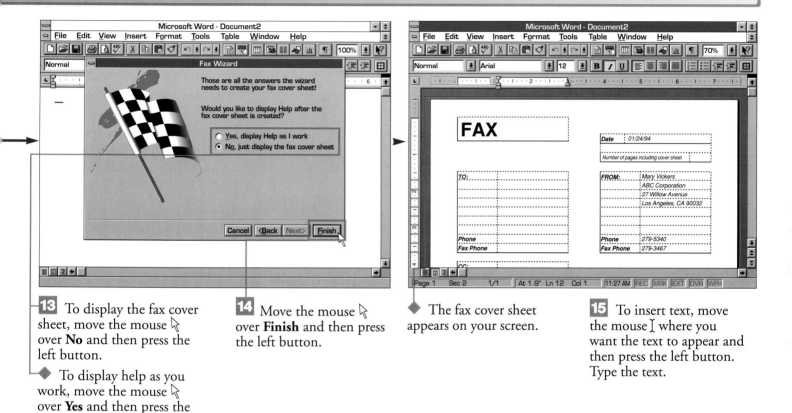

13 To display the fax cover sheet, move the mouse � over **No** and then press the left button.

◆ To display help as you work, move the mouse � over **Yes** and then press the left button.

14 Move the mouse � over **Finish** and then press the left button.

◆ The fax cover sheet appears on your screen.

15 To insert text, move the mouse ⌶ where you want the text to appear and then press the left button. Type the text.

Overview

CUSTOMIZE WORD

Record a Macro

Run a Macro

Create Your Own Toolbar

◆ This chapter will show you how to customize Word so you can work more efficiently. You will learn how to use macros and create your own toolbar.

RECORD
A MACRO

A macro saves you time by combining a series of commands into a single command.

Record a Macro

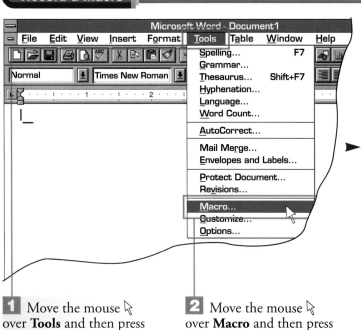

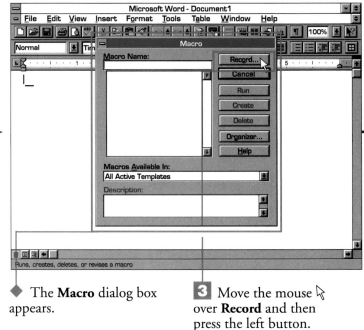

1 Move the mouse ⌖ over **Tools** and then press the left button.

2 Move the mouse ⌖ over **Macro** and then press the left button.

◆ The **Macro** dialog box appears.

3 Move the mouse ⌖ over **Record** and then press the left button.

WORKING WITH WORD

| Format Characters | Format Paragraphs | Format Pages | Smart Formatting | Working With Tables | Using Graphics | Using Templates and Wizards | **Customize Word** | Merge Documents | Sharing Data |

Record a Macro
Run a Macro
Create Your Own Toolbar

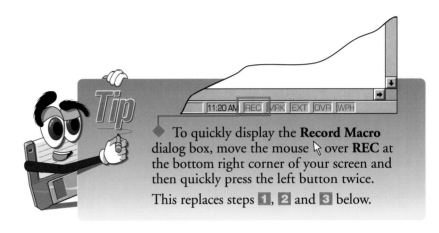

◆ To quickly display the **Record Macro** dialog box, move the mouse ⌐ over **REC** at the bottom right corner of your screen and then quickly press the left button twice.

This replaces steps **1**, **2** and **3** below.

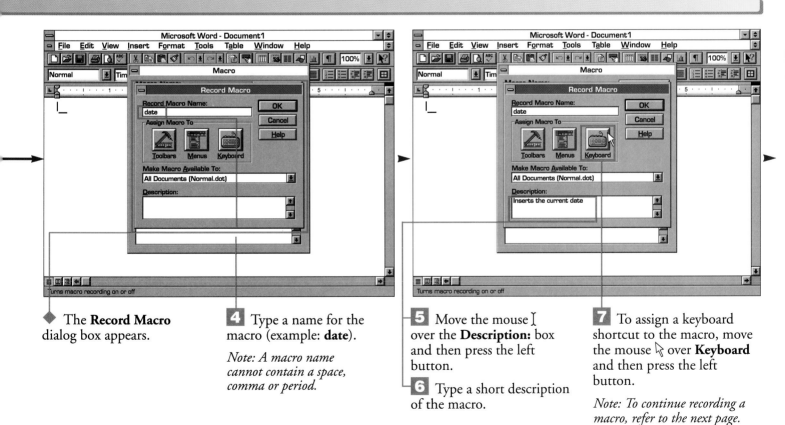

◆ The **Record Macro** dialog box appears.

4 Type a name for the macro (example: **date**).

Note: A macro name cannot contain a space, comma or period.

5 Move the mouse I over the **Description:** box and then press the left button.

6 Type a short description of the macro.

7 To assign a keyboard shortcut to the macro, move the mouse ⌐ over **Keyboard** and then press the left button.

Note: To continue recording a macro, refer to the next page.

203

Record a Macro (Continued)

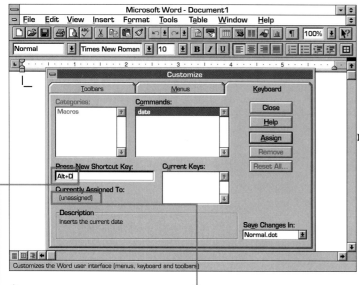

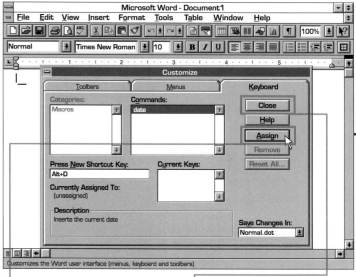

◆ The **Customize** dialog box appears.

8 Press the shortcut key combination you want to assign to the macro (example: Alt + D).

Select one of the following:

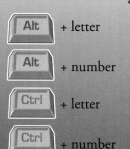

Alt + letter

Alt + number

Ctrl + letter

Ctrl + number

◆ The word **[unassigned]** appears.

Note: If the word [unassigned] did not appear, the shortcut key combination is assigned to another macro. Press ◆Backspace and then try another key combination.

9 To assign the shortcut key combination to the macro, move the mouse ⍉ over **Assign** and then press the left button.

10 Move the mouse ⍉ over **Close** and then press the left button.

WORKING WITH WORD

Format Characters | Format Paragraphs | Format Pages | Smart Formatting | Working With Tables | Using Graphics | Using Templates and Wizards | **Customize Word** | Merge Documents | Sharing Data

Record a Macro
Run a Macro
Create Your Own Toolbar

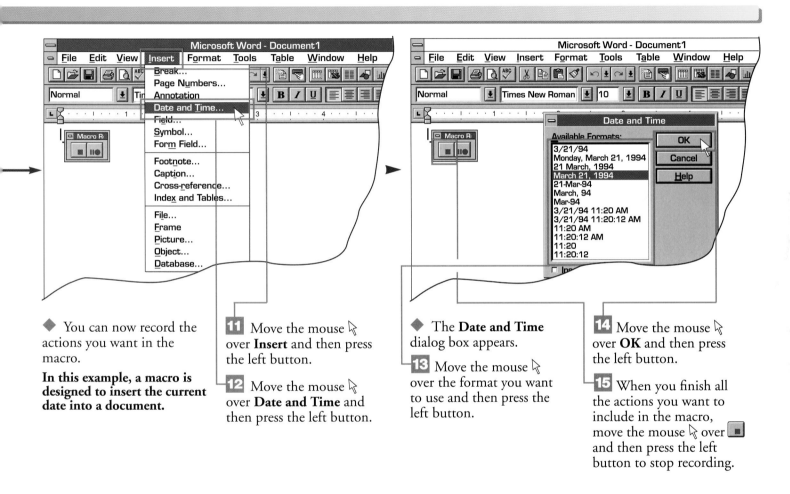

◆ You can now record the actions you want in the macro.

In this example, a macro is designed to insert the current date into a document.

11 Move the mouse ⌖ over **Insert** and then press the left button.

12 Move the mouse ⌖ over **Date and Time** and then press the left button.

◆ The **Date and Time** dialog box appears.

13 Move the mouse ⌖ over the format you want to use and then press the left button.

14 Move the mouse ⌖ over **OK** and then press the left button.

15 When you finish all the actions you want to include in the macro, move the mouse ⌖ over ■ and then press the left button to stop recording.

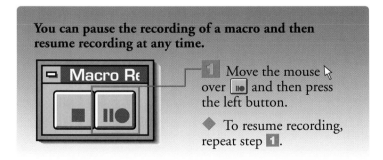

You can pause the recording of a macro and then resume recording at any time.

1 Move the mouse ⌖ over ⏸ and then press the left button.

◆ To resume recording, repeat step **1**.

RUN A MACRO

When you run a macro, Word automatically performs the series of commands you assigned to the macro.

Run a Macro

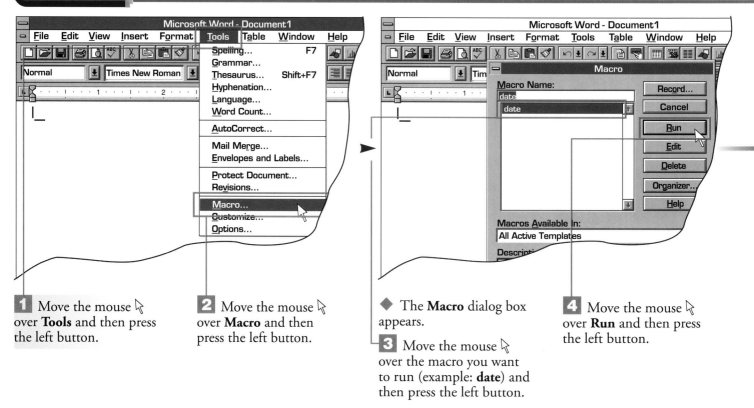

1 Move the mouse ⓚ over **Tools** and then press the left button.

2 Move the mouse ⓚ over **Macro** and then press the left button.

◆ The **Macro** dialog box appears.

3 Move the mouse ⓚ over the macro you want to run (example: **date**) and then press the left button.

4 Move the mouse ⓚ over **Run** and then press the left button.

Format
Characters

Format
Paragraphs

Format
Pages

Smart
Formatting

Working
With Tables

Using
Graphics

Using
Templates
and Wizards

Customize
Word

Merge
Documents

Sharing
Data

WORKING WITH WORD

Record a Macro
Run a Macro
Create Your Own Toolbar

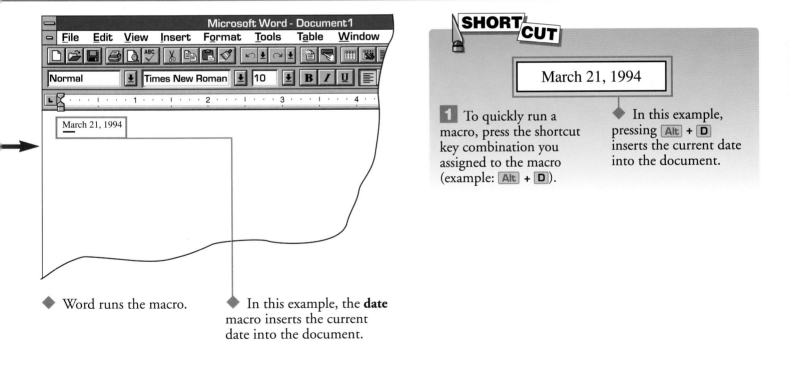

SHORT CUT

March 21, 1994

1 To quickly run a
macro, press the shortcut
key combination you
assigned to the macro
(example: `Alt` + `D`).

◆ In this example,
pressing `Alt` + `D`
inserts the current date
into the document.

◆ Word runs the macro.

◆ In this example, the **date**
macro inserts the current
date into the document.

CREATE YOUR OWN TOOLBAR

You can create your own toolbar to provide quick access to the commands you use most often.

Create Your Own Toolbar

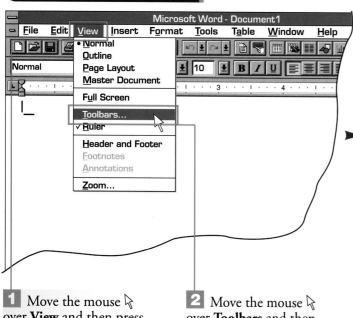

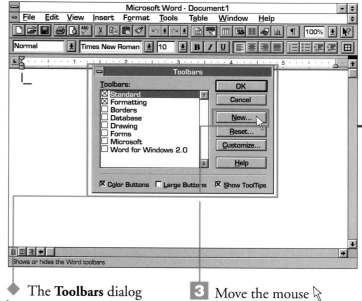

1 Move the mouse � over **View** and then press the left button.

2 Move the mouse ⍨ over **Toolbars** and then press the left button.

◆ The **Toolbars** dialog box appears.

3 Move the mouse ⍨ over **New** and then press the left button.

Format
Characters

Format
Paragraphs

Format
Pages

Smart
Formatting

Working
With Tables

Using
Graphics

Using
Templates
and Wizards

Customize
Word

Merge
Documents

Sharing
Data

Record a Macro
Run a Macro
Create Your Own Toolbar

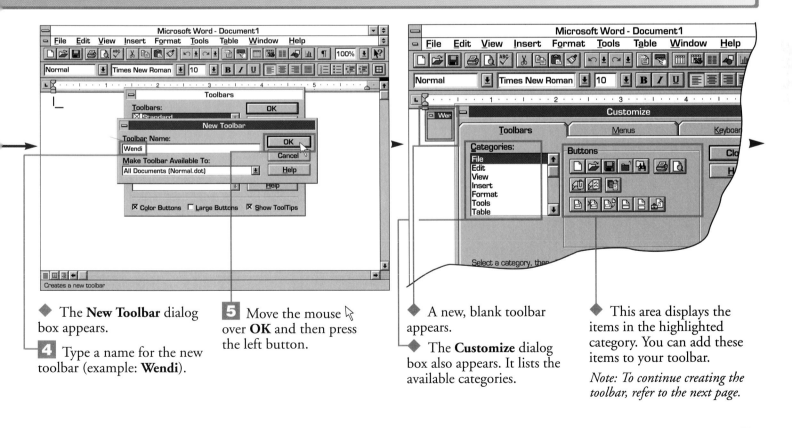

◆ The **New Toolbar** dialog box appears.

4 Type a name for the new toolbar (example: **Wendi**).

5 Move the mouse ⌖ over **OK** and then press the left button.

◆ A new, blank toolbar appears.

◆ The **Customize** dialog box also appears. It lists the available categories.

◆ This area displays the items in the highlighted category. You can add these items to your toolbar.

Note: To continue creating the toolbar, refer to the next page.

209

Create Your Own Toolbar (Continued)

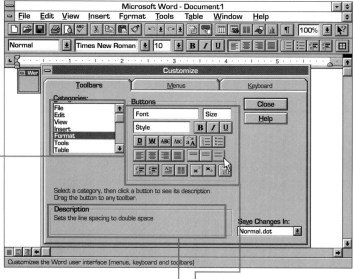

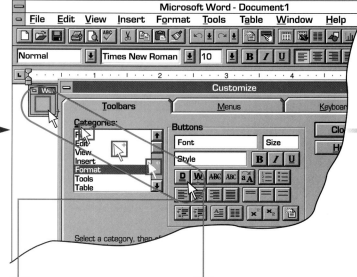

◆ To view more categories, move the mouse ▸ over ▼ or ▲ and then press the left button.

6 To display the items in another category, move the mouse ▸ over the category (example: **Format**) and then press the left button.

◆ All the items in the category appear.

7 To view a description of an item, move the mouse ▸ over the item and then press the left button.

◆ A description appears.

8 To add an item to your toolbar, move the mouse ▸ over the item and then press and hold down the left button.

9 Still holding down the button, drag the item to the toolbar.

Format
Characters

Format
Paragraphs

Format
Pages

Smart
Formatting

Working
With Tables

Using
Graphics

Using
Templates
and Wizards

Customize
Word

Merge
Documents

Sharing
Data

WORKING WITH WORD

Record a Macro
Run a Macro
Create Your Own Toolbar

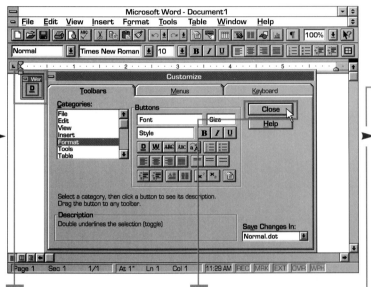

10 Release the button and the item appears in the toolbar.

11 Repeat steps **6** to **10** for each item you want to add.

12 When you finish adding items to the toolbar, move the mouse ⊠ over **Close** and then press the left button.

You can position the toolbar anywhere on your screen.

13 To move the toolbar, position the mouse ⊠ over an empty area on the toolbar and then press and hold down the left button.

14 Still holding down the button, drag the toolbar to a new location. Then release the button.

Note: To display or hide a toolbar, refer to page 104.

You can make changes to your toolbar at a later date. To do so, you must first display the Customize dialog box.

1 To display the **Customize** dialog box, move the mouse ⊠ over **Tools** and then press the left button.

2 Move the mouse ⊠ over **Customize** and then press the left button. The **Customize** dialog box appears.

3 To add an item to your toolbar, perform steps **6** to **11** above.

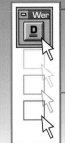

4 To remove an item from your toolbar, move the mouse ⊠ over the item and then press and hold down the left button.

5 Still holding down the button, drag the item off the toolbar. Then release the button.

Overview

MERGE DOCUMENTS

◆ This chapter will show you how to produce personalized letters and envelopes for each person on your mailing list.

INTRODUCTION

You can use the Merge feature to produce personalized letters for each person on your mailing list. To do this, you must create a Main Document and a Data Source.

Create the Main Document

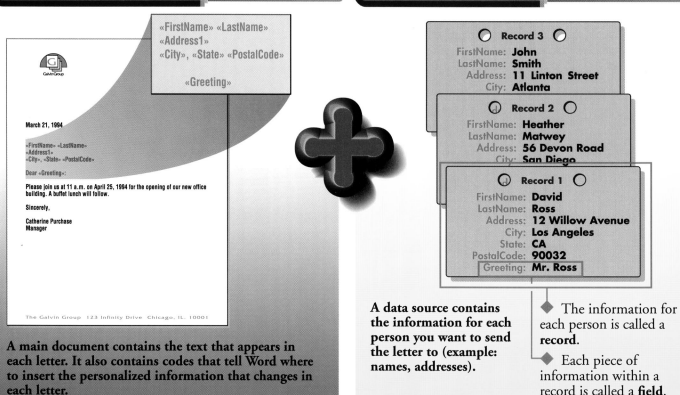

A main document contains the text that appears in each letter. It also contains codes that tell Word where to insert the personalized information that changes in each letter.

Create the Data Source

A data source contains the information for each person you want to send the letter to (example: names, addresses).

◆ The information for each person is called a **record**.

◆ Each piece of information within a record is called a **field**.

Merge the Main Document and Data Source

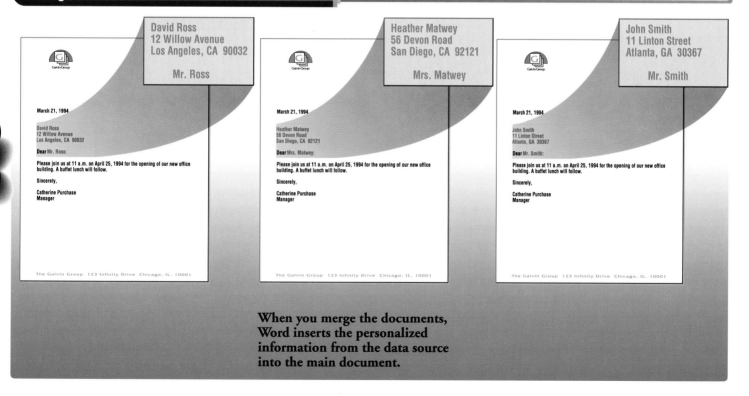

When you merge the documents, Word inserts the personalized information from the data source into the main document.

CREATE A MAIN DOCUMENT

The main document contains the text that appears in each letter. It also contains codes that tell Word where to insert the personalized information from the data source.

STEP 1 — Create a Main Document

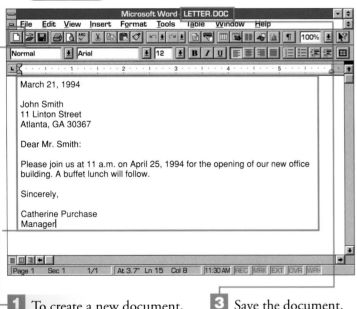

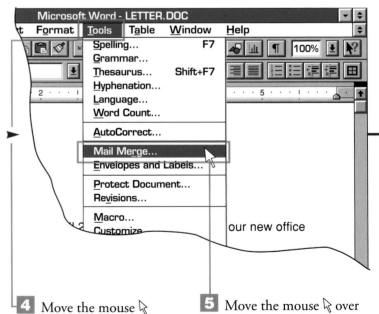

1 To create a new document, move the mouse ⇧ over 🗋 and then press the left button.

2 Type a letter for one of the customers on your mailing list.

3 Save the document. In this example, the document was named **letter.doc**.

Note: To save a document, refer to page 64.

4 Move the mouse ⇧ over **Tools** and then press the left button.

5 Move the mouse ⇧ over **Mail Merge** and then press the left button.

WORKING WITH WORD

Format Characters	Format Paragraphs	Format Pages	Smart Formatting	Working With Tables	Using Graphics	Using Templates and Wizards	Customize Word	**Merge Documents**	Sharing Data

Introduction   Complete the Main Document
Create a Main Document Merge Documents
Create a Data Source   Using Merge to Print Envelopes

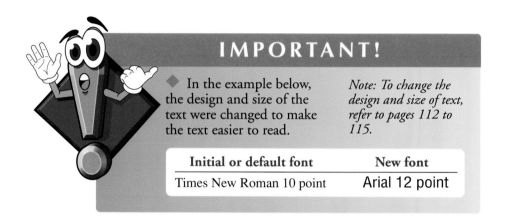

IMPORTANT!

◆ In the example below, the design and size of the text were changed to make the text easier to read.

Note: To change the design and size of text, refer to pages 112 to 115.

Initial or default font	New font
Times New Roman 10 point	Arial 12 point

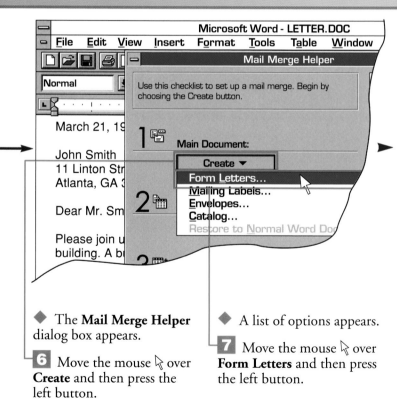

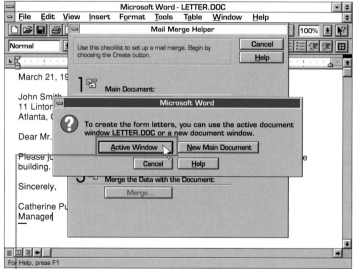

◆ The **Mail Merge Helper** dialog box appears.

6 Move the mouse ⌖ over **Create** and then press the left button.

◆ A list of options appears.

7 Move the mouse ⌖ over **Form Letters** and then press the left button.

8 To make the document displayed on your screen the main document, move the mouse ⌖ over **Active Window** and then press the left button.

◆ To continue the merge process, refer to the next page.

CREATE A DATA SOURCE

The data source contains the information for each person you want to send a letter to. This file may include information such as names and addresses.

Record 3

FirstName: **John**
LastName: **Smith**
Address: **11 Linton Street**
City: **Atlanta**
State: **GA**
PostalCode: **30367**
Greeting: **Mr. Smith**

Field Names
To create a data source, you must divide your information into different categories and provide a term that describes each one. These terms are known as field names.

STEP 2 Create a Data Source

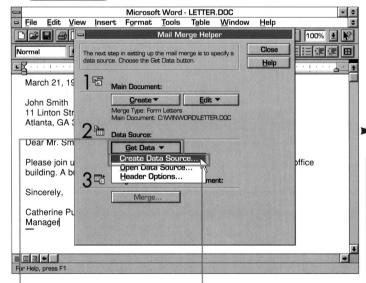

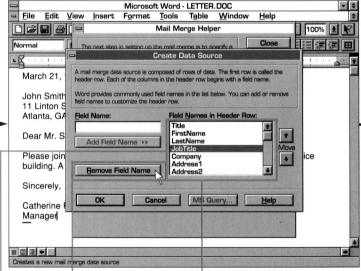

1 Move the mouse ⇧ over **Get Data** and then press the left button. A list of options appears.

*Note: If you previously created a data source, refer to **Open an Existing Data Source** at the top of page 219.*

2 Move the mouse ⇧ over **Create Data Source** and then press the left button.

◆ The **Create Data Source** dialog box appears.

◆ Word provides a list of field names commonly used in letters.

3 To view all the field names in the list, move the mouse ⇧ over 🔽 or 🔼 and then press the left button.

4 To remove a field name you will not use in your letter, move the mouse ⇧ over the name (example: **JobTitle**) and then press the left button.

5 Move the mouse ⇧ over **Remove Field Name** and then press the left button.

WORKING WITH WORD

Format
Characters

Format
Paragraphs

Format
Pages

Smart
Formatting

Working
With Tables

Using
Graphics

Using
Templates
and Wizards

Customize
Word

**Merge
Documents**

Sharing
Data

Introduction
Create a Main Document
Create a Data Source

Complete the Main Document
Merge Documents
Using Merge to Print Envelopes

OPEN AN EXISTING DATA SOURCE

**You only have to create a data source once. To use a data source
you previously created, perform the following steps.**

1 Perform step **1** on page 218.

2 Move the mouse ▷ over **Open Data
Source** and then press the left button.

3 Move the mouse ▷ over the name of
the data source you want to use and then
quickly press the left button twice.

4 Move the mouse ▷ over **Edit Main
Document** and then press the left button.

◆ The main document appears on your
screen. To continue the merge process,
refer to **Complete the Main Document** on
page 224.

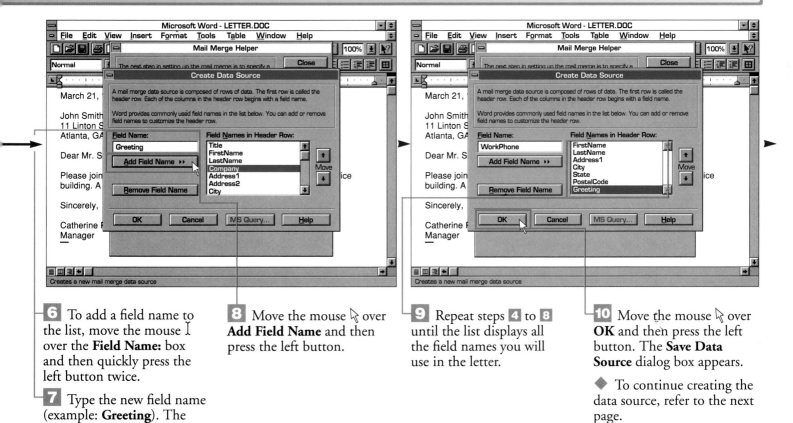

6 To add a field name to
the list, move the mouse I
over the **Field Name:** box
and then quickly press the
left button twice.

7 Type the new field name
(example: **Greeting**). The
name cannot contain spaces
and it must begin with a
letter.

8 Move the mouse ▷ over
Add Field Name and then
press the left button.

9 Repeat steps **4** to **8**
until the list displays all
the field names you will
use in the letter.

10 Move the mouse ▷ over
OK and then press the left
button. The **Save Data
Source** dialog box appears.

◆ To continue creating the
data source, refer to the next
page.

STEP 2 Create a Data Source (Continued)

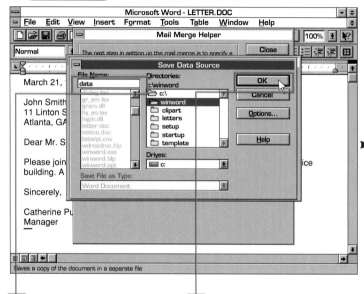

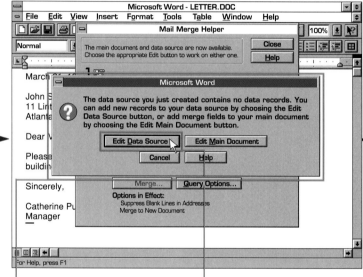

11 Type a name for the data source (example: **data**).

*Note: To make it easier to find the document later on, do not type an extension. Word will automatically add the **doc** extension to the file name.*

12 To save the document, move the mouse ⏳ over **OK** and then press the left button.

◆ This dialog box appears.

13 To enter customer information, move the mouse ⏳ over **Edit Data Source** and then press the left button.

◆ The **Data Form** dialog box appears.

WORKING WITH WORD

| Format Characters | Format Paragraphs | Format Pages | Smart Formatting | Working With Tables | Using Graphics | Using Templates and Wizards | Customize Word | **Merge Documents** | Sharing Data |

Introduction | Complete the Main Document
Create a Main Document | Merge Documents
Create a Data Source | Using Merge to Print Envelopes

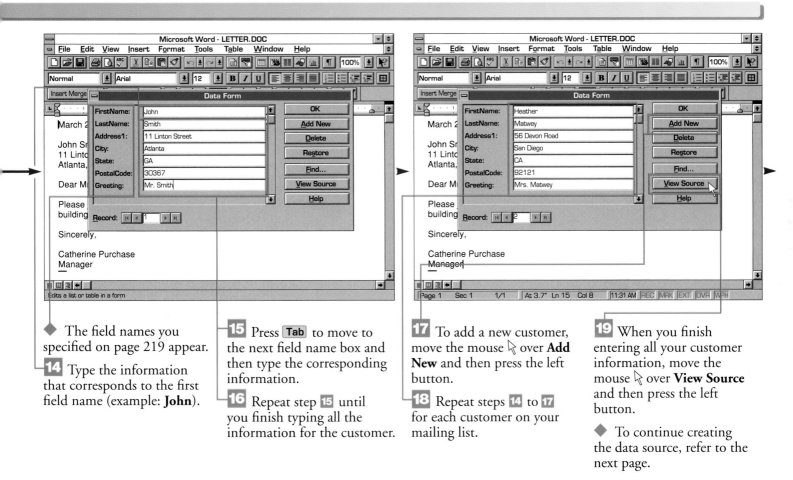

◆ The field names you specified on page 219 appear.

14 Type the information that corresponds to the first field name (example: **John**).

15 Press **Tab** to move to the next field name box and then type the corresponding information.

16 Repeat step **15** until you finish typing all the information for the customer.

17 To add a new customer, move the mouse ⬚ over **Add New** and then press the left button.

18 Repeat steps **14** to **17** for each customer on your mailing list.

19 When you finish entering all your customer information, move the mouse ⬚ over **View Source** and then press the left button.

◆ To continue creating the data source, refer to the next page.

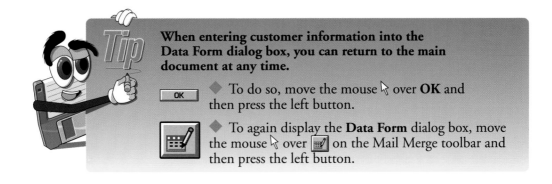

When entering customer information into the Data Form dialog box, you can return to the main document at any time.

OK ◆ To do so, move the mouse ⬚ over **OK** and then press the left button.

◆ To again display the **Data Form** dialog box, move the mouse ⬚ over ▦ on the Mail Merge toolbar and then press the left button.

CREATE A DATA SOURCE

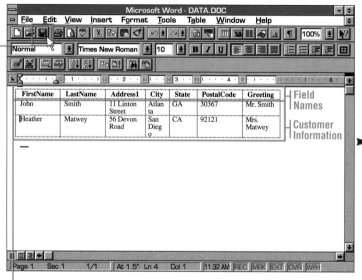

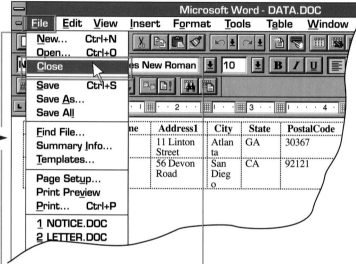

◆ The information you entered appears in a table.

20 To save the document, move the mouse ⇖ over 🖫 and then press the left button.

◆ Each row in the table displays information for one customer.

21 To close the data source, move the mouse ⇖ over **File** and then press the left button.

22 Move the mouse ⇖ over **Close** and then press the left button.

◆ The main document appears on your screen.

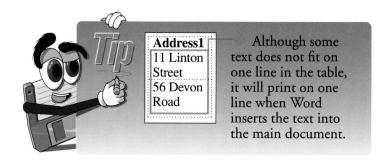

Although some text does not fit on one line in the table, it will print on one line when Word inserts the text into the main document.

WORKING WITH WORD

Format Characters	Format Paragraphs	Format Pages	Smart Formatting	Working With Tables	Using Graphics	Using Templates and Wizards	Customize Word	**Merge Documents**	Sharing Data

Introduction	Complete the Main Document
Create a Main Document	Merge Documents
Create a Data Source	Using Merge to Print Envelopes

Edit the Data Source

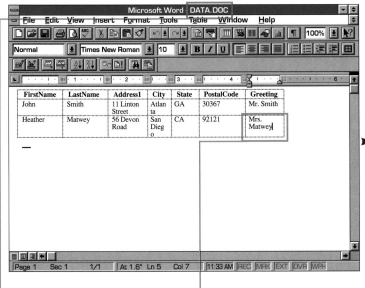

After you create the data source, you can open the document to add or change customer information.

1 Open the data source document.

Note: To open a document, refer to page 72.

2 To add a new customer, position the insertion point in the bottom right cell of the table.

3 Press **Tab** to add a new row.

4 Type the information that corresponds to the first field name (example: **David**).

5 Press **Tab** to move to the next field name area and then type the corresponding information.

6 Repeat step **5** until you finish typing all the information for the customer.

7 Perform steps **20** to **22** on page 222 to save and then close the document.

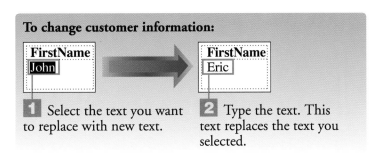

To change customer information:

1 Select the text you want to replace with new text.

2 Type the text. This text replaces the text you selected.

223

COMPLETE THE MAIN DOCUMENT

To complete the main document, you must tell Word where you want the information from the data source to appear. You accomplish this by adding merge fields to the main document.

STEP 3 — Complete the Main Document

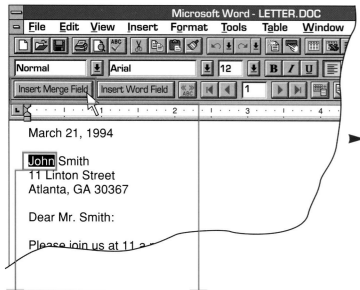

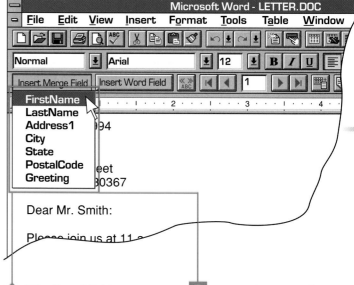

1 Select the text you want to replace with information from the data source.

Note: Make sure you do not select the space before or after the text since this can affect the spacing of the merged document.

2 Move the mouse ⊕ over **Insert Merge Field** and then press the left button.

◆ The list of field names you specified on page 219 appears.

3 Move the mouse ⊕ over the field name you want to insert into your document (example: **FirstName**) and then press the left button.

WORKING WITH WORD

| Format Characters | Format Paragraphs | Format Pages | Smart Formatting | Working With Tables | Using Graphics | Using Templates and Wizards | Customize Word | **Merge Documents** | Sharing Data |

Introduction
Create a Main Document
Create a Data Source

Complete the Main Document
Merge Documents
Using Merge to Print Envelopes

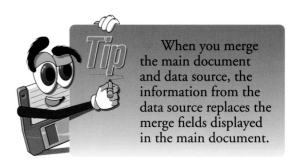

Tip

When you merge the main document and data source, the information from the data source replaces the merge fields displayed in the main document.

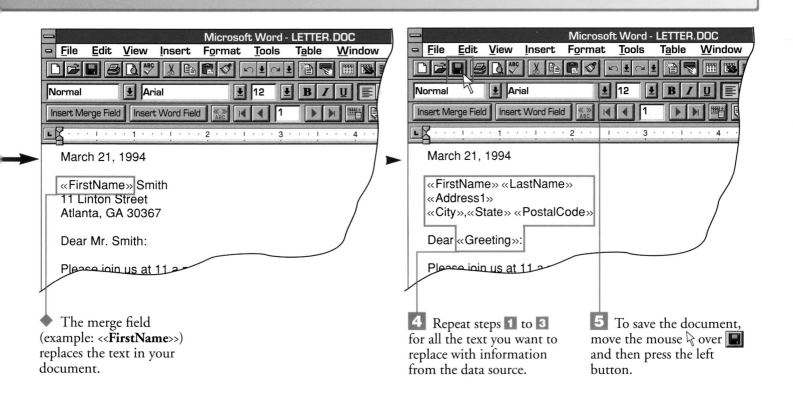

◆ The merge field (example: <<**FirstName**>>) replaces the text in your document.

4 Repeat steps **1** to **3** for all the text you want to replace with information from the data source.

5 To save the document, move the mouse ⬚ over 💾 and then press the left button.

225

MERGE DOCUMENTS

You can combine the main document and data source to create a personalized letter for each person on your mailing list.

STEP 4 — Merge the Main Document and Data Source

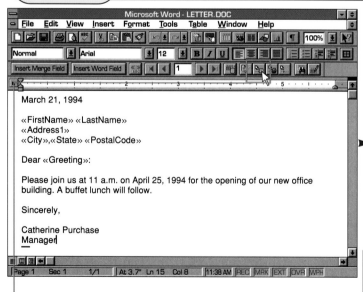

```
Microsoft Word - LETTER.DOC
File  Edit  View  Insert  Format  Tools  Table  Window  Help
Normal        Arial         12    B  I  U
Insert Merge Field   Insert Word Field   ◄◄ ◄ 1 ► ►►

March 21, 1994

«FirstName» «LastName»
«Address1»
«City», «State» «PostalCode»

Dear «Greeting»:

Please join us at 11 a.m. on April 25, 1994 for the opening of our new office
building. A buffet lunch will follow.

Sincerely,

Catherine Purchase
Manager

Page 1   Sec 1   1/1   At 3.7"  Ln 15  Col 8   11:38 AM  REC  MRK  EXT  OVR  WPH
```

1 To merge the main document and data source, move the mouse ♙ over ▣ and then press the left button.

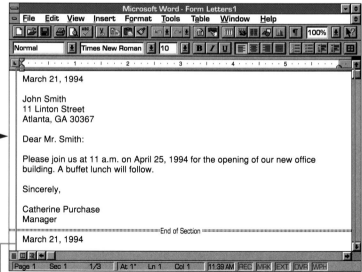

```
Microsoft Word - Form Letters1
File  Edit  View  Insert  Format  Tools  Table  Window  Help
Normal        Times New Roman   10    B  I  U

March 21, 1994

John Smith
11 Linton Street
Atlanta, GA 30367

Dear Mr. Smith:

Please join us at 11 a.m. on April 25, 1994 for the opening of our new office
building. A buffet lunch will follow.

Sincerely,

Catherine Purchase
Manager
═══════════════ End of Section ═══════════════
March 21, 1994

Page 1   Sec 1   1/3   At 1"  Ln 1  Col 1   11:39 AM  REC  MRK  EXT  OVR  WPH
```

◆ Word creates a personalized letter for each customer.

2 To ensure no errors have occurred, press **Page Down** on your keyboard to view the letters.

◆ You can edit and print this document as you would any document.

WORKING WITH WORD

| Format Characters | Format Paragraphs | Format Pages | Smart Formatting | Working With Tables | Using Graphics | Using Templates and Wizards | Customize Word | **Merge Documents** | Sharing Data |

Introduction   Complete the Main Document
Create a Main Document   **Merge Documents**
Create a Data Source   Using Merge to Print Envelopes

◆ To conserve hard disk space, do not save the merged document after you print it.

Print the Merged Document

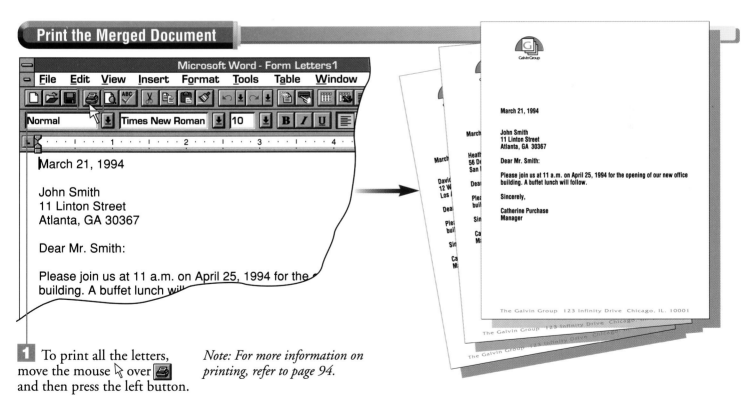

1 To print all the letters, move the mouse ⇱ over 🖨 and then press the left button.

Note: For more information on printing, refer to page 94.

227

> You can quickly print an envelope for every customer on your mailing list by using the merge feature.

Using Merge to Print Envelopes

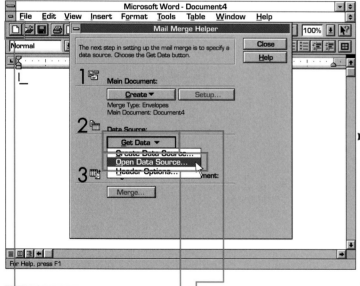

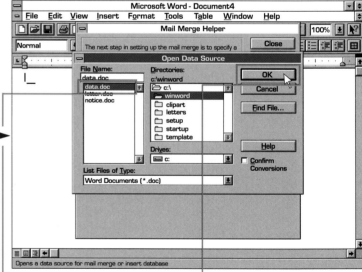

1 To create a new document, move the mouse ⍉ over ☐ and then press the left button.

2 Perform steps **4** to **8** on pages 216 and 217, except select **Envelopes** in step **7**.

3 Move the mouse ⍉ over **Get Data** and then press the left button.

Note: To create a data source, refer to page 218.

4 Move the mouse ⍉ over **Open Data Source** and then press the left button.

◆ The **Open Data Source** dialog box appears.

5 Move the mouse ⍉ over the name of the data source you want to use (example: **data.doc**) and then press the left button.

6 Move the mouse ⍉ over **OK** and then press the left button.

WORKING WITH WORD

| Format Characters | Format Paragraphs | Format Pages | Smart Formatting | Working With Tables | Using Graphics | Using Templates and Wizards | Customize Word | **Merge Documents** | Sharing Data |

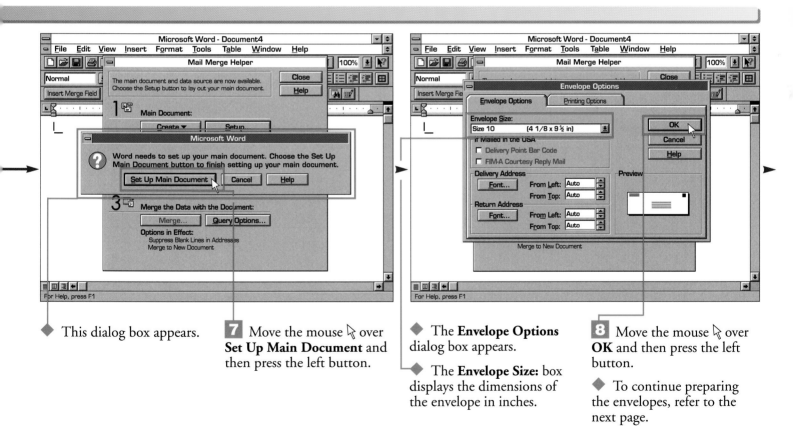

◆ This dialog box appears.

7 Move the mouse ⌖ over **Set Up Main Document** and then press the left button.

◆ The **Envelope Options** dialog box appears.

◆ The **Envelope Size:** box displays the dimensions of the envelope in inches.

8 Move the mouse ⌖ over **OK** and then press the left button.

◆ To continue preparing the envelopes, refer to the next page.

USING MERGE TO PRINT ENVELOPES

Using Merge to Print Envelopes (Continued)

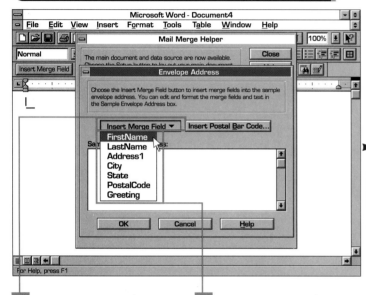

9 Move the mouse ⟍ over **Insert Merge Field** and then press the left button.

◆ The list of field names you specified on page 219 appears.

10 Move the mouse ⟍ over the field name you want to include on your envelopes (example: **FirstName**) and then press the left button.

◆ The merge field appears (example: ‹‹**FirstName**››).

11 To insert the next merge field on the same line, press the **Spacebar**.

◆ To insert the next merge field on the following line, press Enter .

12 Repeat steps **9** to **11** for each merge field you want to insert.

13 Move the mouse ⟍ over **OK** and then press the left button.

14 Move the mouse ⟍ over **Close** and then press the left button.

230

WORKING WITH WORD

| Format Characters | Format Paragraphs | Format Pages | Smart Formatting | Working With Tables | Using Graphics | Using Templates and Wizards | Customize Word | **Merge Documents** | Sharing Data |

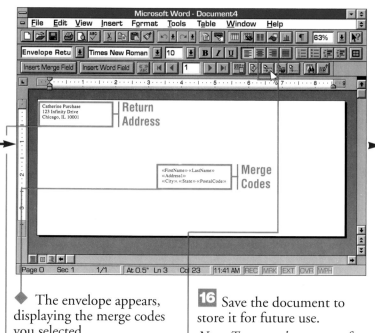

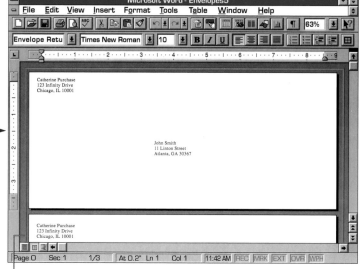

◆ The envelope appears, displaying the merge codes you selected.

15 To edit the return address, select the text you want to change and then type the new text.

16 Save the document to store it for future use.

Note: To save a document, refer to page 64.

17 To create an envelope for each customer, you must merge this document with the data source. To do so, move the mouse ⌖ over 🖳 and then press the left button.

◆ Word creates an envelope for each customer.

18 To ensure no errors have occurred, press **PageDown** on your keyboard to view the envelopes.

◆ You can edit and print the envelopes as you would any document.

Overview

SHARING DATA

◆ This chapter will show you how to place information from another application into a Word document. You will also learn how to edit the information while working in Word.

> You can easily place information from another application into a Word document.

SOURCE DOCUMENT

◆ A source document supplies objects that you place in the Word document.

DESTINATION DOCUMENT

◆ Word is the destination document that accepts objects from other applications.

OBJECT

An object is the information you transfer between applications, such as a chart, a table, text or graphics.

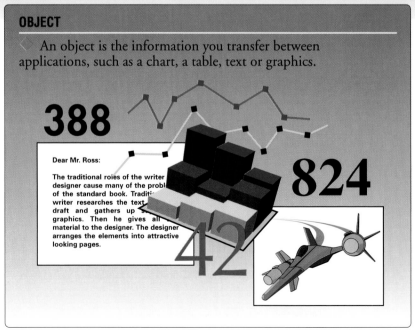

WORKING WITH WORD

| Format Characters | Format Paragraphs | Format Pages | Smart Formatting | Working With Tables | Using Graphics | Using Templates and Wizards | Customize Word | Merge Documents | **Sharing Data** |

Introduction
Embed an Object
Edit an Embedded Object

Embed an Object

You can embed an object in a Word document. The Word document will then contain a copy of the object.

◆ When you embed an object in a Word document, the object becomes part of the document. This makes the document portable since it does not require a connection to the source document. You can edit the object directly in the Word document.

LINK AN OBJECT

◇ When you link an object to a Word document, Word receives a "screen image" of the object. The real object still resides in the source application. When changes are made to the object in the source application, all documents linked to the object will automatically change.

For example, if you distribute a monthly sales report to all your regional managers, you can link the current sales data to each report. This way, each time you update the sales data, the reports will include the most current sales information.

Note: For more information on linking objects, refer to your Microsoft Word for Windows manual.

Sales Data

Source Document

Word Documents

EMBED
AN OBJECT

You can place an object from another application in a Word document. To do so, you must first start the application that contains the object.

Embed an Object

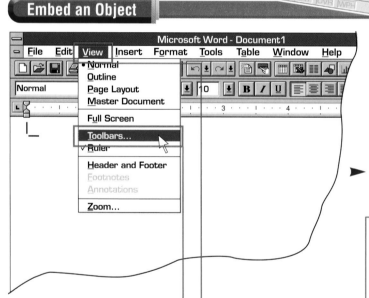

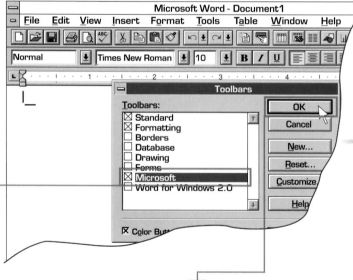

This example demonstrates how to start a Microsoft application while in Word.

Note: To start another application, refer to its manual.

■1 To display the Microsoft toolbar, move the mouse ⇗ over **View** and then press the left button.

■2 Move the mouse ⇗ over **Toolbars** and then press the left button.

◆ The **Toolbars** dialog box appears.

■3 Move the mouse ⇗ over **Microsoft** and then press the left button (☐ becomes ⊠).

■4 Move the mouse ⇗ over **OK** and then press the left button.

WORKING WITH WORD

Format Characters | Format Paragraphs | Format Pages | Smart Formatting | Working With Tables | Using Graphics | Using Templates and Wizards | Customize Word | Merge Documents | **Sharing Data**

Introduction
Embed an Object
Edit an Embedded Object

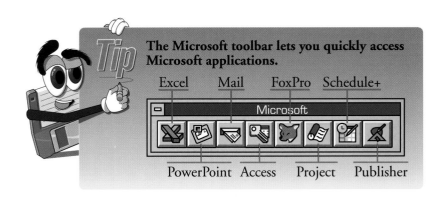

The Microsoft toolbar lets you quickly access Microsoft applications.

Excel   Mail   FoxPro   Schedule+

Microsoft

PowerPoint   Access   Project   Publisher

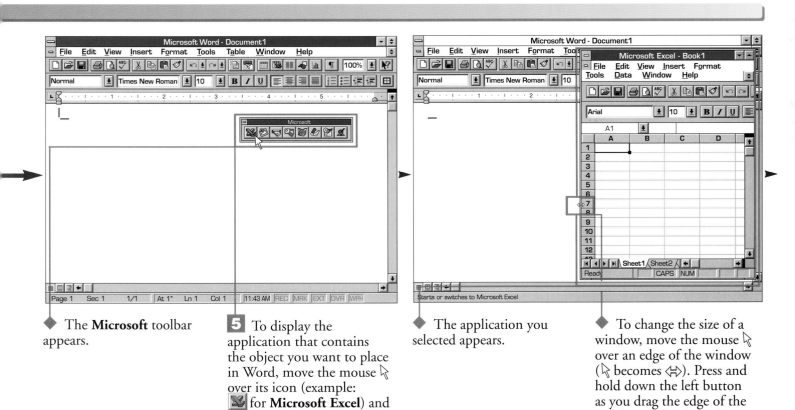

◆ The **Microsoft** toolbar appears.

5 To display the application that contains the object you want to place in Word, move the mouse �)⟍ over its icon (example: ▨ for **Microsoft Excel**) and then press the left button.

◆ The application you selected appears.

◆ To change the size of a window, move the mouse �)⟍ over an edge of the window (�)⟍ becomes ⟨↔⟩). Press and hold down the left button as you drag the edge of the window to the desired size. Then release the button.

Note: To continue the embed process, refer to the next page.

Embed an Object (Continued)

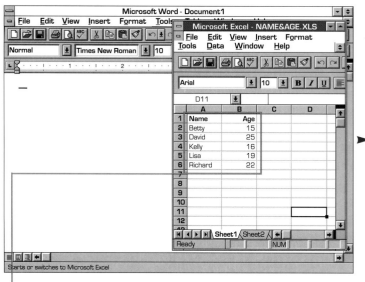

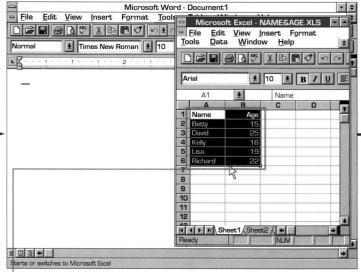

6 Open the file containing the object you want to place in the Word document.

Note: To open a file, refer to page 72.

7 Select the object.

WORKING WITH WORD

| Format Characters | Format Paragraphs | Format Pages | Smart Formatting | Working With Tables | Using Graphics | Using Templates and Wizards | Customize Word | Merge Documents | **Sharing Data** |

Introduction
Embed an Object
Edit an Embedded Object

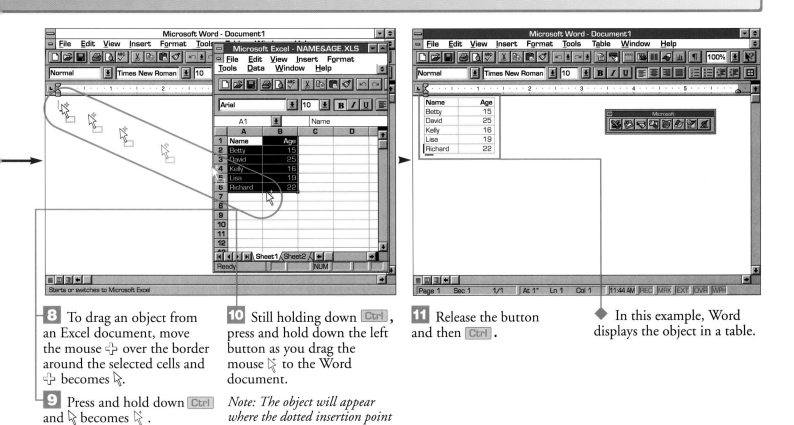

8 To drag an object from an Excel document, move the mouse ⊹ over the border around the selected cells and ⊹ becomes ↖.

9 Press and hold down Ctrl and ↖ becomes ↖⁺.

10 Still holding down Ctrl, press and hold down the left button as you drag the mouse ↖⁺ to the Word document.

Note: The object will appear where the dotted insertion point appears on your screen.

11 Release the button and then Ctrl.

◆ In this example, Word displays the object in a table.

IMPORTANT!

The drag and drop method of exchanging objects between applications only works with applications that support OLE 2.0. These applications currently include:

◆ CorelDraw 5.0
◆ Microsoft Access 2.0
◆ Microsoft Excel 5.0
◆ Microsoft PowerPoint 4.0

◆ Microsoft Publisher 2.0
◆ Microsoft Word 6.0
◆ Microsoft Works 3.0

Note: If you are not sure the application you are using supports OLE 2.0, check its manual.

You can edit an embedded object while working in Word.

Edit an Embedded Object

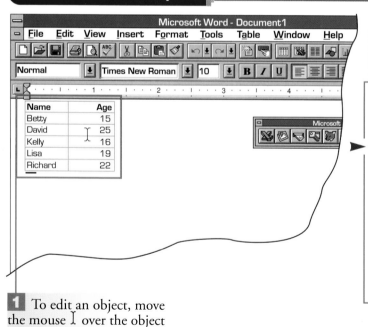

1 To edit an object, move the mouse I over the object and then quickly press the left button twice.

◆ In this example, the Excel menus and toolbars temporarily replace the Word menus and toolbars. This lets you access all of the Excel commands while working in the Word document.

WORKING WITH WORD

| Format Characters | Format Paragraphs | Format Pages | Smart Formatting | Working With Tables | Using Graphics | Using Templates and Wizards | Customize Word | Merge Documents | **Sharing Data** |

Introduction
Embed an Object
Edit an Embedded Object

IMPORTANT!

You can only edit an object directly in the document (as shown below) if the applications you are using support OLE 2.0.

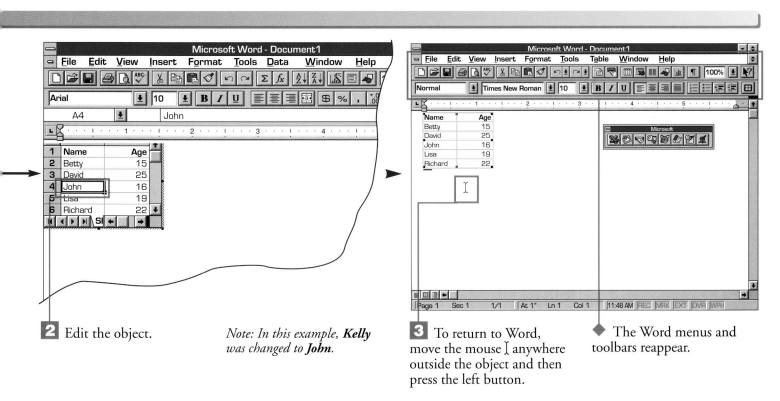

2 Edit the object.

*Note: In this example, **Kelly** was changed to **John**.*

3 To return to Word, move the mouse I anywhere outside the object and then press the left button.

◆ The Word menus and toolbars reappear.

INDEX

IDG BOOKS ®

TRADE & INDIVIDUAL ORDERS

Phone: **(800) 762-2974** *or* **(317) 895-5200**
(8 a.m.–6 p.m., CST, weekdays)
FAX : **(317) 895-5298**

CORPORATE ORDERS FOR 3-D VISUAL™ SERIES

Phone: **(800) 469-6616** *ext.* **206**
(8 a.m.–5 p.m., EST, weekdays)
FAX : **(905) 890-9434**

Qty	ISBN	Title	Price	Total

Shipping & Handling Charges

	Description	First book	Each add'l. book	Total
Domestic	Normal	$4.50	$1.50	$
	Two Day Air	$8.50	$2.50	$
	Overnight	$18.00	$3.00	$
International	Surface	$8.00	$8.00	$
	Airmail	$16.00	$16.00	$
	DHL Air	$17.00	$17.00	$

Subtotal _____

*CA residents add
applicable sales tax* _____

*IN, MA and MD
residents add
5% sales tax* _____

*IL residents add
6.25% sales tax* _____

*RI residents add
7% sales tax* _____

*TX residents add
8.25% sales tax* _____

Shipping _____

Total _____

Ship to:

Name_____

Address_____

Company _____

City/State/Zip _____

Daytime Phone_____

Payment: ☐ Check to IDG Books (US Funds Only)

☐ Visa   ☐ Mastercard   ☐ American Express

Card # _____ Exp. _____ Signature_____

IDG Books Education Group
Jim Kelly, Director of Education Sales – 9 Village Circle, Ste. 450, Westlake, TX 76262
800-434-2086 Phone • 817-430-5852 Fax • 8:30-5:00 CST

IDG BOOKS WORLDWIDE REGISTRATION CARD

RETURN THIS
REGISTRATION CARD
FOR FREE CATALOG

Title of this book: Word 6.0 For Windows Simplified

My overall rating of this book: ❏ Very good [1] ❏ Good [2] ❏ Satisfactory [3] ❏ Fair [4] ❏ Poor [5]

How I first heard about this book:

❏ Found in bookstore; name: [6] _____ ❏ Book review: [7] _____

❏ Advertisement: [8] _____ ❏ Catalog: [9] _____

❏ Word of mouth; heard about book from friend, co-worker, etc.: [10] _____ ❏ Other: [11] _____

What I liked most about this book:

_____
_____
_____

What I would change, add, delete, etc., in future editions of this book:

_____
_____
_____

Other comments:

_____
_____

Number of computer books I purchase in a year: ❏ 1 [12] ❏ 2-5 [13] ❏ 6-10 [14] ❏ More than 10 [15]

I would characterize my computer skills as: ❏ Beginner [16] ❏ Intermediate [17] ❏ Advanced [18] ❏ Professional [19]

I use ❏ DOS [20] ❏ Windows [21] ❏ OS/2 [22] ❏ Unix [23] ❏ Macintosh [24] ❏ Other: [25]_____
(please specify)

I would be interested in new books on the following subjects:
(please check all that apply, and use the spaces provided to identify specific software)

❏ Word processing: [26] _____ ❏ Spreadsheets: [27] _____

❏ Data bases: [28] _____ ❏ Desktop publishing: [29] _____

❏ File Utilities: [30] _____ ❏ Money management: [31] _____

❏ Networking: [32] _____ ❏ Programming languages: [33] _____

❏ Other: [34] _____

I use a PC at (please check all that apply): ❏ home [35] ❏ work [36] ❏ school [37] ❏ other: [38] _____

The disks I prefer to use are ❏ 5.25 [39] ❏ 3.5 [40] ❏ other: [41] _____

I have a CD ROM: ❏ yes [42] ❏ no [43]

I plan to buy or upgrade computer hardware this year: ❏ yes [44] ❏ no [45]

I plan to buy or upgrade computer software this year: ❏ yes [46] ❏ no [47]

Name: _____ Business title: [48] _____ Type of Business: [49] _____

Address (❏ home [50] ❏ work [51]/Company name: _____)

Street/Suite# _____

City [52]/State [53]/Zipcode [54]: _____ Country [55] _____

❏ **I liked this book!** You may quote me by name in future
IDG Books Worldwide promotional materials.

My daytime phone number is _____

IDG BOOKS

THE WORLD OF
COMPUTER
KNOWLEDGE

❏ YES!

Please keep me informed about IDG's World of Computer Knowledge.
Send me the latest IDG Books catalog.